Virgil's Map

Bloomsbury Studies in Classical Reception

Bloomsbury Studies in Classical Reception presents scholarly monographs offering new and innovative research and debate to students and scholars in the reception of Classical Studies. Each volume will explore the appropriation, reconceptualization and recontextualization of various aspects of the Graeco-Roman world and its culture, looking at the impact of the ancient world on modernity. Research will also cover reception within antiquity, the theory and practice of translation, and reception theory.

Virgil's Map

Geography, Empire, and the Georgics

Charlie Kerrigan

BLOOMSBURY ACADEMIC
LONDON • NEW YORK • OXFORD • NEW DELHI • SYDNEY

BLOOMSBURY ACADEMIC
Bloomsbury Publishing Plc
50 Bedford Square, London, WC1B 3DP, UK
1385 Broadway, New York, NY 10018, USA
29 Earlsfort Terrace, Dublin 2, Ireland

BLOOMSBURY, BLOOMSBURY ACADEMIC and the Diana logo are trademarks of Bloomsbury Publishing Plc

First published in Great Britain 2020
This paperback edition published in 2022

Cover design: Terry Woodley
Cover image © Ethiopia, Shoa Province, Ethiopian highlands © James Baigrie/Getty Images

A SMALL PLACE by Jamaica Kincaid. Copyright © 1988, Jamaica Kincaid,
used by permission of the Wylie Agency (UK) Limited.

Library of Congress Cataloging-in-Publication Data
Names: Kerrigan, Charlie, author.
Title: Virgil's map : geography, empire, and the Georgics / Charlie Kerrigan.
Other titles: Bloomsbury studies in classical reception.
Description: London ; New York : Bloomsbury Academic, 2020. | Series: Bloomsbury studies in classical reception |
Based on the author's dissertation (doctoral)–Trinity College, 2018. | Includes bibliographical references and index. |
Summary: "Virgil's Georgics depicts the world and its peoples in great detail, but this geographical interest has received
little detailed scholarly attention. Hundreds of years later, readers in the British empire used the poem to reflect upon their
travels in acts of imagination no less political than Virgil's own. Virgil's Map combines a comprehensive survey of the
literary, economic, and political geography of the Georgics with a case study of its British imperial reception c. 1840–1930.
Part One charts the poem's geographical interests in relation to Roman power in and beyond the Mediterranean; shifting
readers' attention away from Rome, it explores how the Georgics can draw attention to alternative, non-Roman histories.
Part Two examines how British travellers quoted directly from the poem to describe peoples and places across the world,
at times equating the colonial subjects of European empires to the 'happy farmers' of Virgil's poem, perceived to be
unaware, and in need, of the blessings of colonial rule. Drawing attention to the depoliticization of the poem in scholarly
discourse, and using newly discovered archival material, this interdisciplinary work seeks to re-politicize both the poem
and its history in service of a decolonizing pedagogy. Its unique dual focus allows for an extended exploration, not just of
geography and empire, but of Europe's long relationship with the wider world"– Provided by publisher.
Identifiers: LCCN 2020018745 (print) | LCCN 2020018746 (ebook) | ISBN 9781350151505 (hardback) |
ISBN 9781350151512 (ebook) | ISBN 9781350151529 (epub) Subjects: LCSH: Virgil. Georgica. | Imperialism in literature. |
Power (Social sciences) in literature. | Geography in literature. | Rome–In literature. | Virgil–Appreciation–Great Britain–
History–19th century. | Virgil–Appreciation–Great Britain–History–20th century.
Classification: LCC PA6804.G4 K47 2020 (print) | LCC PA6804.G4 (ebook) | DDC 871/.01—dc23
LC record available at https://lccn.loc.gov/2020018745
LC ebook record available at https://lccn.loc.gov/2020018746

ISBN: HB: 978-1-3501-5150-5
        PB: 978-1-3501-9490-8
        ePDF: 978-1-3501-5151-2
        eBook: 978-1-3501-5152-9

Series: Bloomsbury Studies in Classical Reception

Typeset by RefineCatch Limited, Bungay, Suffolk

To find out more about our authors and books visit www.bloomsbury.com and sign up for our newsletters.

Contents

Acknowledgements

The work for this book was done at Trinity College, Dublin, first as a non-foundation scholar and later as a research fellow in the Department of Classics. As such it owes a lot not just to friends and colleagues in the Department, but to many in the wider TCD community. The Irish material in Chapter 7 was first published as 'Virgil's *Georgics* and Nineteenth-Century Ireland' in *Classics Ireland* 25 (2018): my thanks to the editor Shane Wallace for his support. Special thanks to Monica Gale, David Scourfield, Anna Chahoud and Winifred Ryan; to Stephen Harrison and Susanna Braund; to Alice Wright, Georgina Leighton and Lily Mac Mahon at Bloomsbury; and to all those who read, reviewed and helped in production. Matthew Leigh's training at Oxford in 2013–14, though it pre-dates this project, helped me a great deal. This book would not be the book it is without Ciarán, Rob, Nandini and Nita; it wouldn't have been written without the support of my family – Mum and Dad, Olivia and Jack – to whom I dedicate it now.

Abbreviations

Abbreviations of Greek and Latin authors and their works correspond to those used in the *Oxford Classical Dictionary* (see *OCD*, below); abbreviations of journal titles are those used in *L'Année philologique*.

CIL   *Corpus Inscriptionum Latinarum*, 1863–present, Berlin: Berlin-Brandenburgische Akademie der Wissenschaften.

Hansard   *The Official Report of Parliamentary Debates*, 1803–present, London: The Stationary Office, online edn, last accessed via hansard.parliament.uk, 28 November 2019.

ILS   Dessau, H., ed. (1892–1916), *Inscriptiones Latinae selectae*, 3 vols., Berlin: Weidmann.

ILLRP   Degrassi, A., ed., *Inscriptiones Latinae liberae rei publicae*, 2 vols., first volume second edition (1965) and second volume first edition (1963), Florence: La nuova Italia.

OCD   S. Hornblower, A. Spawforth and E. Eidinow, eds (2012), *The Oxford Classical Dictionary*, 4th edn, Oxford: Oxford University Press.

OLD   P. G. W. Glare, ed. (2012), *The Oxford Latin Dictionary*, 2 vols., 2nd edn, Oxford: Oxford University Press.

RE   A. F. von Pauly et al. (1894–1980), *Real-Encyclopädie der classischen Altertumswissenschaft*, Stuttgart and Munich: J. B. Metzler, A. Druckenmüller.

TLL   *Thesaurus linguae Latinae*, 1900–present, Munich: Bayerische Akademie der Wissenschaften.

Introduction

This book is a history of Virgil's *Georgics*. In Part One I chart the poem's geographical interests and argue for the political nature of those interests. Four chapters examine its literary, economic, civil war and Italian geography, while an appendix of all the peoples and places it names is provided so that readers can explore this geography according to their own interests. But what I really want to suggest is that there is a way of reading the *Georgics* against the grain, in sympathy with the colonized rather than the colonizing power.[1] On my reading the *Georgics* is Virgil's map, a document both creative and political, which imagines the world from a particular point in time and space, saying to its first readers, 'Here is the world, and here is Rome's place in it.'[2] That imagined world testifies to Roman power in and beyond the Mediterranean, but also to the endless diversity of the world at large, its peoples and places. Read in this way, the poem both promotes and undermines the universalizing rhetoric of empire, reminding us that, for all Rome's power in the world, the world was always bigger, 'Incorrigibly plural.'[3]

What I try to demonstrate here are the poem's politics in terms of Italian society beyond Rome, and of the peoples and places of the wider world that were subject to real or imagined Roman power. The geography of the *Georgics* offers an expansive picture of Roman power in the world, but does not instruct its readers in their reading. Certain peoples and places evoke not only Roman victory and success, but also its civil wars and its wars in the Italian Peninsula. It is worth considering, that is, how the poem's first readers (or listeners – in any case, I mean the elite Roman audience of the 20s BCE) would have received this at once confident and ambivalent evocation of their world. For today's readers, this geography can help us to imagine non-Roman experience, in particular the experiences of those communities caught up in, and at times destroyed by, Rome's consistent military aggression. Such an act of imagination is important in trying to counteract both the paucity of evidence for these communities in the historical record, and – not unrelated – the cumulative biases of 'Roman' history, which tend to keep the victors' versions of events foremost in our minds.

Part Two draws on a range of archival material *c.* 1840–1930 to investigate the poem's reception in Britain and the British Empire. Like Part One, it is an attempt to politicize the *Georgics* and its tradition, motivated by what I identify in Chapter 5 as an aesthetic trend in the poem's British scholarly reception. The argument is that celebration of the poem as a beautiful masterpiece has, since the time of Joseph Addison, tended to obscure its politics to an unnecessary and unhelpful degree. It is not the appreciation I take issue with, but the resulting imbalance in scholarship, which, while sometimes engaging with the patriotic and imperial aspects of the poem, rarely lingered on the contexts of slavery and imperial violence. Modern scholarship has been talking about the poem's politics for some decades now, but within a Roman, not a post-colonial, framework.[4] This book is thus partly about the history of scholarship, about how agendas and oversights persist from one generation to the next, influencing in a very fundamental sense what a text is taken to be.

Readers in Britain responded with great feeling to Virgil's depictions of the world, and had no difficulty in relating those depictions to their own environment and their own experience. Travelling abroad, they used lines from a Latin poem they knew to make the unfamiliar a little less so: here too the *Georgics* functioned as a kind of map, a useful aid in the negotiation of difference. But readers also used the poem to aestheticize and depoliticize peoples and places that were subject to European colonialism, a practice which, at its worst, justified imperial intervention as the bringing of 'civilization' to willing and needy subjects. As part of a condescending imperial rhetoric, colonial subjects in Australia, Ireland, India and South Africa were cast as the 'happy farmers' of Virgil's poem, unaware of the blessings of British rule, a rhetoric that was in turn satirized and challenged by journalists and politicians in the same Virgilian terms. The *Georgics*, therefore, has an imperial history in British no less than in Roman contexts. A final chapter returns to Britain in order to highlight the politics of the poem's reception during the First World War, and the implication of post-war reconstruction and empire.

This book prioritizes the reader's point of view, and in so doing follows the current practice of thinking about Greek and Latin texts and their influence in terms of reception. If a text is what you make of it, then it can be reimagined over and over again. But two additional points are important. First, this is a politically committed study, and deliberately so; it stems from my thinking not just about Latin literature, but about politics and society in general. I disagree with the idea, put forward by Martindale, that reception is somehow disinterested; I prefer to embrace my own subjectivity, in the hope that a forthright argument, well researched and backed up by plenty of evidence, is more productive in stimulating debate than claiming an objectivity which is inevitably fallacious and which often, paradoxically, disguises a less than disinterested position.[5]

Second, in as much as I want to leave readers to their own relationship with Virgil and his texts, in as much as I prioritize the reader's point of view, the historical aspect of what follows is important. There is a virtue and at times an ethical imperative in gathering the evidence for Roman and British imperialism, in attempting to chart (despite the difficulties) the brutality of both, if only to seek connections and narratives that can make sense of the present. In this approach I am indebted primarily to the work of Walter Benjamin, Edward Said and Adrienne Rich, but also to politically engaged classical scholars and those working on the reception of ancient Greek and Latin literature in the British Empire; this book is, needless to say, built upon the work of many Virgilian scholars.[6] Readers should note that many aspects of the poem's reception history are not covered here, and this is because I have tried to write not a general historical survey, but a politicizing essay.

The underlying framework I have in mind is that of decolonization. As I understand it, decolonization in academic terms is the effort to identify, analyse and challenge the operation and the legacies of imperial power. As such it has not only political, but pedagogical and institutional concerns, and as a metaphor it can usefully denote broader attempts to identify and emancipate oneself from structures of power of different kinds. What follows is meant as a broad and interdisciplinary investigation into empire and its relationship to literature, scholarship and pedagogy; my hope is that it will be of use to those trying to decolonize the study of ancient Greek and Latin literature. The *Georgics*, while bound up in the histories of power, is not prescriptive, and is there to be reimagined by every new reader. 'Since decolonization', writes bell hooks, 'is always a struggle to define ourselves in and beyond the act of resistance to domination, we are always in the process of both remembering the past even as we create new ways to imagine and make the future.'[7]

This double action of remembrance and imagination sums up for me the ability of the *Georgics* to raise questions of the present as much as the past. The most famous part of the poem paints an idyllic picture of Italy, at a time when elite Italian agriculture was reliant on slave labour, and in the immediate aftermath of bitter civil conflict. The identity of Virgil's farmers might not be made clear in the poem, but that does not make the question any less pertinent.[8] Its cast of characters, though full of goddesses, nymphs and female animals, features almost no women, something which speaks to the marginalization of women's agricultural labour in European discourse from Rome to the present day.[9] And it imagines other peoples in exotic and often fantastic ways, at times equating difference with inferiority, with an otherness that is either threatening or supine.[10]

In Britain many landowners, politicians and imperial actors found in the *Georgics* a convenient mirror for their own concerns. Women in Britain did read Virgil in Latin and those who did often recorded their experience of doing so,[11] but that should not allow us to forget the extent to which discriminatory educational practice, in a patriarchal society, restricted women's access to Latin.[12] Virgilian scholarship has been, until very recently, overwhelmingly male. As has been well documented, the classical languages served as passports to a world of elite white male privilege,[13] and we should not underestimate just how fundamentally that world has shaped discourse about the *Georgics*, and thus our understanding of it. And while it is important to distinguish between the modern ideology of race and constructions of difference in ancient Roman contexts,[14] there are certain continuities in the history of European imperial power – among them 'the fierce colonial desire to divide and classify, to create hierarchies and produce difference'[15] – which are common to the Roman and British imperial contexts discussed here. To see the *Georgics* only as a beautiful masterpiece is to limit its educational potential.

Part One

Rome and the Roman Empire, 29 BCE

1

The World and Its Peoples

The *Georgics* presents the reader with a diverse picture of a world.[1] It does this through a series of toponyms and ethnonyms which name cities and peoples, mountains, rivers and lakes from throughout the *orbis terrarum*. The world is brought to the reader: Thule in the far north (according to Pytheas, some six days' sail north of Britain),[2] Iberia and the Balearic Islands, Egypt and the Nile as far south as ancient Ethiopia, Thrace and the Black Sea, Anatolia and the Levant, Iran and the Caucasus, Bactra (now the site of Balkh) in modern Afghanistan, the great river systems of South Asia, even the *Seres*, 'silk people', evoking what is now China. Unsurprisingly, Italy and Greece are the places most often alluded to, from the Cyclades to the Peloponnese and Macedonia, through the whole Italian Peninsula to the Alps. There are mythical or semi-mythical places like Thule and the islands of Panchaia; there is a magical hall of rivers and a journey to the underworld. Virgil's apparent inaccuracies – like putting the river Hydaspes in Media (*G.* 4. 211) and India as the source of the Nile (*G.* 4. 293) – can be considered poetic licence or geographical confusion; my focus here is on his geography's imaginative potential.

The poem's geography is intensely literary, and is bound up with the literature and history of the Greek and Roman worlds. Its dense network of allusion (or reference, or intertextuality)[3] is often presented in geographic terms: readers will find their own examples to match the ones mentioned here. So Virgil describes his poem as an *Ascraeum carmen* (*G.* 2. 176; an 'Ascraean song'), which denotes the town of Ascra on Mt Helicon in Boeotia and, by extension, the town's most famous resident, Hesiod. Mt Ida and Gargara may evoke for some readers the Homeric poems,[4] while the description of the sands of Libya in Book 2 may recall the same image in Catullus 7.[5] It has also been suggested that Virgil's *Medus Hydaspes* (*G.* 4. 211), referring to what is now the river Jhelum in Pakistan, is an allusion to a fragment of Posidippus, which begins: Ἰνδὸς Ὑδάσπης ('Indian Hydaspes').[6] A fragment of Eratosthenes' *Hermes*,[7] meanwhile, is echoed in Virgil's description of the heavenly zones:

> quinque tenent caelum zonae: quarum una corusco
> semper sole rubens et torrida semper ab igni;
> quam circum extremae dextra laeuaque trahuntur
> caeruleae, glacie concretae atque imbribus atris;
> has inter mediamque duae mortalibus aegris
> munere concessae diuum

G. 1. 233–8

Five bands occupy the sky: one of these is always red from the blazing sun and always scorched by its fire; around it on the left and right edges stretch two blue ones, hardened by ice and black showers; between these two and the middle zone are two which have been given to poor mortals by the gods' gift[8]

Moreover, the poem describes not just places but peoples: Scythians, Libyans, Indians, Iberians, Dacians, Britons and many Italian peoples, among others. In its sustained depictions of foreign peoples – particularly of the Scythians wintering out and of the Libyan herdsman in Book 3 – the influence of the ethnographic tradition in Greek and Latin literature can be detected, elucidated by Thomas.[9] As we shall see, such descriptions can be considered highly political if one places them in their proper historical contexts.

This literary geography reaches levels of considerable sophistication, with complex references as well as periphrases and apparent neologisms. When Virgil recounts his meeting with the old man from Corycus in Book 4 he names Tarentum by periphrasis: 'under the towers of an Oebalian citadel', referencing the Spartan king Oebalus and hence the Spartan origins of the town.[10] The phrase 'Cecropian bees' (*Cecropias . . . apes*: G. 4. 177) evokes the legendary King Cecrops of Athens and so means something like 'Attic' or 'Athenian' bees.[11] The ancient commentator Servius says that by the 'groves of Molorchus' (*G.* 3. 19) Virgil means Nemea, referencing the story of the poor host of Hercules and, by extension, Callimachus's *Aetia*, in which this story featured;[12] Gigante, meanwhile, has argued that the description of 'the shore close to Vesuvius's slope' (*uicina Vesaeuo / ora iugo*: G. 2. 224–5) is a periphrasis for Herculaneum.[13] 'The happy people of Pellaean Canopus' (*G.* 4. 287) relies on the reader's knowledge of Pella in Macedonia for the reference to the Ptolemies and Ptolemaic Egypt, and Ceres is referred to at *G.* 1. 163 in a two-word periphrasis as 'Eleusinian mother' (*Eleusinae matris*), recalling her religious role at Eleusis near Athens.

Two further examples highlight the complexity of this literary geography. The adjective *Narycius* (*G.* 2. 438) refers primarily to Narycum in Locris (*OLD* s.v.), but by extension connotes its colony of Locri Epizephyrii in the *ager Bruttius* (modern Calabria), Italy, whose groves Virgil names. This is one of five examples where the *Georgics* provides the first extant instance of a toponym or ethnonym in Latin, and while it cannot be said for certain whether these words are neologisms or merely our first references, this does point, I think, to the innovative nature of Virgil's picture of the world.[14] Arcadia is referred to eight times in the poem, twice by name and six times by a periphrasis. At a basic level it evokes the central Peloponnese and by extension Greece. For a reader of Virgil, ancient and modern, Arcadia may recall the *Eclogues*; for a modern reader, Arcadia can summon up the whole range and complexity of the pastoral tradition in Renaissance and modern poetry and art.[15] This particular example neatly points out how many layers of potential meaning a toponym can have for different readers, something relevant to the poem's literary geography as a whole.

Cultural appropriation

The *Georgics'* pervasive allusions to Greek and Latin literature often take a geographical form. But the poem's literary geography can also be taken to represent a process of cultural appropriation familiar to readers of Latin poetry, whereby a Latin poem offers a confident assertion of its mastery of Greek literature.[16] It is important to realize that behind this cultural appropriation lies Rome's political dominance of the Mediterranean, and, in particular, of the Greek world. The two processes are interrelated and interdependent. Polybius recognized Rome's swift rise to dominance over Greece in the second century BCE,[17] and Horace provided the most well-known, and ambivalent, commentary on the cultural aspect of Roman imperialism.[18]

At two moments in the *Georgics* this appropriation becomes strikingly visible. Firstly, in the poem's opening lines, Virgil invokes twelve deities from the Greek and Italian worlds, in a passage whose ostensible model is Varro's *De Re Rustica*.[19] Italian deities Liber, Silvanus and the *Fauni* appear alongside Minerva, Triptolemus, Neptune, Dryads and, in particular, Pan, who is called on to leave Arcadia and be present at the opening of the poet's song:

> ipse nemus linquens patrium saltusque Lycaei
> Pan, ouium custos, tua si tibi Maenala curae,
> adsis, o Tegeaee, fauens

G. 1. 16–18

> *As you yourself leave your native forest and the woodlands of Mt. Lycaeus, Pan the shepherd, if you care for your Maenalus, then come, o Tegean one, and be propitious*

For Virgil, Nelis and Nelis-Clément argue: 'Greece is a place of cultural origins, but it is also a part of the world ruled by Rome and it is a place in which the fate of Rome is played out.'[20] This act of translation from Greece to Italy foreshadows the opening to Book 3, the passage in which all Greece comes to the banks of the river Mincius at Mantua to witness the poet's procession, games and newly built temple:[21]

> cuncta mihi Alpheum linquens lucosque Molorchi
> cursibus et crudo decernet Graecia caestu

G. 3. 19–20

> *All Greece as it leaves the Alpheus and the groves of Molorchus will compete for me in foot races and rough boxing contests*

Wilkinson's analysis of this passage highlights the influence of Pindar and of the Roman triumph;[22] the green plain (*G.* 3. 13) is, Spencer notes, 'saturated in the civic Roman imagery of conquest and imperialism'.[23] The whole passage neatly highlights the political dominance which underlies Roman appropriation of Greek culture, in particular the use of the verb *deducere* in line 11, whose root meaning is 'to lead away' or 'to carry off', but which can be used both for taking captives to Rome for triumphal processions *and* for the act of writing poetry:[24]

primus ego in patriam mecum, modo uita supersit,
Aonio rediens deducam uertice Musas

G. 3. 10–11

I shall be the first, provided my life endures, to bring back the Muses with me as I return from Helicon's peak to my own land

We have seen that *lucos Molorchi* can refer to Nemea and can be taken as a reference to Callimachus's *Aetia*. A further geographical reference to the Cyrenean poet can perhaps be detected in the phrase *Cinyphii . . . hirci* at G. 3. 312. *Cinyphius* denotes the river Cinyps, the modern Wadi Ka'am in western Libya, which appears in a fragment of Callimachus's epinician poem for Sosibios.[25] There may also have been a town of the same name nearby.[26] What has been called 'Callimachus's aesthetics of learned elegance'[27] is perhaps what many readers will think of when considering the sophistication of the *Georgics'* literary geography, but it would be truer to say that the poem owes a great deal to the intellectual culture of the Hellenistic world more generally, to figures like Callimachus, Eratosthenes and Aratus. Nevertheless, Acosta-Hughes and Stephens note the structural and thematic similarities between the *Aetia* and the *Georgics*,[28] and how Callimachus can be seen to engage in an act of cultural translation similar to Virgil. The *Aetia's* 'Libya-centric geography', they argue, is a deliberate strategy, one which reorientates the Greek world towards Ptolemaic Alexandria, in order to reflect the fact that that city had superseded others as the political and cultural capital of the Greek world.[29] Virgil in the *Georgics* goes one step further in bringing that world to Italy and to Rome.

Peoples and places

Many of the peoples and places described in the *Georgics* are directly involved in the history of Roman imperialism, the 'extraordinary bellicosity'[30] of the Roman state as it came to dominate the Italian Peninsula and, in the decades following the Second Punic War, gained control of more and more of the Mediterranean world. The civil conflicts of the first century BCE did little to dampen this foreign aggression, which continued throughout Virgil's lifetime and the Principate.[31] So as well as appreciating the imaginative, aesthetic and literary qualities of Virgil's geography, we must also consider the relationship between empire and geographical knowledge – what it means for a Roman poet to describe places of Roman conquest and aggression in picturesque terms. One could see such literary portrayals as facilitating the power of the Roman state, as a confident assertion of its dominance. At the very least, one can see how, without proper knowledge of important historical contexts, the reader might fail to see how political many of the poem's descriptions are.

At *G.* 3. 24–5 an image of Britons (*Britanni*) appears at the poet's celebration by the Mincius, woven into the fabric of a stage curtain as it rises to cover the stage. The people described in *Eclogue* 1 as 'cut off from the whole world'[32] have been transported to the green plain, with its imagery of imperial conquest, in another example of the centripetal dynamic of the *Georgics'* literary geography. But there is a real political context here too. Octavian, Dio reports, planned an expedition to Britain on at least three occasions – 34, 27 and 26 – none of which went ahead.[33] These years are contemporary with the composition and completion of the *Georgics*, and Octavian's planned expeditions are but one part of a much longer history of Roman imperialism in Britain, beginning with Julius Caesar. Britain will become a centre of empire in later centuries, but in the *Georgics* the *Britanni* are very much imagined subjects of Roman power, their appearance on stage much more than an imaginative flourish. This reinforces the fact that the rhetoric of Roman imperialism under Octavian often outstripped its actual military activity. 'The regime', Gruen argues, 'persistently projected the impression of vigour, expansionism, triumph and dominance.'[34]

Thrace

One landscape which features prominently in the *Georgics* is Thrace, the area corresponding roughly to modern Bulgaria and southern Romania. Reference is made to the rivers Hebrus, Strymon and Hister (Danube), the mountain ranges of Rhodope and Haemus, wine from Mt Ismarus, the *Bisaltae* and the *Getae*. The whole Thracian landscape mourns Eurydice:

at chorus aequalis Dryadum clamore supremos
impleuit montis; flerunt Rhodopeiae arces
altaque Pangaea et Rhesi Mauortia tellus
atque Getae atque Hebrus et Actias Orithyia

G. 4. 460–3

But a chorus of Dryads, her companions, filled the mountain tops with a cry;
Rhodopeian peaks weep and high Pangaeum, the warlike land of Rhesus, the
Getae, the Hebrus, and Attic Orithyia

and is then one setting for Orpheus's final wanderings and death in the frozen
wilderness:

nulla Venus, non ulli animum flexere hymenaei:
solus Hyperboreas glacies Tanaimque niualem
aruaque Riphaeis numquam uiduata pruinis
lustrabat, raptam Eurydicen atque inrita Ditis
dona querens. spretae Ciconum quo munere matres
inter sacra deum nocturnique orgia Bacchi
discerptum latos iuuenem sparsere per agros.
tum quoque marmorea caput a ceruice reuulsum
gurgite cum medio portans Oeagrius Hebrus
uolueret, Eurydicen uox ipsa et frigida lingua,
a miseram Eurydicen! anima fugiente uocabat:
Eurydicen toto referebant flumine ripae.

G. 4. 516–27

No love nor any marriage interested him. Alone he used to cross the
Hyperborean ice and the snowy Don, and lands which are never without
Riphaean hoar frost, complaining of the theft of Eurydice and the useless gifts
of Dis. Offended by this behaviour, Ciconian women, during the rituals of the
gods and the nocturnal rites of Bacchus, scattered the young man's butchered
body across the broad fields. Even still, as the Oeagrian Hebrus bore along in
mid-stream a head severed from a marble-white neck, his very voice and cold
tongue, as their life ebbed away, were calling out 'Eurydice', 'oh poor Eurydice!',
and the banks all along the river's course echoed back 'Eurydice.'

These two passages are vivid and dramatic, with many literary and mythical
associations: Rhesus, the Thracian king killed by Diomedes in *Iliad* 10; Orithyia,
the daughter of Erechtheus, raped by Boreas and brought to Thrace; 'Hyperborean'
ice, referencing perhaps the mythical people who lived 'beyond the north wind'.[35]

Dexter has explored how the second passage quoted here relates to a fragment of the Alexandrian poet Phanocles;[36] nor should we expect a factual, scientific topography. But this depiction of a wild, cold and warlike land should be contrasted with Roman activity in the area in the late first century BCE.

The extant summaries to Livy's 135th and 140th books, covering the years 28–25 and 13–11 respectively, record campaigns in Thrace:

> Bellum a M. Crasso adversus Thracas et a Caesare adversus Hispanos gestum refertur, et Salassi, gens Alpina, perdomiti.[37]

> *The war waged against Thracians by Marcus Crassus and against Spaniards by Caesar is reported, and the subjugation of the Salassi, an Alpine people.*

> Thraces domiti a L. Pisone, item Cherusci Tencteri Chauci aliaeque Germanorum trans Rhenum gentes subactae a Druso referuntur.[38]

> *The subjugation of Thracians by Lucius Piso, and likewise the subjugation by Drusus of Cherusci, Tencteri, Chauci and other German peoples beyond the Rhine are reported.*

Such notices highlight the breadth of Roman military activity in these years. Marcus Licinius Crassus, the proconsul of Macedonia, spent 29–27 fighting the *Bastarnae*, a Scythian people who had crossed into Thrace, and was awarded a triumph 'over Thrace and the *Getae*' (*ex Thraecia et Geteis*) in 27.[39] Lucius Piso's suppression of rebellion in Thrace is recorded by Velleius Paterculus and by Dio.[40] In the years directly following the *Georgics'* appearance, then, Thrace remained an area in which people were actively resisting Roman rule. This is perhaps as much as can be said given the dearth of evidence, but it is an important observation nonetheless. The details of Velleius's and Dio's accounts hint at the brutality of Rome's treatment of rebellion, something we can all too easily gloss over when reading Roman accounts of Roman victories: huge loss of life, ravaged landscapes, enslaved captives. Virgil's depiction of the 'warlike land of Rhesus' can thus take on a highly political dimension.

North Africa

In Book 3 of the *Georgics* there is a description of North African desert life and a nomadic African herdsman, *armentarius Afer*:

Quid tibi pastores Libyae, quid pascua uersu
prosequar et raris habitata mapalia tectis?
saepe diem noctemque et totum ex ordine mensem
pascitur itque pecus longa in deserta sine ullis
hospitiis: tantum campi iacet. omnia secum
armentarius Afer agit, tectumque laremque
armaque Amyclaeumque canem Cressamque pharetram;
non secus ac patriis acer Romanus in armis
iniusto sub fasce uiam cum carpit, et hosti
ante exspectatum positis stat in agmine castris.

G. 3. 339–48

What need for me to tell you in verse of the shepherds and pastures of Libya, its settlements occupied by scattered huts? Often day and night the whole month through the herd grazes and travels in great deserts lacking any shelters: so far the plain extends. The African herdsman takes everything with him, his roof and his hearth, his weapons, his Amyclaean dog and his Cretan quiver – not unlike the fierce Roman carrying his nation's arms, when he moves along the road under an unfair burden, and having set up camp stands in the line before he is expected by the enemy.

This passage can be divided into three sections: a description of North African nomadism (vv. 339–43), a sketch of the herdsman (vv. 343–5) and a simile comparing him to a Roman soldier (vv. 346–8). The first section emphasizes the harshness of the environment. The herdsman is depicted as carrying all his possessions with him, including a Spartan hunting dog (from Amyclae in Laconia) and a Cretan quiver. While literary imagery does not require an explanation, these particular items are striking. 'Unseasonable reminiscences … the Numidian was not likely to be thus equipped', Conington commented.[41] Thomas suggests they are 'absurd it taken literally', but imply 'a moral strength which contrasts with the miserable conditions of Libya'.[42] And there may be an allusion to Nicander.[43]

I suggest another way of reading this passage is to think of it in terms of contemporary history. In particular, to read the lines with one eye on the imperial contexts of Rome's long involvement in North Africa, including the sack of Carthage in 146, the colonization plans of C. Gracchus, the wars with Jugurtha and Caesar's civil war campaigns in North Africa.[44] Five proconsuls were awarded triumphs *ex Africa* in the years 34–19, including the very last triumph recorded by the *Fasti Triumphales*, awarded to L. Cornelius Balbus against the Garamantes, a Berber people who appear in *Aeneid* 6.[45] Africa was also a vital economic resource for Rome: Cicero had called it one of the three pillars of the Roman grain supply,[46] while Julius Caesar was able to impose a tax of one million litres of olive oil on Tripolitania.[47]

North Africa, at the time of the *Georgics'* composition, had been a site of Roman imperialism for over a century. In a certain sense, these lines aestheticize an imperial location and an imperial subject. Libya is a land of endless desert, and the herdsman is given literary equipment. The otherness of Africa is rendered less strange by the poetic register of the epithets. The word *Lar*, used of the herdsman's hearth or fire, further assimilates him into the Roman world by connoting the *Lares*, the traditional household deities in Roman life – so one way of reading these lines is to see poetry echoing history. As indigenous North African history has been continually subsumed beneath the history of its colonizers (not just Roman, but Arab, French and Italian), so indigenous experience is depicted here in literary, and Roman, terms by a Roman poet writing for a Roman audience. It is this metropolitan perspective that makes life in North Africa seem so strange and inhospitable. The lines become an example of Roman poetry's relationship to Roman imperialism. As those five African triumphs were being awarded between 34 and 19, Virgil was writing the *Georgics* and the *Aeneid*, where, on the shield of Aeneas, Octavian is predicted to bring Roman *imperium* beyond the Garamantes and the Indians.[48]

That said, the poem allows for a further level of interpretation. The African herdsman is depicted in military terms. Far from a passive figure, he is like a Roman legionary on the march. This image can be seen as part of the Romanizing language just described, but it can also suggest the violence and militarism of the Roman presence in North Africa. This is a land where Roman armies do march, subjugating local peoples. Perhaps the poem itself, therefore, supplies a hint to the reader to consider the imperial context behind the life of the *armentarius Afer*, and the possibility of local resistance to Roman rule.

Iberia

In Book 3 the reader is also advised that guard dogs will ensure that one's property and livestock remain safe:

Nec tibi cura canum fuerit postrema, sed una
uelocis Spartae catulos acremque Molossum
pasce sero pingui. numquam custodibus illis
nocturnum stabulis furem incursusque luporum
aut impacatos a tergo horrebis Hiberos.

G. 3. 404–8

Don't let care for dogs be the least of your priorities, but feed the swift Spartan pups and the fierce Molossian together on fattening whey. With those dogs guarding your stalls you'll never tremble because of a thief in the night, or an attack of wolves or unsubdued Iberians at your back.

The inclusion of 'unsubdued Iberians' in this list of threats to the farm is striking. Most modern commentators (Conington, Page, Mynors, Thomas, Erren) quote Varro, who, in a discussion of things to be wary of in choosing the location of a farm, cites the 'brigandage of local people', of a kind he associates with Spain.[49] Page suggests the phrase gives 'a local colouring';[50] Thomas, that the *Hiberi* may simply be 'generic'.[51] For Richter, as for Fairclough, *Hiberos* is a straightforward equivalent to 'robber' or 'brigand'.[52]

Of interest is the explanation given by Servius's commentary in relation to the passage, both for its stereotyping and its confusion:

HIBEROS abactores; fere enim Hispani omnes acerrimi abactores sunt. et aliter: Hiberi gens in Ponto; sed magis de Hispanis intellegendum, quorum in latrociniis fama praeponderat.[53]

IBERIANS *cattle thieves; for almost all Spaniards are the most violent cattle thieves. Another interpretation: Iberians are a people in Pontus; but it is better to understand this as referring to Spaniards, who had more of a reputation for brigandage.*

The depiction of the *Hiberi* as thieves reflects, the Servian tradition suggests, historical fact. Taking *Hiberos* at G. 3. 408 as referring to the inhabitants of the Iberian Peninsula, it is worth imagining how the line might have struck the poem's first, elite Roman audience.[54] Were there those with property in Spain among its first readers or listeners? How would reference to the dangers to the colonial farm have been met by those in the imperial metropolis? We can't know, but it is worth considering that the inclusion of the *Hiberi* can be read as something other than a touch of poetic colour: however the reader judges the tone of the passage, its highly politicized nature becomes clear once contemporary imperial contexts are borne in mind. As in the example of the *armentarius Afer*, the hint to the reader to consider such contexts comes from the poem itself: the *Hiberi* are 'unsubdued', 'unpacified'.

This rebellious characterization cannot be understood without an awareness of the extraordinary history of resistance to Roman rule in the Iberian Peninsula, stretching from 218 and the beginning of the Second Punic War, through the second century and to, at least, the very end of the first century BCE.[55] This history is best exemplified by the town of Numantia (now Garray, near Soria), which was attacked repeatedly in the second century – perhaps by Cato in 195, by Q. Fulvius Nobilior (153), M. Claudius Marcellus (152), Q. Pompeius (140) and Hostilius Mancinus (137), before finally falling to Scipio Aemilianus.[56] The city's final defeat drew from Appian a eulogy for its citizens, who records that Scipio took fifty captives for his triumph, sold the rest and razed the city to the ground.[57]

In Virgil's time, too, Spain provoked Rome into action. Triumphs were awarded for victories in Spain in 36, 34, 33, 28 and 26.[58] The Cantabrian and Asturian War, against the peoples of north-western Spain whose names survive in two provinces of the Spanish state, prompted Octavian to reopen the doors of the Temple of Janus and proceed to Spain in order to personally direct the war there in 26.[59] Gruen highlights the propaganda value of the campaign, which formed the concluding part of Octavian's autobiography.[60] But Octavian's efforts did not pacify the region, and there were further rebellions in 24, 22, 19 and 16.[61] Of particular note are the actions of L. Aemilius, the governor of Spain, in response to further rebellion of the *Cantabri* and *Astures* immediately after Octavian had departed the province. Dio records that in revenge for the murder of Roman hostages, Aemilius pillaged the countryside, razed forts and cut off the hands of captives.[62] This history of Iberia in response to Roman rule is an extremely important context for the reader who comes across *impacati Hiberi* among the many dangers to the farm. It is occasionally noted by commentators, but is nowhere dwelt upon. Rather than following uncritically the metropolitan viewpoint preserved in the exegetical tradition, which associates the *Hiberi* primarily with cattle theft, the lines can instead prompt us to consider those who resisted, rather than those who exercised, Roman power in Europe.

Illyria

Then there is the setting of the plague in Book 3, where Virgil takes several lines to establish the areas affected and impress on the reader the gravity of the event:

> tum sciat, aërias Alpis et Norica si quis
> castella in tumulis et Iapydis arua Timaui
> nunc quoque post tanto uideat, desertaque regna
> pastorum et longe saltus lateque uacantis.
>
> G. 3. 474–7

Should anyone see even now, so long afterwards, the lofty Alps, the hilltop garrisons of Noricum and the fields by the Iapydian Timavus, the deserted kingdoms of shepherds and the woodlands empty far and wide, then they would know.

We are in the area of modern Trieste: the Alps and north-east Italy, southern Austria, Slovenia and north-west Croatia. As Foster notes, 'Virgil's plague may have owed more to Lucretius 6 than to unvarnished historical fact, but the hostility to Rome of the peoples in the area where it is set certainly is historical.'[63] At the time of the *Georgics'* composition, this area was not an inert and willing partner in Roman politics, and the historical record, slim as it may be, offers evidence of resistance to Roman rule. Again it is Appian who provides the relevant information: Octavian's campaigns against numerous peoples in Illyricum 35–33, for which he claimed the first of his three triumphs in 29,[64] as well as the resistance of the *Salassi* and the *Iapydes*.

> Those who gave him the most trouble were the *Salassi*, the transalpine *Iapydes*, the *Segestani*, the Dalmatians, the *Daesitiatae*, and the Pannonians, far distant from the *Salassi*, who occupy the higher Alpine mountains, difficult of access, the paths being narrow and hard to climb. For this reason they had not only preserved their independence, but had levied tolls on those who passed through their country.[65]

According to Appian (*Ill.* 52–3), the *Iapydes* repelled the Romans twice in twenty years, overran Aquileia (near modern Trieste) and attacked the Roman colony of Tergestus, before Octavian's army defeated them.

Iapydes do appear in the *Georgics* in connection with the river Timavus; not so the *Salassi*. Nevertheless, the *Salassi*'s Alpine homeland does, both in the lines quoted above and as one of the threats to a Rome weakened by civil war: 'the Alps shook with strange disturbances' (*G.* 1. 475).[66] They controlled the Little and Great St Bernard Passes in the western Alps and imposed tolls on travellers; they also worked local gold mines, which the Romans took over once the *Salassi* had been expelled from the area.[67] They were subject to three Roman campaigns in ten years, led by C. Antistius Vetus, by Messalla Corvinus and finally by Terentius Varro in 25, who imposed a tribute and sold captives into slavery.[68] The best of their land became the new foundation of Augusta Praetoria, now Aosta.[69] The Alps continued to resist, and occasioned the joint campaign of Tiberius and Drusus *c.* 15 against peoples in Raetia and Noricum:[70] eventual Roman dominance was emphatically advertised by a monument at what is now La Turbie, above Monte Carlo, set up *c.* 7, listing all the conquered tribes by name – a list recorded by Pliny the Elder.[71] So there is evidence that across the whole Alpine region there were people actively resisting Roman rule in the final decades of the first century BCE, something which provides historical context for the location of the plague described in the poem, and which introduces an ambiguity into the phrase *deserta regna pastorum*: ostensibly a countryside laid low by a devastating animal plague, but also, for the historically minded reader, evocative of the relentless progress of Roman imperialism, its targets, and histories of resistance which we can only glimpse.

The literary geography of the *Georgics* is multifaceted. It evokes the world, but also engages with a variety of influences from Greek and Latin literature. It is a confident act of translation, centring the Mediterranean world on Italy and, by extension, on Rome; this translation echoes and expresses the political shift which saw Rome become the major power in that world. But by appreciating this geography only for its literary or descriptive qualities, the reader can lose sight of important political contexts. On one level, the poem's descriptions serve to obscure, and so facilitate, the operation of Roman imperial power in the Mediterranean. We know barely anything about the peoples described above; our only information in most cases is that recorded from a Roman point of view. Yet on another level, those descriptions invite their own critique, mapping out not just the triumphalist history of Rome, but the places and peoples caught up in its wake.

2

Provincializing Rome

The growth of Roman power in the Mediterranean in the second and first centuries BCE had a profound impact on the Roman economy. Of the period 133–31, Nicolet writes of 'the establishment of a whole new map of production, consumption and exchange', as Rome's economic influence increased in concert with its political influence.[1] Harris identifies some salient features of this development, including the financial gains of foreign wars, the influx of vast amounts of tax revenue to Rome and the increased presence of Roman and Italian landowners in the provinces.[2] Without examining this complex process in detail, some of the evidence can nevertheless be highlighted.[3] This includes the abolition of the *tributum*, a direct tax on the land of Roman citizens, in 167 after the end of the Macedonian Wars,[4] the law of C. Gracchus which gave *publicani* the right to bid for contracts to collect the tax of the province of Asia,[5] evidence for the manufacture and export of Italian goods all over the Mediterranean – what Potter calls 'an extraordinary boom in the export market of later Republican Italy'[6] – as well as epigraphic evidence for the presence of Italian merchants at Alexandria and at Delos in the late second century.[7] Delos in the late second and early first century was a major hub for the Mediterranean slave trade, and a place where Italian businessmen were conspicuous and successful.[8] Rome's wars created an abundance of new slaves for this market and catered for the slave economy of Roman Italy.[9]

In tandem with this Mediterranean context, it should be borne in mind that Rome was part of a global network of trade, whose workings can only be faintly discerned.[10] It was apparently only in the late second century BCE that Ptolemaic Egypt gained knowledge of the monsoon winds, the winds which blow from the south-west across the Arabian Sea in summer and then from the north-east in winter, which allowed Greek ships to reach the west coast of

India and then return safely to Egypt.[11] By the late first century BCE, and after Rome's annexation of the Ptolemaic kingdom, Strabo reports that 120 ships were making the trip from Myos Hormos in Egypt to India.[12] This trading network, incorporating the east coast of Africa, the Arabian Sea and the coasts of Pakistan and India, is revealed by a document of the first century CE, the *Periplus Maris Erythraei*. This source, dating to between 40 and 70 CE, is a guide for traders, written by an Egyptian Greek, which gives information on ports and goods along the network just described, from Egypt to Sri Lanka and as far as the mouth of the Ganges. Casson notes the belatedness of Greek and Roman sailors' arrival into what was a centuries-old network of Indian Ocean trade, and that the *Periplus* alludes to a trade in commodities, not luxury goods, in which Roman traders played little part: in contrast to the Mediterranean, this was a world in which Rome was by no means the major player.[13]

As well as this ocean network, there was the trade over land between China and Europe, via Bactria, Parthia and Mesopotamia.[14] The impetus for this trade was the expansive foreign policy of Han China under Emperor Wu in the final two decades of the second century BCE. The Han court began sending delegations to Parthia, Rome, Mesopotamia and India along a network that included what became known as the Silk Road: from western China, along either side of the Tarim Basin, through central Asia, to Parthia and the Mediterranean.[15] And while most of the evidence we have for this system of global trade dates to the decades and centuries after the composition of the *Georgics*, late-Republican Rome was by no means isolated from this world. In fact, the *Georgics* evokes Asia and Asian trade on a number of occasions. For the moment, it is sufficient to note that, as Fitzpatrick argues,[16] the Roman economy should not be seen as residing within a hermetically sealed Mediterranean world, but rather as one part of a much larger Eurasian and African system of trade.

Products and produce

As part of the world it presents to the reader, the *Georgics* depicts a range of produce from across the *orbis terrarum*. While bearing in mind the literary and imaginative elements of this geography – taking into account, that is, Virgil's poetic licence – it can still be seen as reflective of Rome's relationship with the wider world, and, with the help of some context, as evocative of Roman economic imperialism. Many plants and products are associated with different places. There are ties for vines from Ameria in southern Etruria (*G.* 1. 265), oysters from Abydos at the entrance to the Hellespont (*G.* 1. 207), lentils from Pelusium[17] at the eastern edge of the Nile Delta (*G.* 1. 228) and slingshots from the Balearic Islands (*G.* 1. 309). There are olives from Mt Taburnus near Beneventum (*G.* 2. 38), pears from Crustumerium (north of Rome) and Syria[18] (*G.* 2. 88), boxwood from Mt Cytorus in Pontus (*G.* 2. 437), Jupiter's acorns from Chaonia in Epirus (*G.* 2. 67), myrtle from Paphos (*G.* 2. 64), Persian citrons to cure bad breath (*G.* 2. 126–35), timber from the Caucasus (*G.* 2. 440) and yew bows from Palestine (*G.* 2. 448). There is bronze from Corinth (*G.* 2. 464), dye from Assyria (*G.* 2. 465) and Tyre (*G.* 2. 506), as well as a catalogue of wines from Thasos, Lesbos and Rhodes in the Aegean, Egypt, Pontus and Italy (*G.* 2. 89–108). And there are palms from Idumaea in Judea (*G.* 3. 12), fleeces from Miletus (*G.* 3. 306, 4. 334) and marble from Paros (*G.* 3. 34).

Some of these toponyms have literary or cultural associations: Chaonian acorns and Paphian myrtle, for instance, recall the oracle of Jupiter at Dodona in Epirus and Venus respectively.[19] Others, like Ituraean bows and Idumean palms, have, as we shall we presently, political contexts. Something is known of the reputation of Corinthian bronzeware and Parian marble as luxury products in the Roman world,[20] while some of the items mentioned, like the wines, olives and pears, perhaps reflect real origins of produce consumed in Rome in the late first century. The *Georgics* can thus be said to map the world in economic terms, reflecting the economic aspect of Rome's rise to political pre-eminence in the Mediterranean. And given the historical contexts to be discussed here, it further demonstrates that, in terms of empire, politics and economics go hand in hand.

Arabian frankincense

On two occasions an extended passage explicitly references products and their places of origin. The first is at *G.* 1. 56–9:

nonne uides, croceos ut Tmolus odores,
India mittit ebur, molles sua tura Sabaei,
at Chalybes nudi ferrum uirosaque Pontus
castorea, Eliadum palmas Epiros equarum?

G. 1. 56–9

Don't you see how Tmolus exports fragrant saffron, India ivory, the soft Sabaeans their frankincense, but the naked Chalybes export iron, Pontus rank castor, and Epirus the palms for Elean mares?

These lines are used to illustrate regional variety, the fact that different places produce different crops. The instruction to look (*nonne uides*) is a familiar didactic trope found in Aratus and Lucretius,[21] but it is also a stimulus to the reader to engage with the poem's imaginative geography (smells, good and bad, heighten the sensory aspect of these lines). Literary and cultural references are discernible: the *Chalybes*, a people of the south-eastern coast of the Black Sea, appear in literature as archetypal forgers of iron;[22] the palms of Epirus are prizes for horses at Olympia in Elis.[23] Yet there are political connotations here too, some of which we can recover. India in contemporary Latin poetry and in the *Georgics* can evoke Alexander, and, as part of the hyperbolic rhetoric of Roman imperialism, the fiction of Octavian's world power, to be discussed in Chapter 3. For now it is sufficient to note the vagueness of the toponym, covering as it does a vast area and one associated primarily with luxury produce and trade.[24]

The latent politics of these lines are most clearly apparent in the case of the Sabaeans, the people of southern Arabia who were known to the Romans as producers of myrrh and frankincense. Pliny (*HN* 12. 51–65) describes the frankincense-producing district of the Sabaeans, Sariba, and describes the route the finished product took to reach the Mediterranean. In spite of Roman military operations in Arabia, however, the appearance of the plant which produced frankincense was still a mystery.[25] Pliny mentions explicitly only the invasion of C. Caesar, Octavian's grandson, in 1 CE, but in 26 Aelius Gallus had led a campaign from Egypt which besieged Mariba (modern Ma'rib, Yemen).[26] Cooley discusses the debate surrounding the motives of this campaign, which may well have been economic.[27] Within a few years of the *Georgics*' appearance, then, the homeland of the Sabaeans was directly attacked by a Roman army. In the poem they are soft (*molles*), a word which conjures up stereotypes with a long history in European depictions of Asia: weakness, effeminacy, passivity.[28] By juxtaposing this description with the subsequent Roman invasion, the cultural imperialism of Octavian's Rome becomes apparent: a people described as weak and passive in poetry are simultaneously a target for political control, and that control appears to have been motivated, at least in part, by economic considerations.

The Levant: balsam, bows, palms

In Book 2 the poem turns to the variety of trees in the world:

> aspice et extremis domitum cultoribus orbem
> Eoasque domos Arabum pictosque Gelonos:
> diuisae arboribus patriae. sola India nigrum
> fert hebenum, solis est turea uirga Sabaeis.
> quid tibi odorato referam sudantia ligno
> balsamaque et bacas semper frondentis acanthi?
> quid nemora Aethiopum molli canentia lana,
> uelleraque ut foliis depectant tenuia Seres?

G. 2. 114–21

Look too at the world conquered by far-off farmers, the eastern homes of Arabs and the painted Geloni: countries differ in their trees. Only India yields black ebony, the sprig of frankincense is the Sabaeans' alone. What need for me to tell you of balsam oozing from fragrant wood, and the fruit of the ever-flowering acanthus? Or the woods of the Ethiopians, white with soft wool, and how the Seres comb soft fleeces from leaves?

The first thing to note is the geographic range of these lines: Scythia, Arabia, India, Ethiopia, China. There are several continuities with the first example. The emphasis on sight (*aspice*) kindles the reader's geographic imagination, as do the descriptions of foreign peoples. There are also literary models to be borne in mind, particularly in the description, immediately following these lines, of Persian citron trees and their fruit, indebted to Theophrastus.[29] But taking a hint from line 114, with its instruction to look at a conquered world, my focus is again on some instructive political contexts.

Virgil cites India as the sole producer of ebony (*hebenum*), something which Pliny says (*HN* 12. 20) was first seen in Rome at the triumph of Pompey in 61.

Balsam, we learn, was native only to a small area of Judea near Jericho.[30] What is more, Pliny describes the plant in explicitly political terms. During the First Jewish Revolt (66–70 CE), Jews sabotaged balsam plantations in resistance to Roman rule; now (i.e. when Pliny was writing) the plant is a subject of Rome, just like the Jewish population in Judea:

> ostendere arborum hanc urbi Imperatores Vespasiani, clarumque dictu, a Pompeio Magno in triumpho arbores quoque duximus. servit nunc haec ac tributa pendit cum sua gente . . . saeviere in eam Iudaei sicut in vitam quoque suam; contra defendere Romani et dimicatum pro frutice est; seritque nunc eum fiscus, nec umquam fuit numerosior.[31]

> *Vespasian and Titus showed this tree to the City and, famously, since the triumph of Pompey we have also led trees in triumph. Now it is a subject and pays levies along with its people . . . The Jews vented their rage upon it as they did against their own life; but the Romans defended it, and there was fighting over a plant. Now the Treasury cultivates it, and it has never been more abundant.*

Pliny gives further information on what seems to have been an economic benefit resulting from Rome's (re)conquest of Judea between 66 and 70: within five years of the conquest, balsam shoots sold for 800,000 sesterces.[32] And there are further contexts to be added, from the decades preceding the composition of the *Georgics*: Pompey stopping in the balsam-producing area of Judea before the capture of Jerusalem in 63,[33] and Crassus's stripping of the gold from the temple in advance of his Parthian expedition.[34] Balsam, as a luxury product associated very specifically with Judea, thus has very political connotations, and can summon up a long history of Roman brutality in the region.

Two further toponyms heighten these political connotations. The Ituraeans were Bedouin Arabs who fought with Caesar in North Africa and provided the bodyguard of archers which protected Antony in Rome in 43, described in Cicero's attack as 'the most barbaric of all peoples'.[35] And it is archery with which the Ituraeans are associated in the *Georgics*, when its discussion of different timbers describes yew trees bent into Ituraean bows (*G.* 2. 448). But again, a stereotypical literary depiction can be related to a near-contemporary political campaign, in that there is also epigraphic evidence for the suppression of the Ituraeans in 6 CE.[36] Palms from Idumaea in southern Judea – Pliny notes the fame of Judean palms[37] – recall the birthplace of Herod (*c.* 73–4), who had supported Antony, but who, after Actium, met and was reconciled with Octavian at Rhodes.[38] Octavian was returning from Egypt to Italy for the first time since the battle, and on his return Virgil is said to have read him the poem at Atella – all of which gives *Idumaeas palmas* (*G.* 3. 12) an acute contemporary relevance. The appearance of these palms amid the triumphal imagery which opens *Georgics* 3 can perhaps be seen to evoke this settlement as another aspect of Octavian's comprehensive victory, especially when it is noted that the dedication of a palm is part of the triumphal formula found on the *Fasti Barberini*.[39] Thus the political connotations of the poem's Judean topography would also have been clear, I think, to its first readers, indicative not so much of long-term Roman foreign policy as of a very recent and controversial political settlement after bitter civil conflict.

Ethiopian wool, Chinese silk

Ethiopia in ancient Greek and Roman geography implied (as best we can tell) not modern Ethiopia, but rather the area of the upper Nile in what is now northern Sudan. As early as the *Odyssey*, it is a land characterized by its remoteness.[40] The *Georgics* tells of its 'woods white with soft wool', which is to say, its cotton plants, noted also by Pliny (*HN* 13. 90). Does this imply that Ethiopian cotton was to be found in late-Republican Italy? We cannot say, but the poem invites such speculation. And this descriptive picture of the Ethiopians' cotton groves can again be contrasted with political reality. A trilingual *stele* or monument set up by Cornelius Gallus in 29 proclaims his defeat of rebellions in the Nile Delta and in the Thebaid, his unprecedented progress upriver and his reception of ambassadors from Ethiopia.[41] In 25 P. Petronius suppressed an Ethiopian revolt, attacked and captured the royal residence of Napata and sent one thousand prisoners to Octavian in Rome.[42] So in the years after the *Georgics*' composition, Ethiopia was not just a picturesque and far-off destination, but a site of Roman military action.

The most remote ethnonym in the *Georgics* is *Seres*, a derivation from the Chinese *suu*, meaning 'silk people'.[43] The silk trade from China to Europe seems to have begun in earnest only upon the initiative of the Han court at the end of the second century BCE. It was in the 30s BCE that silk first began to appear in

Roman literature: *Seres* is first here (*G.* 2. 121), but Horace in the *Epodes* writes of silk cushions, and there are later instances in the *Odes*, in Propertius and in Ovid.[44] It has been argued that *Seres* must refer not to Chinese, but to intermediary peoples or traders along the Silk Road.[45] Whatever the knowledge of China in Rome in the 30s (and it may well have been greater than we can tell), *Seres* is an inherently imaginative word, which seems to me to suggest the makers, rather than the traders, of silk. This is reinforced by the poem's imagining of the process of silk production as one of combing from trees. The *Seres* thus evoke the most remote place in the *Georgics*' geography, a people at the furthest extremes of the *orbis terrarum* who provide a unique product to Rome. Unlike Arabia, Judea and Ethiopia, eastern Asia was far beyond the range of Roman military intervention; unlike southern Asia, eastern Asia did not have associations with Alexander. The *Seres* and their unique product, rather, evoke the location in the *Georgics* farthest from Rome – a useful reminder of the limits of Roman imperialism, and of Rome's place within a larger world beyond the Mediterranean.

Triumphal geography

The *Georgics*, then, has an economic geography. On two occasions, when the poem considers regional variation of crops and trees, this economic geography comes into particular focus. The visual emphasis in both passages, coupled with the political contexts discernible for some of the items, suggests an analogous process. The Roman triumph brought people, products and even geography to the city, allowing spectators to see the world and Rome's dominant position within it. Beard writes of the triumph as 'a microcosm of the very processes of imperial expansion',[46] while Murphy highlights its 'imperial geography'.[47] The *Georgics* brings the peoples and products of the world to the reader in a way which asserts a confident, Rome-centric worldview. The triumph appears in the poem at *G.* 1. 504 and at 2. 148, when sacrificial animals bathed in the river Clitumnus are pictured at the head of a triumphal procession. But the opening of Book 3 is also full of triumphal imagery: in what is perhaps the most imperialistic moment in the poem, Rome's abject and defeated enemies appear on the temple doors (*G.* 3. 26–33). Ebony (*G.* 2. 117) can recall the triumph of Pompey, when trees appeared in a triumphal procession for the first time;[48] Idumean palms (*G.* 3. 12) and balsam (*G.* 2. 118–19) recall the brutality of Roman imperialism in Judea, most famously represented by the reliefs on the Arch of Titus: Jewish captives, their holy objects and even the river Jordan brought in humiliation to Rome.[49]

This geographic aspect of the triumph is echoed by the *Georgics'* depiction of defeated or resistive rivers and mountains: Mt Niphates in Armenia (*G.* 3. 30), the flooded Nile (*G.* 3. 28–9) and the Euphrates, along which Octavian thunders at the poem's end (*G.* 4. 561).[50] One can think back to *G.* 2. 114, when the reader is asked to look at a conquered world. Whereas the *Georgics* only imagines Rome's defeated global enemies, the triumph had historically brought them to the heart of the city. Dacians, who appear threateningly crossing the Danube at *G.* 2. 497, fought in mass combat in Rome in 29, the year in which it is assumed the *Georgics* was completed.[51] One can perhaps imagine the first Roman readers of the *Georgics* reading of this Dacian threat and then going to view Dacian prisoners fighting in the city.

Provincializing Rome

There is a tension in the *Georgics* between its explicit didactic theme – the harsh rural life of 'unskilled country people' (*G.* 1. 41) – and the range of often exotic produce it describes from across the world, between the small-scale life of the farmer and a vast international network of trade. The poem makes such tension explicit at certain points, in particular at the end of Book 2, where luxurious modernity is contrasted with the blessings of country life. Yet any sense of the condemnation of luxury that might be detected there can be contrasted with the very cosmopolitan world which is continually evoked in the poem. As Geue has argued, the *Georgics* can be read as dramatizing a very particular economic moment, when, with the annexation of Ptolemaic Egypt, the Roman imperial economy kicked into a higher gear and its elite reaped the rewards; this is a poem directed not so much at labourers or even at the supervisors of labour, but at absentee proto-capitalists, ruthless extractors of value in a system based on slavery and imperial expropriation, one 'where many are forced to work for few, while those few do not have to work at all'.[52]

The poem's economic geography on one level fits well with this view, dramatizing as it does the implication of economics and empire, mapping a whole network of products and produce now known in, available in or for the imperial centre, and backed by expansive political influence. But I don't think that is the only thing it does. Read in conjunction with a text like the *Periplus Maris Erythraei*, its imagining of Persian citron trees, Indian ebony and Chinese silk is not prescriptive. Rather, it highlights the fact that Rome was only ever one part of a wider, more complex world of trade and exchange, regardless of what Roman hyperbole, or indeed Latin poetry, claimed. The challenge is, in the words of Fitzpatrick's 2011 article, to try to provincialize Rome, to see it not on its own inflated terms, but in proper and reduced perspective. And that seems to me to be a first step in any decolonizing approach to Latin literature. Given that the symbiotic relationship between capital and empire remains one of the most fundamental factors shaping a globalized twenty-first-century world, it also makes the *Georgics* a very contemporary poem.

3

Civil War

It is in the early first century that evidence begins to appear for the imagining of Roman power in universal terms, as being commensurate with the *orbis terrarum*.[1] It appears first in the *Rhetorica ad Herennium*, is present in Cicero's speeches and becomes prominent in the poetry of the late first century BCE.[2] The globe appears on Roman coins of that period,[3] and in statues like the male nude now at the Palazzo Spada in Rome. This figure, which has long been thought to represent Pompey, stands beside a palm trunk and holds a globe in its outstretched hand.[4] This idea that Rome's power embraced the entire inhabited world had, by Octavian's time, become what Vogt calls 'a firm component of national identity', at least for the Roman elite, something traceable in Livy and in Ovid, and in the *Aeneid*'s image of 'empire without end' (*imperium sine fine*).[5]

One precedent for such universal power was the campaigns of Alexander, who three hundred years earlier had conquered the *orbis terrarum* and reached Punjab. As Green notes, imitation of Alexander is more easily assumed than proven, and he was by no means an unproblematic model for Roman generals.[6] Nevertheless, it seems clear that Pompey cultivated the comparison.[7] The only evidence for Caesar's thoughts on Alexander is the story of his melancholy reflection on seeing the Macedonian's statue at Cadiz: while Green is sceptical as to Caesar's conscious imitation of Alexander, Krebs argues that Alexander and Pompey are models to be outdone in Caesar's own account of his campaigns in Gaul.[8] Here it is important that Octavian does seem, as Antony had before him,[9] to have cultivated comparison with the Macedonian general. There is circumstantial evidence, like Octavian's private seal bearing Alexander's image or the paintings of Alexander placed in the *Forum Augustum*, as well as Octavian's enormous mausoleum, which Nicolet argues was designed in conscious imitation of Alexander.[10]

Where the comparison seems clear, however, and where it links with the idea of universal Roman power, is in the *Res Gestae Diui Augusti*, Octavian's record of his political career. The Latin text begins with an explicit notice, that these are deeds 'by which the world was subjected to the power of the Roman people'.[11] The text is also full of geography: fifty-five toponyms and ethnonyms particularly prominent in Chapters 26–33, chapters 'liberally sprinkled with the exotic names of places and persons, calculated to inspire awe and to evoke the ends of the earth'.[12] 'The *Res Gestae*', writes Nicolet, 'asserts from the very first line that there was Roman control of the inhabited world (*orbis terrarum*). And it proves this methodically, without symbolism, by using a series of topographic lists that correspond to precise geographical knowledge.'[13] Certain parts of the *Res Gestae* can be seen, Cooley argues, to evoke the achievements of Alexander: Octavian's claim to have conquered from Cadiz to the Elbe (*RG* 26. 2), his restoration of artworks to Asia Minor (*RG* 24. 1) and his reception of ambassadors from India while at Tarraco (now Tarragona), Spain (*RG* 31. 1).[14] India, in particular, is a toponym which may have evoked the achievements of Alexander, and the imagined (if not actual) subservience of the most remote peoples of the *orbis terrarum* to Roman rule.

In the *Georgics* there can be traced both a universal conception of Roman power and an implicit comparison between Octavian and Alexander. At the beginning of the poem, Octavian is portrayed as ruler, not just of the *orbis terrarum*, but of the whole natural world:

> tuque adeo, quem mox quae sint habitura deorum
> concilia incertum est, urbisne inuisere, Caesar,
> terrarumque uelis curam, et te maximus orbis
> auctorem frugum tempestatumque potentem
> accipiat cingens materna tempora myrto;
> an deus immensi uenias maris ac tua nautae
> numina sola colant, tibi seruiat ultima Thule,
> teque sibi generum Tethys emat omnibus undis

G. 1. 24–31

And you too, Caesar, since it is unclear in what role the gods are soon going to receive you, whether you want care of the earth and to watch over the cities, and the great world accepts you as augmenter of crops and lord of the seasons, ringing your brow with your mother's myrtle; or whether you come as god of the immense ocean and sailors worship your divinity alone, farthest Thule obeys you, and Tethys buys you for her son-in-law with all the waves[15]

In these complex lines, Octavian is imagined deciding as to the realm of his power: whether he will rule the land or the sea or (in lines not quoted here) whether he will become a star in the sky. In lines 26–7 it is the entire world (*maximus orbis*) which may accept him as controller of agriculture and of the seasons: it is a strikingly capacious conception of his power, and one which matches the poet's theme. In the lines which imagine Octavian's marine power, 'farthest Thule' is his subject, a semi-mythical toponym connoting the very north-west of Europe, a place reported by Pytheas,[16] whose location is unclear. The poem thus imagines one man's power as straining at the very limits of the known world.[17]

Harrison suggests that the opening lines of the *laudes Italiae* (*G*. 2. 136–8) echo Alexander's career.[18] India, as we shall see presently, is a prominent location in the poem, not least in the image of the defeated *Gangaridae* on the doors of the temple in the proem to Book 3. Furthermore there are two references to the conquest of Asia and its people,[19] as well as the lines which imagine Octavian in the east:

> et te, maxime Caesar,
> qui nunc extremis Asiae iam uictor in oris
> imbellem auertis Romanis arcibus Indum.
>
> G. 2. 170–2

And you, Caesar, greatest of all, who now turn back from the hills of Rome the unwarlike Indian, a victor on the farthest shores of Asia.

This hyperbolic image can be seen to be part of the rhetoric of Octavian's Actian victory, as Rome's universal ruler went no further east than Egypt and Syria.[20] The poem imagines what in reality did not occur: Octavian's progress to India in emulation of Alexander.

This can also be seen in the poem's final lines, with their martial image of Octavian on the Euphrates, dispensing Roman rule to willing subjects. Note that Octavian is here given the epithet *magnus*, which Catullus gave to Octavian's adoptive father, which Pompey adopted and which Plautus first gave in Latin to Alexander:[21]

Haec super aruorum cultu pecorumque canebam
et super arboribus, Caesar dum magnus ad altum
fulminat Euphraten bello uictorque uolentis
per populos dat iura uiamque adfectat Olympo.

G. 4. 559–62

These things I was singing about the care of fields and livestock and trees, while
great Caesar thundered by the deep Euphrates, and, a victor in war, gave laws
to suppliant peoples, and sought a path to Olympus.

The geography of the *Georgics* thus imagines Roman power in universal terms
and can, furthermore, be seen to construct an implicit comparison between
Octavian and Alexander. This is the poem's geography at its most hyperbolic
and imperial. However, to see how this picture of the world is threatened and
then, paradoxically, brought to its fullest extent, we need to examine the
Georgics' geography of civil war.

The geography of civil war

The end of *Georgics* 1 contains a famous depiction of the evils of civil war, as
Virgil's discourse on weather signs shifts into a history of recent conflict. Some
future farmer is imagined unearthing the bones of dead combatants (*G. 1.*
493–7). In stark contrast to the confident imperial rhetoric just discussed, the
Roman world is under threat from external enemies – Parthia to the east and
Germany to the north[22] – as war seems to embrace the entire *orbis terrarum*:

hinc mouet Euphrates, illinc Germania bellum;
uicinae ruptis inter se legibus urbes
arma ferunt; saeuit toto Mars impius orbe

G. 1. 509–11

From here the Euphrates, from there Germany incites war; neighbouring cities
take up arms, their treaties broken; unholy Mars rages across the entire world

It is a famous passage, and yet one not without irony. During the decades of
civil conflict, Rome was never existentially threatened by foreign enemies. As
outlined in Chapter 1, its foreign campaigns continued unabated, and many of
the peoples perceived in the poem as threats – Alpine peoples, Dacians,

Iberians – were defeated. One has to contrast the anxiety of *G.* 1. 489–514 with the confident assertions of imperial power elsewhere in the poem. When the doors of the Temple of Janus were closed in January 29, in a very public demonstration of the end of war, Dio notes that many foreign wars were still ongoing (the doors were open again before long, to mark the renewal of wars in Spain).[23] We have to consider, that is, the narrow metropolitan viewpoint of these lines, and compare the evidence for contemporary resistance to Roman rule in Europe. One of the central ironies of the poem is that while war is a cause for horror, it is also a cause for triumphal celebration, over both civil and foreign enemies.

At the end of Book 1 Virgil references two major battles in the civil wars: Pharsalus, fought in 48 between the forces of Julius Caesar and Pompey, and Philippi, fought in 42 between the forces of Brutus and Cassius, Caesar's killers, and Octavian and Antony, his avengers. The former battle took place in Thessaly in central Greece, the latter in Thrace (what is now north-eastern Greece). Virgil appears to have conflated the two locations:[24]

> ergo inter sese paribus concurrere telis
> Romanas acies iterum uidere Philippi;
> nec fuit indignum superis bis sanguine nostro
> Emathiam et latos Haemi pinguescere campos.

G. 1. 489–92

And so Philippi for a second time saw Roman armies matched in strength do battle with each other; nor did it seem shameful to the gods to enrich for a second time Emathia and the broad plains of Haemus with our blood.

The first readers of the *Georgics*, many of whom may have been veterans of either conflict, find Pharsalus and Philippi included in the poem's geography. Further locations can also evoke the battles: the river Enipeus (*G.* 4. 368), for example, which ran along the site of Pharsalus, or the river Strymon (*G.* 1. 120, 4. 508), some forty-five miles west of the battlefield at Philippi.[25] Thrace is thus not merely the scene for Orpheus's final wanderings, but also the site of a climactic moment of civil war. A reference to the wine of the island of Thasos (*G.* 2. 91), meanwhile, may have evoked the part played by that island in the Philippi campaign, as both the store depot for Brutus and Cassius's army and the first point of escape for defeated survivors.[26]

Other locations include those affected by the land distributions agreed by the triumvirs at Bononia in 43 and put into effect after the victory at Philippi. Capua (*G.* 2. 224) was one of the eighteen towns included for settlement,[27] and while Mantua was not, it suffered by its proximity to Cremona: 'such land as unhappy Mantua lost'.[28] In Book 2 there are lines which describe Agrippa's engineering works at the Lucrine Lake, works designed to provide safe anchorage while a new fleet was built for Octavian in the fight against Sextus Pompeius, defeated by Agrippa off Naulochus in 36:[29]

> an memorem portus Lucrinoque addita claustra
> atque indignatum magnis stridoribus aequor,
> Iulia qua ponto longe sonat unda refuso
> Tyrrhenusque fretis immittitur aestus Auernis?
>
> G. 2. 161–4

Or should I recall the ports and the barriers added to the Lucrine Lake, and the sea raging with great crashes, where a Julian lake shut off from the ocean resounds far and wide, and the Tyrrhenian tide is directed into the channels of Lake Avernus?

The geography of the *Georgics* includes, therefore, locations which were closely associated with the civil conflicts between 49 and 31. Because of the fleeting nature of such references, they are non-prescriptive, a kind of ambivalent geographic register of recent national history which could evoke, for the poem's first readers, all sides of the conflicts. Most of all, they serve to highlight that the *Georgics* is a post-war poem, and thus cannot simply be a poem which celebrates peace. Rather, Octavian's reported burning of documents related to the civil wars[30] should remind us of the tensions inherent in any post-war society, of the competing narratives of the victorious and the defeated. In this light, the *Georgics'* themes of land and homeland seem all the more audacious.

India

The culmination of the civil wars at Actium in 31, and the role that battle went on to play in the ideology of Octavian's political power, lead to two further, complex locations. South Asia is evoked eight times in the poem, and I again note the generalization inherent in a toponym like 'India', which then, as now, refers to a large geographical area full of many diverse languages and cultures.[31] The river Hydaspes appears at *G.* 4. 211 but is called a Median, not an Indian river. It is the modern Jhelum in Pakistan, which Alexander's army crossed in 326.[32] The words 'India' or 'Indian' occur six times in the poem, in ways which reveal the biases of representation. In one sense, images like the one of trees in Indian forests higher than the range of an arrow shot (*G.* 2. 122–4) highlight the imaginative aspect of the poem's geography, well captured by Steinmayer.[33]

But India is also a remote and exotic place, a source of ivory and ebony, its people described in terms of skin colour, climate and perceived passivity.[34] This description of India and Indians is, as Thomas shows, part of an ancient Greek and Roman tradition of ethnographical writing, which described foreign peoples and places according to a standard set of geographical and ethnological features.[35] To my mind, however, all ethnography is in some sense political, especially when the place described is imagined in the poem, however vaguely, as being subject to Roman power. Skin colour appears, at times, to have played a role in Roman writers' construction of difference, important as it is to distinguish between those constructions and the modern ideology of race.[36] Indians in the *Georgics* are both 'unwarlike' and 'coloured', and the question for readers is to what extent this is, if not racist language, then, to use Isaac's formulation, 'proto-racist' language.[37] In any case, the poem's depictions of a people in supine terms make for an interesting case study in pre-modern constructions of difference. They can be related to the much more aggressive othering that is found in the *Aeneid*, in contemporary Latin poetry's descriptions of Cleopatra and, before both of those instances, on the temple doors in *Georgics* 3.[38]

The most complex Indian ethnonym in the poem is *Gangaridae*, a people (or peoples) who appear on the temple doors:

> in foribus pugnam ex auro solidoque elephanto
> Gangaridum faciam uictorisque arma Quirini

G. 3. 26–7

> *On the doors I shall fashion from gold and solid ivory the battle of the*
> *Gangaridae and the arms of victorious Quirinus*

At this point I should note that Pieri has questioned the prevailing interpretation of these lines, which takes *Gangaridum* with *pugnam*, and which is reflected in my translation above; she instead argues that *Gangaridum* should be read with *ex auro solidoque elephanto*, giving not 'the battle of the *Gangaridae*', but a depiction of the battle of Actium (*pugnam*) made 'from the gold and solid ivory of the *Gangaridae*'.[39] I want to incorporate this reading alongside – not in place of, given that the lines admit both interpretations – the one followed here. Taken in Pieri's sense, it is the economic aspect of the *Gangaridae* which features, their land a place of ivory and gold, and those commodities, by incorporation on the temple doors, implicitly within Rome's reach.

Gangaridae evoke the story of Alexander, who was forced to turn back at the Hyphasis River (the modern Beas in northern India) in 326. Three sources – Diodorus, Curtius Rufus and Plutarch – say that Alexander heard of two peoples beyond the river Ganges, one of whom are the *Gangaridae*.[40] Pliny (*HN*. 6. 66) stresses the size – and the elephants – of the *Gangaridae* army which Alexander would have had to face. Diodorus in Book 2 says that this people had never been conquered, and that when Alexander heard they had 4,000 elephants he gave up his campaign against them. In Book 17 he says something different: that Alexander wanted to lead his men against the *Gangaridae*, but they refused.[41] Bosworth regards any suggestion that Alexander planned to reach the Ganges as pure fiction, but it is important to note that this did become part of the Alexander legend.[42]

Pliny and Ptolemy locate the *Gangaridae* on the lower course of the river Ganges, in what is today Bengal and Bangladesh.[43] And it should be said that Roman knowledge of the Bay of Bengal did exist. Strabo's account of India dates from the last decades of the first century BCE, and he notes that some merchants did travel from Egypt as far as the Ganges,[44] while the *Periplus Maris Erythraei* reports information as far as the Ganges' delta. To add to the confusion, the word is similar to two other toponyms: *Gandaris* in Punjab and *Gandaritis* or *Gandhara* in modern-day Pakistan.[45] This latter region appears in Achaemenid sources, was home to a flourishing Buddhist tradition and gave its name to a famous artistic tradition.[46] Most of the relevant manuscripts give *Gandaridae* (two *d*s) rather than *Gangaridae*, and Kiessling suggests that *Gandaridae* became *Gangaridae* by an easy association with the great river.[47] So, the first thing to note is that the meaning of this word, and any historical people(s) behind it, are very unclear to us.

What are *Gangaridae* doing in the *Georgics*? Apart from Valerius Flaccus's *Argonautica*,[48] the word occurs only here in Latin poetry. One option is to see them as part of the hyperbolic rhetoric of Actium, where Octavian is seen to save Rome from the Eastern forces of Antony and Cleopatra, as part of an attempt to cast a civil conflict as a war against vague and effeminate (yet threatening) oriental forces.[49] This is something which reaches fever pitch in the eighth book of the *Aeneid* and which inspired, as David Quint shows, a whole tradition in later European epic.[50] Syme put it like this:

> The official Roman version of the cause of the War of Actium is quite simple, consistent, and suspect – a just war, fought in defence of freedom and peace against a foreign enemy: a degenerate Roman was striving to subvert the liberties of the Roman People, to subjugate Italy and the West under the rule of an oriental queen. An expedient and salutary belief. Octavianus was in reality the aggressor, his war was preceded by a *coup d'état*: Antonius had the consuls and the constitution on his side. It was therefore necessary to demonstrate that Antonius was 'morally' in the wrong and 'morally' the aggressor.[51]

Another option is to see them as evoking Alexander and, implicitly, as portraying Octavian in Alexander-like terms. In Diodorus's version of the story, remember, which is roughly contemporary with the *Georgics*, the *Gangaridae* intimidate Alexander and his men: in the *Georgics* they are added to the list of Octavian's conquests.[52] It is possible that Virgil is referring to a specific and well-defined people, known to him but not to us. Yet leaving aside attempts at clear identification, we can note the rhetorical aspect of this people's appearance in the *Georgics*. They are the epitome of foreignness and of the threat of the 'East', the most exotic of the peoples against whom Octavian defends Rome. The doors of the temple (made partly from ivory) prefigure the triple triumph of *Aeneid* 8, where the conquered peoples of the world are led in triumph through the streets of Rome.[53] Both moments stand at the head of a long European tradition of ignorance and speculation about the 'East', and indeed about most of the world beyond Europe, a tradition which has often gone hand in hand with imperial violence and exploitation.[54]

Egypt

Egyptian peoples and places occur eight times in the poem. There are vines from the Maerotic Lake on Alexandria's southern edge (*G.* 2. 91), lentils from

Pelusium at the easternmost point of the Nile delta (*G.* 1. 228) and a Callimachean theme among those deemed clichéd at the start of Book 3: the altars of Busiris (*G.* 3. 5: *Busiridis aras*).[55] The most concentrated reference to Egypt is in Book 4, where it is the setting for bugonia, the strange ritual whereby Aristaeus's bees are regenerated from the carcass of a bull:

> nam qua Pellaei gens fortunata Canopi
> accolit effuso stagnantem flumine Nilum
> et circum pictis uehitur sua rura phaselis,
> quaque pharetratae uicinia Persidis urget, 　　　290
> et diuersa ruens septem discurrit in ora 　　　292
> usque coloratis amnis deuexus ab Indis, 　　　293
> et uiridem Aegyptum nigra fecundat harena, 　　　291
> omnis in hac certam regio iacit arte salutem.

G. 4. 287–94[56]

For where the fortunate people of Pellean Canopus live by the pools of the flooded Nile, and are carried round their fields in painted boats, and where the proximity of the quivered Persian threatens, and the Nile, having made its way down from the coloured Indians, runs into seven different channels and, as it hurries along, makes green Egypt fertile with its black silt: the whole region puts its sure safety in this art.

These are picturesque lines, full of colour and geography, as the reader imagines boatmen on the flooded Nile. And yet such vivid description does not mention, and can obscure for the modern reader, the fact that Egypt had, since August 30 and the suicide of Antony and Cleopatra, been annexed by Octavian and was to remain under his personal control.[57] The third of Octavian's three triumphs in 29 was dedicated to this Egyptian victory, as Cleopatra's children were paraded, alongside an effigy of their mother, through the streets of Rome.[58] Coins proclaimed the conquest.[59] What the ancient sources remark upon is the impact of Octavian's personal theft of Ptolemaic treasure: money became so abundant in Rome that interest rates fell and property prices rose.[60]

At the time of the *Georgics*' completion, therefore, Egypt was a place of the most recent and the most intense political relevance. In contrast to the conquest of India, vaguely imagined in the poem, the conquest of Egypt was very real. The Nile appears with the *Gangaridae* on the temple doors:

atque hic undantem bello magnumque fluentem
Nilum ac nauali surgentis aere columnas.

G. 3. 28–9

And here [I shall fashion] the Nile in spate and surging with war, and columns standing tall with naval bronze.

These lines appear to refer to the captured prows from Actium which Octavian had placed in the *Forum Romanum*.[61] The Nile appears on the temple doors on the banks of the Mincius, alongside 'the conquered cities of Asia' (*G. 3. 30*). On the one hand, this scene (to my mind) exemplifies the ugly imperial hyperbole which reappears at the end of *Aeneid* 8 but which is first in Virgil here. Yet on the other hand, the river as it appears on the temple doors is not placid but is 'surging with war'. There is evidence of resistance to Roman rule in Egypt at this time. Dio refers to inhabitants who resisted the Roman annexation, and the suppression of rebellions in Egypt by C. Gallus was discussed in Chapter 2.[62] All of which can introduce ambiguity into the description of the Egyptians as a *gens fortunata*, a fortunate people. The Latin word can, in a secondary sense, mean wealthy or rich, evoking perhaps the wealth taken from that country to Rome in 29.[63] The word is used, in its primary sense, of the farmers and of the lover of the countryside in Book 2, who are seen to lead a frugal and carefree life.[64] Are we supposed to picture the people of Ptolemaic Egypt in similarly utopian terms? A knowledge of contemporary Egyptian history provides the reader with cause for doubt, for while India may have been beyond the reach of Roman power, Egypt and its people were not.

'All Italy'

The *Georgics* evokes locations across the length and breadth of the Italian Peninsula, including mountains, rivers and lakes, as well as wines and other produce. There are rural vignettes – the Etruscan flute-player (*G.* 2. 193) and the revelries of the *Ausonii* (*G.* 2. 385–9) – and extended scenes in particular locations: the Calabrian snake (*G.* 3. 425–34) and the old man's garden by the Galaesus (*G.* 4. 125–46). One of the most famous parts of the whole poem is the passage in praise of Italy, the *laudes Italiae* (*G.* 2. 136–76). This passage proclaims the fertility and bounty of Italy, its temperate climate and its supremacy over other lands. It is partly what Thomas calls 'a rhetorical set-piece', one of many passages in Greek and Latin literature praising the author's native land.[1] It can also be seen within the ancient ethnographical tradition, a miniature study of Italy and its people in keeping with the other ethnographic passages in the poem.[2] Most strikingly, its tone of idealizing celebration is at odds with the realism elsewhere in the *Georgics*, when the existential struggles which the farmer faces on the land are made clear.[3]

Partly to account for this discrepancy, perhaps, Ross and Thomas read the *laudes Italiae* ironically,[4] identifying details in the passage (and in the rest of the poem) which contradict the sunny picture of Italian life, what Thomas calls 'obvious fictions, demonstrably in conflict with the reality of Italy as it exists in the "technical" sections of the poem'.[5] Alternatively, the patriotic tone of the passage can be read unironically, as part of Virgil's interest in the histories, peoples and geography of the peninsula which so animate the second half of the *Aeneid*.[6] The political nature of this Italian interest in the *Georgics* is noted by Harrison, who shows how the praise of Italy as superior to (specifically) Eastern lands engages with the politics of the 30s BCE.[7] Regardless of how readers judge the tone of the passage, my concern here is with how the *Georgics* can be seen to portray the diversity of the Italian Peninsula and its history, even as it suggests Rome's pre-eminence in that same history.[8]

Italian landscapes: the *ager Bruttius*, Lucania, Campania

Roman imperialism began in the Italian Peninsula, as Rome expanded its power first in Latium and then further afield. This extremely complex process was by no means complete by the beginning of the first century BCE, and was only arguably so at its end.[9] A glance at the *Fasti Triumphales* for the sixth to third centuries BCE gives a list of seemingly endless triumphs over the peoples of Italy: Etruscans and Sabines, *Aequi* and *Volsci*, Gauls and Samnites.[10]

The area in the extreme south-west of the Italian Peninsula is now Calabria, but to the Romans it was known as *ager Bruttius* and its inhabitants as *Bruttii*. In the centre of this area is the mountainous plateau of La Sila, which in antiquity was heavily forested and a valuable source of timber and pitch. It is here that Virgil sets the battle of two bulls, rivals in love:

> pascitur in magna Sila formosa iuuenca:
> illi alternantes multa ui proelia miscent
> uulneribus crebris; lauit ater corpora sanguis,
> uersaque in obnixos urgentur cornua uasto
> cum gemitu; reboant siluaeque et longus Olympus.

G. 3. 219–23

> *A beautiful heifer grazes on great Sila: two bulls join battle, each in turn, with great force and constant blows; black blood soaks their bodies, and each one's horns are turned and shoved against the opponent with a desolate moan; the woods and the whole sky resound.*

The *Bruttii* revolted against Rome during the war with Pyrrhus (280–275), and again during Hannibal's occupation of southern Italy in 216.[11] A fragment of Dionysius of Halicarnassus records that, in the aftermath of the Pyrrhic War, they ceded voluntarily to Rome one half of La Sila.[12] We are not in a position to say how voluntary this was, but the history of resistance to Rome in the *ager Bruttius* is cause for scepticism. Toynbee and Brunt assume that the rest of La Sila was annexed by Rome in retribution after the end of the Second Punic War, but this is an assumption for which evidence is lacking.[13]

Dionysius, a contemporary of Virgil writing at Rome, speaks in the present tense of a thriving forestry industry, of woods populated with fir, poplar, pine, beech, oak and ash and producing enough timber to supply the demands of the entire peninsula for shipbuilding and construction.[14] Pliny says (*HN* 14. 127) that Bruttian pitch was sought after for sealing wine casks, and Virgil refers to the pitch pine groves of Locri Epizephyrii.[15] The Dionysius fragment thus offers a window onto the expansion of Roman control in the south of the peninsula, and the economic incentives and rewards of that control. But the wider historical record shows too the often violent nature of this process. The poem's sensitivity to ecological violence is exemplified in its lines about the angry ploughman felling woodland for cultivation.[16] The violence of the bulls, meanwhile, can evoke for the reader not just an animal contest or even the conflicts of human love, but also the history of Rome and the *ager Bruttius*. Readers of the *Aeneid* will note that this scene, in the same setting, is reworked to describe Aeneas and Turnus as they begin their final duel – the founding act of violence, as imagined by the poem, between settler and native.[17]

Ancient Lucania comprised the modern regions of Basilicata and southern Campania, and, as in the *ager Bruttius*, there was active resistance to Rome here during both the war with Pyrrhus and the war with Hannibal.[18] A succession of Roman colonial foundations across southern Italy in the 190s points to the extension of Roman control after the defeat of Hannibal,[19] and further evidence of Roman colonization is visible. In the Vallo di Diano, one of the main thoroughfares of Lucania, evidence exists for the activities of Gracchan land surveyors, who, under the *lex Sempronia* of 133, surveyed and demarcated areas of state land, or *ager publicus*. Inscriptions survive from a number of boundary stones (*termini*) in the area, near the sites of Atina, Cosilinum and Tegianum, recording the activities of the surveyors.[20] As well as representing increased Roman involvement in the south of the peninsula, the state repossession and redistribution of lands facilitated by the *lex Sempronia* aroused major political opposition from Rome's allied landholders.[21]

And it is in the Vallo di Diano, too, that Virgil sets the lines about the *asilus*, the pest which annoys cattle:

> est lucos Silari circa ilicibusque uirentem
> plurimus Alburnum uolitans, cui nomen asilo
> Romanum est, oestrum Grai uertere uocantes,

asper, acerba sonans, quo tota exterrita siluis
diffugiunt armenta; furit mugitibus aether
concussus siluaeque et sicci ripa Tanagri.

G. 3. 146–51

There is, around the groves of Silarus and Mt Alburnus green with its holm-oaks, a very common insect, for which the Roman name is 'asilus', but the Greeks use a different name, calling it 'oistros'. It is angry and makes a harsh sound, and makes the whole herd flee terrified from the woods. The air seethes, excited by bellowing cattle, so too the woods and the bank of the dried-up Tanager.

This part of Lucania is also where a famous inscription was found, recording the achievements of a Roman magistrate who, among other things, declares that he built a road *ab Regio ad Capuam*, that is, from the Straits of Messina to the Bay of Naples.[22] The identity of the magistrate and the road he built are much debated and decisive evidence is lacking.[23] Nevertheless, this road can tell us something about Rome's relationship with this part of Italy in the late second century. Roads are means of communication, but also means of control in their facilitation of the movements of armies and in their opening up of territories to outside influence.

The announcement of this road's construction on an inscription in Lucania, as such, can prompt consideration of the complex processes of Roman imperialism at an important moment in its history. This is highlighted by the other details provided by the inscription: the capture of fugitive slaves, building projects, a policy favouring arable over pastoral farming on the *ager publicus*. All of which reinforces what has been called 'the impression of multiple, complementary lines of antagonism between representatives of the Roman state and exploiters and inhabitants of land in Lucania' given by the inscription.[24] On my reading, then, Virgil's lines about La Sila and the Vallo di Diano are not simply descriptive Italian vignettes. In Ireland under English (and later British) rule, roads were also built as a means of exerting control over a native population, while the island's trees were felled on such a scale as to leave Ireland among the most deforested places in Europe.[25] If one reads the poem, as I do here, with a conscious effort to imagine the experience of the colonized, then such historical contexts naturally animate its Italian geography.

In Book 2 there is a pair of lines depicting Capua and the surrounding area. We are in the fertile landscape of Campania:

talem diues arat Capua et uicina Vesaeuo
ora iugo et uacuis Clanius non aequus Acerris.

G. 2. 224–5

Such land rich Capua ploughs, and the shore close to Vesuvius's slope, and the Clanius, unfair to empty Acerrae.

Servius notes that the river Clanius was prone to inundate the town of Acerrae and so is 'unfair'.[26] Gigante suggests that the phrase *uicina Vesaeuo / ora iugo* is a periphrasis for Herculaneum, a word not admissible in hexameters.[27] But there are also political contexts which may colour our sense of 'empty Acerrae'. Capua, a town successively Etruscan, Oscan and Roman, defected to Hannibal in 216 before being besieged by Roman forces.[28] Livy recounts that Acerrae remained loyal to Rome and was besieged by Hannibal, who razed the town after its inhabitants fled.[29]

Acerrae was also the scene of fighting during the Social War (91–89). During that conflict Rome's Italian allies (mainly those inhabiting the central and southern Apennine region, but there was limited intervention on the rebel side by other groups)[30] went to war against Rome, establishing a capital, Italica, at Corfinium and minting their own coinage in the process.[31] Fighting continued for almost two years before the last rebel stronghold, Asculum, fell in November 89; the *Fasti Triumphales* record the triumph of Pompeius Strabo for the final victory.[32] After the war, all Italians became or could become Roman citizens, a revolutionary process which extended well into the middle years of the first century: 'a progressive integration, lasting over more than two generations, but ... on a very large scale, doubling or trebling the number of citizens during that period'.[33]

In the Social War a series of indecisive engagements appears to have been fought in front of Acerrae between the armies of the consul L. Caesar (*RE* 142) and a rebel army under C. Papius Mutilus (*RE* 12), a Samnite and one of the two main commanders on the rebel side.[34] Acerrae was an important strategic town in the fight for control of Campania, and for the Romans it provided a key link between the base of Capua and the Latin colony of Beneventum. Gabba calls it 'the keystone of the Roman defence'.[35] When Caesar came to relieve the town from Papius's siege, a force of *Marsi* attacked the Romans, were repulsed and took shelter in a vineyard, but they were then, according to Appian, routed as they tried to escape.[36] The *Marsi* appear in the *Georgics* as one of the hardy, primitive peoples of Italy. But this double historical context, the war with Hannibal and, in particular, the Social War, can introduce an ambiguity into the phrase 'empty Acerrae'. The town's political history, something not mentioned by modern commentators on this line,[37] can suggest not just a town prone to flooding, but its destruction by Hannibal, the violence of an Italian war and the violence of the complex process by which Rome became the pre-eminent power in the peninsula.

The peoples of Italy: Volscians and Ligurians

Towards the end of the *laudes Italiae*, several Italian peoples appear in the *Georgics*. Italy is the land that bore them and they are the precursors of Roman greatness:

> haec genus acre uirum, Marsos pubemque Sabellam
> adsuetumque malo Ligurem Volscosque uerutos
> extulit, haec Decios Marios magnosque Camillos,
> Scipiadas duros bello et te, maxime Caesar,
> qui nunc extremis Asiae iam uictor in oris
> imbellem auertis Romanis arcibus Indum.

G. 2. 167–72

This land bore a fierce breed of men, the Marsi and the Sabellian youth, the Ligurian accustomed to trouble and the spear-wielding Volsci; this land bore the Decii and men like Marius and great Camillus, the two Scipios harsh in war and you, Caesar, greatest of all, who now turn back from the hills of Rome the unwarlike Indian, a victor on the farthest shores of Asia.

The evidence for these peoples and their history is extremely limited, and what evidence we do have is mainly from an external (i.e. Roman) point of view.[38] I am interested here in the characterization of these peoples in the poem, and how that relates to what is said about them by Roman sources roughly contemporary with the *Georgics*: Diodorus, Strabo, Livy. What we find is a picture of primitive, hardy and warlike peoples. Needless to say, this can be seen as a strikingly political view.

The *Volsci* occupied southern Latium in the early fifth century BCE, as part of a broader movement of peoples all over the peninsula at this time.[39] They appear repeatedly in historical sources (primarily in Livy and in the *Fasti Triumphales*) for the first half of the fifth century, most famously under their (renegade Roman) leader Cn. Marcius Coriolanus.[40] So by the time Livy and Virgil are writing, the *Volsci* are enemies from Rome's far-distant past. They appear in the *Georgics* carrying a type of short spear, the *uerutum*. In Livy they are one of three peoples who, at different points in the narrative of the first ten books, are so thoroughly defeated in battle by the Romans that they are represented as being almost (and in one case, completely) wiped out. These notices are regarded as historical exaggeration by Ogilvie and Oakley, but, if so, they are interesting for precisely that reason.[41] As Hopkins notes,[42] Roman historiography is remarkable in its sanitization of the uglier, bloodier aspects of warfare, and Livy's casual, genocidal notices about the *Volsci*, *Ausoni* and *Aequi* are a striking feature of this narrative about Rome's rise to universal dominion.[43] In the thirties and twenties BCE both Livy and Virgil are writing, in different ways, the history of Roman Italy.[44] The *Volsci* by this time are no longer a threat to Rome and so can be safely depicted as a warlike people who, in the *Georgics* at least, become part of a grand narrative of Roman history.

The *Ligures* were an ethnic group of north-western Italy whose name survives in the modern province of Liguria. Something is known of the different Ligurian peoples and perhaps even the name they called themselves.[45] Of the history of Roman intervention and imperialism in the area there is limited evidence, chiefly in Livy,[46] but the concerted Roman efforts to subdue the entire Alpine region as late as the final decades of the first century, discussed in Chapter 1, should be borne in mind. A clear picture of Rome's relationship with the *Ligures* at this time, and of potential Ligurian resistance to Rome, is inaccessible to us, but their depiction in contemporary Roman sources is of interest. In Livy they are 'born to maintain Roman military discipline' during long periods without war.[47] No other military arena, we are told, provided the things necessary to keep Roman soldiers alert and focused: rough terrain, a mobile enemy and a dearth of provisions owing to the poor quality of the land.[48] The poverty of the *Ligures* and their land is thus depicted as a boon to the Roman state.

Diodorus depicts a people skilled in hunting, quarrying and seafaring, whose strength and endurance stems from the poor quality of their land and thus from the necessities of survival. The harshness of their environment has made their women like men and their men like wild beasts.[49] Strabo's account depicts the *Ligures* as pastoralists, traders and good fighters, known for their bronze shields.[50] This image of a hardy people is echoed in the *Georgics*, where the Ligurian is 'accustomed to toil' (*G*. 2. 168). This is how Servius glosses the phrase,[51] and such a translation can be seen primarily as a reflection of the harshness of their environment, matching the accounts of Diodorus and Strabo. Yet the word *malum* allows for ambiguity: alternative translations such as 'trouble', 'harm' or even 'evil' could in fact evoke the history of Roman aggression in the area.[52]

Like the *Volsci*, the *Ligures* are pictured in the *Georgics* not as a threat to Rome, but as a constituent part of Roman history. These characterizations can raise questions about the way Roman writers at the end of the first century BCE imagined the peoples of Italy and their histories. Does depiction of the *Volsci* and *Ligures* in primitive (and sometimes animalistic, supine) terms serve to make their subjugation by Rome appear less problematic? Does the *Georgics'* portrayal of these peoples as proto-Romans achieve, by opposite means, the same end? Or do these lines (*G*. 2. 167–72) in fact hint at the violence of Roman imperialism in the peninsula from the perspective of its victims? The complexity of the poem admits multiple interpretations.

The peoples of Italy: *Marsi*, Samnites and the Social War

Then there is the half-line at *G*. 2. 167: *Marsos pubemque Sabellam* ('the *Marsi* and the Sabellian youth'). *Sabellus*[53] first appears in extant sources in a fragment of Varro's Menippean satires, preserved in Servius's commentary to this line of the *Georgics*, where he says that, as the Etruscans occupy Etruria, so the *Sabelli* occupy Samnium.

> de Sabellis Varro in age modo sic ait 'terra culturae causa attributa olim particulatim hominibus, ut Etruria Tuscis, Samnium Sabellis.'[54]

> *About Sabelli Varro in* age modo *says this: 'Once land for farming was given to different peoples: as Etruria was to the Etruscans, so Samnium to the Sabelli.'*

Scholars argue that the word is a late-Republican coinage, a new ethnonym used by Roman writers as a collective name for the Oscan-speaking peoples of south-central Italy.[55] Dench suggests that *Sabellus* was a Roman coinage designed to soften the foreignness of the Samnites and the other Social War belligerents now incorporated into the Roman state, specifically by associating them with the more northerly Sabines.[56]

While the word is used by further sources to denote Samnites specifically,[57] there is confusion (ancient and modern) between *Sabelli*, Samnites and Sabines. Ancient tradition seems to have held that the Samnites originated from the Sabines, with whom they are related linguistically and ethnographically.[58] This has introduced an ambiguity into the translation of *Sabellus*, which is often taken, incorrectly, to mean 'Sabine', and is translated thus by many older and modern sources.[59] The first point to be made, then, is that we know precariously little about the history and meaning of *Sabellus*, and indeed about the self-expression of the peoples of Italy more generally, including the names they used for themselves.[60]

The phrase 'Marsos pubemque Sabellam' names together the two major groups who went to war against Rome in 91.[61] The *Marsi*, who inhabited the area surrounding the Fucine Lake in the central Apennines were, according to Diodorus, the first to rebel;[62] their importance in the conflict is attested by the fact that certain sources refer to the Social War as the 'Marsic War'.[63] The phrase 'Sabellian youth' evokes the other major belligerent grouping, the Oscan-speaking peoples of the southern Apennines, including, but not limited to, Samnites. Samnites were not only prominent in the Social War, but also in the Roman civil wars of the 80s, when there were, according to Appian, three separate massacres of Samnites by Sullan forces: at Sacriportus, at the Villa Publica on the Campus Martius and at Praeneste.[64] For the historically minded reader of the *Georgics*, I suggest that the Social War is doubly evoked in Book 2, both by the ambiguity of 'empty Acerrae', a key battle site of the conflict, and by the naming together at *G. 2. 167* of the *Marsi* and the Sabellian youth. Readers interested in wordplay in Latin literature might even consider the possibility of a double pun within the half-line, suggesting the conflict between these peoples and Rome – one playing on the etymological link between the *Marsi* and the god of war,[65] the other a near-spelling of the Latin word for war: '**Mars**os pubemque Sa**bellam**'.[66]

In contrast to the *Volsci* and the *Ligures*, the *Marsi* and the Samnites had posed a very serious military threat to Rome within two generations of the composition of the *Georgics*. Barchiesi has argued that the Social War would have been part of the collective memory, not only of the Roman elite in the final decades of the Republic, but also of poets like Horace, Propertius, Ovid and perhaps even Virgil, whose home places either were or may have been sites of resistance to Rome during the conflict.[67] He further suggests that the peculiarities of the catalogue of Italian peoples in *Aeneid* 7, a catalogue which features both a Marsic leader and Samnite weaponry,[68] are best interpreted as evoking the Social War.[69] There the peoples of Italy are both threatening enemies and noble ancestors of the Roman people, an ambivalence which also animates the inclusion of the *Marsi* and the Sabellian youth in the *Georgics*. It is an ambivalence which may also have struck the poem's first readers. Does the poem work to assimilate the peoples of Italy into hardy Roman ancestors, suppressing, in the process, the violence of the 90s and 80s? Or is that violence, rather than being erased, just beneath the surface? The poem leaves interpretation to its readers.

Volsci, Ligures, Marsi and the *pubes Sabella* appear in the *Georgics* together with a list of famous Roman heroes: Camillus, the Decii, Marius, the two Scipios and Octavian. Virgil in *Georgics* 2 is, like Livy, writing the history of the peninsula and its people. This is, in part, a teleological vision of Roman history, as the peoples of Italy are subsumed within a narrative of Rome's greatness. The progression is made clear at the end of Book 2:

> hanc olim ueteres uitam coluere Sabini,
> hanc Remus et frater; sic fortis Etruria creuit
> scilicet et rerum facta est pulcherrima Roma,
> septemque una sibi muro circumdedit arces.

G. 2. 532–5

> *This is the life the old Sabines once lived, and Remus and his brother; in this way Etruria grew to strength and Rome naturally became the fairest place on earth, surrounding for itself seven hills within a single wall.*

The line between the celebration of Italy's diversity and the elision of that diversity within 'Roman' history is a fine one. As *rerum pulcherrima Roma* joined sevens hill within a single wall, so the peoples of Italy are assimilated into a history which culminates in the Roman state. An imperial process that began in Italy reaches its climax as Octavian brings Roman power 'to the furthest shores of Asia' (*G.* 2. 170–2). In the *Res Gestae* Octavian boasted that 'all Italy' (*tota Italia*) swore allegiance to him in 32. What was, in reality, an expedient effort to raise troops for the fight against Antony is portrayed as a moment of quasi-national unity.[70] The oath was voluntary, although scholars are sceptical as to how voluntary it really was.[71] In the *Aeneid* Octavian is depicted leading Italians into battle at Actium.[72] But for the reader of the *Georgics*, the poem's Italian geography, and especially the *laudes Italiae*, can evoke the losers as well as the victors of Roman history, and can highlight, in spite of Octavian's unifying claim, the enormous historical and linguistic diversity of the Italian Peninsula.

Part Two

Britain and the British Empire, *c.* 1840–1930

5

An Aesthetic Trend

Like the *Eclogues* and the *Aeneid*, the *Georgics* has a long reception history in Britain, and has at different times become politicized according to contemporary interests and concerns.[1] This is particularly evident in the eighteenth century, when the poem became a convenient symbol for the aspirations of agrarian capitalists at home and imperialists abroad, inspiring a whole range of georgic poetry in English and influencing discourse on landscape gardening and agriculture.[2] Geography, too, was politicized in this eighteenth-century reception, in, for example, James Thomson's depiction of a South American 'World of Slaves', populated by uncivilized natives in need of the benefits of European civilization (for which, read imperial exploitation).[3] Thomson's binary worldview of European and Other was also found in the House of Commons, where, in a debate on the abolition of the slave trade in 1792, William Pitt quoted from Book 1 of the *Georgics* to illustrate the prospect of Africa's dark continent coming at last into the light of European civilization, masking the self-interest of British foreign policy with a classically informed cliché.[4] But my aim in this chapter is not to write a general history of the poem's reception (much good work has been done), but to trace the origins and development of an aesthetic trend in scholarly reception of the *Georgics*.

By an aesthetic trend I mean the tendency in scholarship for the poem to be lauded as a masterpiece of descriptive beauty and technical perfection, in ways which ignore or obscure any sense of conflict in the *Georgics*, any sense of its agrarian, economic and imperial politics. My problem is not with the appreciation, but with what it leaves out, with its limiting of the poem's interpretative range. And the root of this aesthetic trend, or at least one of its most influential formulations, is, I suggest, to be found in the writings of Joseph Addison (1672–1719). Dryden's judgement of the poem is still quoted – 'the best poem of the best poet'[5] – but it was Addison who, in focusing on the poem's aesthetic achievement, set a course followed by later scholarship. Addison's essay on the *Georgics*, first published as an introduction to Dryden's 1697 translation, argues that the poem is 'Virgil's masterpiece'[6] 'the most complete, elaborate, and finished piece of all antiquity'[7] one which has 'all the perfection that can be expected in a poem written by the greatest poet in the flower of his age, when his invention was ready, his judgement settled, and all his faculties in their full vigour and maturity'[8] All other aspects of the poem are subsumed beneath its aesthetic achievement, the particular challenge in didactic poetry being the marriage of form and content so as to produce something akin to a piece of seamless needlework, whose colours blur imperceptibly together.[9] Moments in the poem which recent scholarship views in more political or darker terms are, for Addison, only an extension of its aesthetics. The passage describing civil war at the end of Book 1 is viewed as an example of how 'beautiful and diverting digressions'[10] ostensibly unrelated to the poem's main subject, are subtly woven into the narrative and are never gratuitous,[11] while the plague at the end of Book 3 'has all the expressiveness that words can give'[12]

Addison's aesthetic reception of the *Georgics* is visible in his other writings. As editor of the *Spectator*, he produced a series of daily articles on aesthetics in the summer of 1712 which quote Latin poets, and the *Georgics* in particular, on a number of occasions.[13] He sets out to inquire about taste and aesthetic appreciation, what it is and how it is acquired.[14] 'Delightful scenes, whether in nature, painting, or poetry', he writes, 'have a kindly influence on the body, as well as the mind, and not only serve to clear and brighten the imagination, but are able to disperse grief and melancholy, and to set the animal spirits in pleasing and agreeable motion.'[15] It is the perfection of nature and its 'scenes . . . most apt to delight the imagination'[16] which attracted Virgil and Horace, while landscape colours Addison's judgement of both the *Aeneid* and the *Georgics*: the former is 'like a well-ordered garden'[17] the latter 'a collection of the most delightful landscapes that can be made out of fields and woods, herds of cattle, and swarms of bees'[18] Such is Virgil's unrivalled aesthetic power, Addison suggests, that his descriptions are often more effective than actual contemplation of the things he describes.[19]

Addison's reception is also seminal in its appreciation of the beauties of Italy, an appreciation formed by travelling in Italy and seeing the places described in the *Georgics*. The early eighteenth century was the heyday of the

Grand Tour, when British men and women of means travelled to Italy to experience the archaeological remains of the Roman Empire.[20] Many of those travelling would have been familiar with the *Georgics*, and, in particular, with its famous praise of Italy in Book 2. Addison himself travelled in Italy between 1701 and 1703, which resulted in his *Remarks on Several Parts of Italy*.[21] The second edition is prefaced by a light-hearted letter to Lord Halifax, and has as its epigraph three lines from *Georgics* 2 in Latin.[22] Italy, for Addison, is not just 'classic ground'[23] but 'Virgil's Italy',[24] and it is clear that Virgil's description of the country is, amid a wide range of classical quotations, a major reference point, both in *Remarks* and in his letters home. 'We saw the Lake Benacus in our way', he writes of his Italian tour, 'which the Italians now call *Lago di Garda*: it was so rough with tempests when we passed by it, that it brought into my mind Virgil's noble description of it.'[25] 'I can't but envy your being among the Alps', he writes from Rome to a friend in Geneva in August 1701, 'where you may see frost and snow in the dog-days. We are here quite burnt up and are at least ten degrees nearer the sun than when you left us. I am very well satisfied 'twas in August Virgil wrote his *O quis me gelidis sub montibus Haemi &c.*'[26]

Addison's depoliticizing characterization is echoed by scholars later in the eighteenth and into the nineteenth century, where he is either quoted by name or implicitly followed. Cambridge scholar John Martyn wrote in 1741 of 'this charming poem', in which Virgil 'has exceeded all other poets in the justness and beauty of his descriptions'.[27] Twenty years later Joseph Warton quoted Addison directly and praised the poem's 'beauty of expression', while for William Mills, writing in 1780, 'to point out all the beauties of the original would far exceed the bounds of a short preface', again quoting Addison in his praise of 'this elegant and beautiful poem'.[28] Robert Hoblyn's 1825 translation of Book 1 leads with Addison's line, quoted above, on the *Georgics* as the most finished piece of all antiquity, while even the more sober view of Thomas Keightley, though critical of 'the artificial character of the style' of the poem, admits that its language is 'uniformly elegant'.[29]

The 'artistic perfection of the Georgics'

One of the most prevalent themes in British scholarship of the second half of the nineteenth century is the poem's perfection, which is to say its beauty and its technical achievement. Merivale calls it 'in point of style the most perfect piece, perhaps, of Roman literature'. Wilkins cites the 'exquisite literary finish' which made it more attractive to schoolboys than the *Aeneid*; Jerram refers to 'the most perfect and artistic production of Virgil's genius', while for Mackail it is 'the most splendid literary production of the Empire'. Sellar argues that the poem 'exhibits the highest perfection of which Latin verse is capable', while for T. E. Page, writing in 1898, 'there is nothing in the Aeneid – or indeed in Latin poetry – which surpasses the artistic perfection of the Georgics'. He continues: 'The characteristic of the Georgics is indeed their consummate art. They cannot, of course, from the nature of their subject exhibit the dramatic power of the fourth Aeneid or the imaginative grandeur of the sixth, but the artistic perfection of their workmanship is of the highest order.'[30]

The poem, then, is renowned for its craft and its perfection in the sense of its finished, polished state. Sellar focuses, like Addison before him, on the poet's achievement in aestheticizing his didactic material. 'The secret of Virgil's power', he writes, 'lies in the insight and long-practised meditation through which he abstracts the single element of beauty from common sights and from the ordinary operations of industry.'[31] Myers uses a musical comparison to emphasize the aesthetic aspect of Virgil's style, 'the hidden music which can give to every shade of feeling its distinction, its permanence, and its charm'.[32] The perfection of the *Georgics* in a literal sense – its finish or its polish – means that, in its own way, it surpasses the *Aeneid*, a poem which famously 'lacks the final touches of the master's hand'.[33] The similarity here with Addison's conception of a masterpiece which successfully aestheticizes its didactic subject matter, and which can be favourably compared to the *Aeneid*, is clear.[34]

Defending Virgil

The defensive tone of *Georgics* scholarship should be seen within the broader context of the defence of Roman literature against a superior contemporary estimation of Greek literature: his aesthetic achievement is one way in which Virgil could be defended against his critics.[35] Myers dismisses German criticisms of Virgil by emphasizing a distinction between history and art: by placing Virgil's poetry in the latter category, and by making history and art mutually exclusive, historical interpretation of the poem is rendered inferior to artistic appreciation.[36] The article on Virgil in the seventh edition of the *Encyclopaedia Britannia*, quoted by Turner,[37] is clear about the imitative nature of Virgil's poetry, claiming that the poet was 'deficient in the highest attribute of genius, in the power of creating and bodying forth original conceptions'.[38] Nevertheless, Virgil makes up for this deficiency by, among other things, his pre-eminence among Roman poets in his powers of description, his appreciation of beauty, and his versification.[39]

Despite the critical consensus which placed Virgil below Homer in the nineteenth century, therefore, the status of the *Georgics* remained high, and this high estimation continued into the twentieth century. The eleventh edition of the *Encyclopaedia Britannia*, published in 1911, describes the poem as 'not only the most perfect, but the most native of all the works of the ancient Italian genius', one which contains 'uniformity of chastened excellence in diction and versification'.[40] Edwardian scholars continued to champion 'the most poetic work ever done in Latin',[41] 'one of the most faultless of poems'[42] and 'the most complete of Latin classics'.[43]

The 'poet of rural life'

Aesthetic appreciation of the *Georgics* becomes problematic when it serves to obscure the politics of the poem. 'All conflict disappears', as John Berger has written in an art-historical context. 'One is left with the unchanging "human condition" and the painting considered as a marvellously made object.'[44] The aesthetic trend incorporates both biographical and Italian emphases which serve to create a rustic and apolitical image of poet and poem. For Mackail, the achievement of the poem is understood through Virgil's concern with 'all that was most beautiful in the most beautiful of lands'.

> His own early years had been spent in the pastures of the Mincio, among his father's cornfields and coppices and hives; and his newer residence, by the seashore near Naples in the winter, and in summer at his villa in the lovely hill-country of Campania, surrounded him with all that was most beautiful in the most beautiful of lands. His delicate health made it easier for him to give his work the slow and arduous elaboration that makes the *Georgics* in

mere technical finish the most perfect work of Latin, or perhaps of any literature.[45]

Other scholars see Virgil primarily as the poet of the *Eclogues* and the *Georgics*, averse to the violence and politics of the *Aeneid*. He is 'the poet of rural life',[46] who 'wrote the *Aeneid* somewhat against the grain'.[47] Scholars focus on the Italian sections of Book 2, but in doing so they idealize uncritically: lines 458–542 become a series of 'idyllic pictures',[48] 'the most perfect passage in all Latin poetry',[49] while the poem's darker moments become, by contrast, regrettable diversions.[50] In imagining the poet as a lover of nature, and the poem as an Italian masterpiece, scholars tended to ignore not just the more violent and darker moments of the original, but the politics of land and landscape as they relate both to the composition and reception of the poem.[51]

It is this tendency to depoliticize that, paradoxically, makes the aesthetic trend political. A poem about nature and about empire reflected the concerns of its British readership.[52] Italy, past and present, is a place of timeless and carefree agriculture,[53] while Virgil is cast as a grateful supporter of Octavian's imperial vision.[54] The beauties of Italy are contrasted with the dangers of the 'East', as scholars reproduce, rather than critique, the East–West binary found in Virgil's own praise of Italy.[55] Merivale's highly influential view of the poem, meanwhile, as 'the glorification of Labour', is elite, Christian and Eurocentric, with little awareness of the politics of work in Roman, British or British imperial contexts.[56] Among nineteenth-century British scholars, it is only W. Y. Sellar who appears attuned to the political implications of agriculture and empire in the poem, noting not just the agrarian and imperial histories of the Italian Peninsula, but also the broader Mediterranean contexts of Roman power.[57]

Scholarship and the First World War (1914–18)

By the second decade of the twentieth century, the *Georgics* was seen as a work of art born from a period of patriotic unity, a simplistic and inaccurate characterization of Italy in the 20s BCE, but one which served as a useful exemplar for Britain in the years before 1914.[58] In the years following the end for the First World War, the aesthetic trend remains in evidence, but in a more sober form. J. W. Mackail's *Virgil and His Meaning to the World of To-day*, published in 1923, reads the post-war context of the *Georgics* as analogous to Europe after the First World War. Mackail is clear about the poem's aesthetic achievement – 'one of the few examples in art of attained perfection'[59] – but this achievement now becomes restorative, offering spiritual and moral guidance to the post-war world. The *Georgics* becomes a poem of peace and reconstruction, as the troubles of ancient Italy are imagined in twentieth-century terms. Virgil is 'the poet and prophet of no mere League of Nations, but of a single world-commonwealth, and of the fulfilment of the divine purpose in an ordered and universal peace'. He continues:

> We stand now, as Virgil stood, among the wreckage of a world; he can give light and guidance to us in the foundation of a new world upon its ruins. Mankind is, above all, human; what it above all needs, not in education only but in the whole conduct of life, is humanism; consciousness of its own past, faith in its own future, the sense of truth, beauty, joy. The human value of all great works of art is not only imperishable but unreplaceable. Virgil is one of the greatest of artists; and it is as such that he finally claims the study which he more than repays, the love which that study increases the further it is pursued and the more largely it is communicated.[60]

Yet any conception of the poem as one of peace needs to distinguish between the end of civil conflict and Rome's continued aggression abroad. The implication, moreover, that Britain is in a phase of peace and reconstruction in 1923 ignores the violence of Britain's post-war foreign policy,[61] and Mackail's reading, compelling as it is, arguably obscures both of these contexts.

W. E. Heitland's *Agricola*, by contrast, first published in 1921, offers what is the one substantive challenge to the aesthetic trend in the scholarship discussed here. While he does allude to the poem's 'finished literary art',[62] there are no lyrical passages extolling the poet's love of nature or the poem's perfection; instead we get an historical analysis of the poem in the light of Roman agriculture. It is hard to say to what extent the war, or Heitland's personal views on the conflict, influenced his picture of the *Georgics*; certainly his preface makes the relevance of the post-war situation clear. As for Mackail, the poem has a moral significance: the importance of agriculture 'was and is not merely economic. Its moral value, as a nursery of steady citizens and, at need, of hardy soldiers, was and still should be recognized by thoughtful men.'[63]

Heitland's originality stems from the attention given to the historical contexts of Roman agriculture. 'The greatest [architectural] works of the ancients', he writes, 'are for the most part silent witnesses to the ruthless employment of forced labour, either that of captives or bought slaves or that of the impressed subjects of an autocrat.'[64] He is one of the few scholars to devote time to the portrayal of rural labour in the poem, to speculate on the status of the many agricultural workers named and to question the picture of the happy farmer at the end of Book 2:

> among the advantages [of country life] he [Virgil] does not omit to reckon the freedom from the extravagance and garish display of city life, the freedom to drowse under trees, the enjoyment of rural sights and sounds, in short the freedom to take your ease with no lack of elbow-room (*latis otia fundis*). This hardly portrays the life of the working farmer, to whom throughout the poem he is ever preaching the gospel of toil and watchfulness.[65]

Heitland identifies, as Spurr would later do, a contemporary Roman readership of the *Georgics* as primarily elite, 'a class dependent on slave-labour in every department of their lives'; he references, too, the impact the proscriptions had on such a land-owning class, of 'large estates bought cheaply in the time of troubles'.[66] Perhaps his most cogent point in relation to the *Georgics* concerns the fallen ox at *G*. 3. 515–19:

> if civilization owed much to the labours of the ox, and if gratitude was due to man's patient helper, what about the human slave? Is it not a remarkable thing that the *Georgics* contain not a word of appreciative reference to the myriads of toiling bondsmen whose sweat and sufferings had been exploited by Roman landlords for at least 150 years? Can this silence on the part of a poet who credits an ox with human affection be regarded as a merely accidental omission?[67]

Heitland's questioning of the poem's aestheticization of labour is an important corrective to the aesthetic trend in British scholarship. The anthropomorphic treatment of animals in Book 3 becomes not just a poetic device but a means of obfuscation. Heitland argues that Virgil suppressed the slave basis of Roman agriculture because of his desire not to provoke confrontation with Maecenas and Octavian: 'it was simpler and safer not to refer to these things'.[68] By focusing on the material side of Roman history in the context of post-war British society, he offers a picture of the *Georgics* unlike that given in print by any other contemporary British scholar, and so challenges the entire tradition of aesthetic reception.

Modern scholarship

An aesthetic trend in British scholarship has fundamentally shaped scholarly discourse surrounding the *Georgics*. If one locates the beginning of modern scholarship on the poem in the 1960s, it becomes clear that aesthetic appreciation, of a kind that can be traced back to Joseph Addison, remained prominent. Wilkinson labelled the *Georgics* 'a descriptive poem', 'the first poem in all literature in which description may be said to be the chief *raison d'être* and source of pleasure'.[69] Superlative judgements about the poem's quality continued to appear – it remained 'Virgil's masterpiece, not only technically but emotionally and intellectually'[70] – while the poem's aesthetic achievement has been consistently imagined in musical terms.[71] If superlative judgements are less conspicuous in the scholarship of more recent decades, literary and aesthetic readings have remained the dominant mode of critical interpretation, particularly in the guise of intertextuality.[72] Thomas has argued that Batstone's article on the poem 'points the way to a sort of didaxis of aesthetics, a spiritual didaxis (such as emerges from contemplation of the failure of Orpheus and Eurydice) that does not directly help us to get along in a world that is deeply problematic, but that impresses us and compensates us through its artistic and aesthetic qualities'.[73] Erren writes of the *Georgics* as belonging among 'the most beautiful and most representative works of Roman literature', while Thibodeau, in introducing his own reading of the poem, also dwells on its aesthetic achievement.[74]

What I have been trying to suggest in this chapter is that there is a long tradition, in scholarship on the *Georgics*, of praising the poem as an aesthetic masterpiece, an outstanding work of art. This tradition is problematic in its narrowing of the scholarly agenda to exclude broader political contexts, in its obscuring of conflict and imperial violence. I do not mean to suggest that scholarship remains apolitical, as in recent decades the politics of the *Georgics* as they relate to Rome and elite Roman society have been much discussed, and darker readings of the poem have been put forward. But I'm interested in the way in which scholarly ideas and agendas pass unquestioned from one generation to the next, in what might be called a continuum of aesthetic reading, traceable back to Addison. To my mind the *Georgics* is a very political text not just in Roman but in post-colonial terms. There is an imbalance in scholarly discourse on the poem, and it is this imbalance that I am seeking to redress.

6

The *Georgics* Abroad

And so all this fuss over empire – what went wrong here, what went wrong there – always makes me quite crazy, for I can say to them what went wrong: they should never have left their home, their precious England, a place they loved so much, a place they had to leave but could never forget.

Jamaica Kincaid, *A Small Place*[1]

In the nineteenth and twentieth centuries, British subjects travelled the world, published their reflections in national newspapers and played key roles in the exercise of British power overseas. A classically based system of elite education goes some way towards explaining both the appearance of the *Georgics* in such reflections, and the tendency for correspondents to be men from privileged backgrounds. Whether in comparisons between Britain and Rome, or in the awareness of Alexander's campaigns in India, or in personal reflection, the classical past was a key reference point in British imperial discourse at this time.[2] More particularly, the *Georgics* was used to aestheticize and depoliticize foreign peoples and locations in ways which demonstrate the condescension of the tourist, an inability or unwillingness to see the larger geopolitical realities that usually lie behind their encounters with deprivation or poverty abroad. The anger of Jamaica Kincaid's *A Small Place* has stayed with me as an instructive guide to the classical tourism described in the next two chapters, in part because the relationship between tourism and empire remains a contemporary one.

Italy

As it had been throughout the eighteenth century, Italy remained a destination for British tourists whose reading of the *Georgics* animated their travels. The beauties of the Italian countryside enhance, and are enhanced by, the beauties of Virgil's poem. Mary Shelley wrote to Maria Gisborne while in Naples in 1819, calling the *Georgics* 'the most beautiful poem I ever read'.[3] 'He wrote it at Baiae', she continues, 'and sitting at the window, looking almost at the same scene as he did, reading about manners little changed since his days, has made me enjoy his poem more, I think, than I ever did any other'.[4] In 1838 Thomas Babington Macaulay climbed to the hilltop town of Narni in Umbria and dwelt in his journal on the 'really glorious'[5] scenery, further enhanced by his reading of Virgil:

> I thought it far finer than that of Matlock or of the Wye, in something of the same style. The pale line of the river which brawled below, though in itself not agreeable was interesting from classical recollections. I thought how happily Virgil had touched the most striking and characteristic feature of the Italian landscape –
>> tot congesta manu praeruptis oppida saxis
>> fluminaque antiquos subter labentia muros.[6]
>> [So many towns built by hand atop sheer cliffs, and rivers gliding beneath ancient walls.]

This sense of familiarity with Italy is highlighted by an account of Italian politics in an article from the *Dublin University Magazine* in 1869. The article discusses the latest developments in the movement for Italian unification and reflects that questions about Italy's future are 'for Englishmen ... peculiarly attractive'.[7] 'Even if we have not all read', it continues, 'the glorious passage in the second "Georgic" where Virgil goes through the capabilities of his country, we all know enough about this "mighty nurse of heroes" to feel more care about her future than we do about that of Bokhara, or even of the Danubian principalities'.[8]

Such receptions point to the way in which aesthetic appreciation of the poem is augmented by readers' travels in Italy. And yet other receptions show how the opinion of the tourist or the journalist can obscure or condescend to the political realities of Italian life. An 1859 article, reporting on a key phase of the campaign for Italian unification in the weeks after the Battle of Solferino (24 June 1859), complained about the politics and people of Italy. Quoting the reports of a French officer, it remarks on:

> the frightful state of misery and disorganisation into which the whole country has been thrown by the war that was to ensure its happiness as well

as its independence. The day has gone by when Italy deserved to be hailed as 'Magna parens virum' [a mighty nurse of heroes]. The day is no more when she can produce

> haec genus acre virum, Marsos pubemque Sabellam
>
> adsuetumque malo Ligurem Volscosque verutos.
>
> [This fierce breed of men, the *Marsi* and the Sabellian youth, the Ligurian accustomed to trouble and the spear-wielding *Volsci*.]

It requires a stronger and more manly race to win and hold their independence.[9]

Modern Italy is thus seen as incapable of emulating Roman Italy, in a period when movements for national unification in Germany and Italy dominated the European political landscape.

William Gladstone, travelling in Sicily in 1838, was struck, in contrast, by how little had changed since Roman times:

> Our road today except four carriageable miles between the wretched village of Vita, and the town or *paese* of Salemi, was rude field path or less. We passed over extensive ranges of grassland, which repose the fifth year after bearing wheat for four. On some of these . . . we did not meet a living soul in our long and slow passage from one extremity to the other, and could scarcely perceive one solitary hut. On others they were ploughing, with a plough ruder than in the days of Virgil: no *aures*, no *dentalia*, the *temo* not of eight feet projection.[10]

Gladstone uses his knowledge of the relevant passage in the *Georgics* – on the construction of a plough – to enforce a particularly strong comparison: the people of Sicily are using equipment not just *as* primitive, but even *more* primitive than that recommended in the poem.[11] The limits of readers' identification with Italy become apparent: in this case the *Georgics* is used to evoke a sense not of familiarity, but of otherness.

This Italian aspect is also present in the period between the two world wars. In 1921 the *Aberdeen Daily Journal* printed a piece entitled 'Italy After the War.' The self-declared motive of the correspondent is to establish the condition of the country after the First World War, 'to see how far the war wounds had healed, and whether the aftermath of revolutionary unrest were as grave a matter as the newspapers made out.'[12] Italy, like many European countries, went through a sustained period of political unrest following the war, and violence was a feature of political life in the period.[13] The piece discusses bread prices and the foreign exchange rate, train travel and fascist rioting. Despite this unsettled post-war climate, however, the correspondent's interest in social and political problems is only cursory: 'a sojourn in Italy is still as delightful as ever'.[14] Indeed, little seems to have changed:

> Certainly, as viewed from the train after the descent from the Alps, things were to all outward appearances the same as they have always been. In the fields the same white oxen were meditatively drawing the same old-fashioned ploughs of Virgil's day; the same farm hands were busy with the spade and the great two-pronged hoe; the same deep runnels, older than the Georgics, had been dug to baffle the blinding heat to come; the same festoonery of vines hung between the trees of the orchards.[15]

The tendency for the *Georgics* to be used in evoking a sense of timeless rural life is present again here. Things are 'the same as they have always been' and, as for William Gladstone in Sicily, it is the plough which most succinctly captures this reality. This Italy is one protected against the challenges of modernity and the ravages of the war by its timeless agriculture, as contemporary political problems are minimized in favour of a literary evocation of the country's charm.

In 1935 an article in *The Times* offered a similar picture of the Italian countryside. The piece informs the reader about the annual vintage in Tuscany, and about the *mezzadria* or sharecropping system, whereby landowners provide capital and land in return for half the tenant's crop. Here, too, the first point of reference for Italian agriculture is Virgil's *Georgics*:

> Late October is the time in Tuscan farms when the wine is made, and to an Englishman brought up on the classics who has not seen it before it is an exhilarating experience. Every scene, every action sends the hexameters of the Georgics racing through his head.[16]

This quotation neatly recalls the social and educational bias on which this study of the *Georgics'* reception is based: it is 'an Englishman brought up on the classics' who can most fully appreciate the poem in an Italian context.

After describing the processes of the vintage, the communal treading of the grapes and the shared operation of the wine-press, the writer muses on the men working:

The men, small and sinewy, in their threadbare clothes, look fine. Hard-working and content with a little, they have the great courtesy and the distinctive facility of expression that come of an old and deep-rooted civilization –

Hanc olim veteres vitam coluere Sabini,

Hanc Remus et frater, sic fortis Etruria crevit . . .

necdum etiam audierant inflari classica, necdum

impositos duris crepitare incudibus ensis.[17]

[This is the life the old Sabines once lived, and Remus and his brother; in this way Etruria grew to strength . . . nor had they yet heard trumpets blare, nor swords sounding on hard anvils.]

The writer's attempt at amateur ethnography occasions another Virgilian reference, this time a direct quotation. It is unclear whether or not the subjects of the piece have themselves been consulted as to their being 'content with a little'. Here we can see the complacency of the tourist, assuming a carefree and conflict-free life for people who are assumed to be happy and prosperous. This impression is reinforced by the article's closing lines, which refer obliquely to the sanctions imposed on Italy by the League of Nations in the aftermath of Italy's invasion of Abyssinia in October 1935.[18] As the writer leaves the pressing room, his 'American-educated host' turns to him and says, 'I guess those guys have had sanctions all their lives.'[19] Italy remains a timeless land of Virgilian agriculture, whose present problems – whether the impact of war or of sanctions – pale in comparison to an aestheticized, classical vision.

A Peloponnesian tour

William Miller (1864–1945) was a classically educated historian and journalist, who in the course of a long career published extensively on the history of Greece and the Balkans.[20] In 1904–5 he contributed a two-part article to *The Westminster Review* entitled 'A Tour Through the Peloponnesos', in which he encouraged readers to stray off the beaten track and to explore the remoter parts of the country. Travel in Greece in the twentieth century, he confidently asserts, requires only three things: 'patience, a working acquaintance with modern Greek, and a small supply of Maggi's soups and Peters' milk chocolate for emergencies.'[21] His tour begins at Nafplio and encompasses many of the major ancient sites in the Peloponnese – Tiryns, Mycenae, Argos, Epidauros, Sparta, Olympia – as well as sites connected with medieval Greek history and the history of the Greek independence movement.

As in the Italian articles just discussed, Greece is presented as a timeless, classical land: 'The Greek boatman is not very different now from what he was in the days of Aristophanes.'[22] Sparta, we are told, is 'much as it was in the times when Thucydides described it'.[23] The reader's interest is thus piqued by a vision of Greece which would have been familiar to those with a classical education (mention of Hercules at Nemea recalls 'that no less Herculean task of our college-days, the Nemean odes of Pindar').[24] But it is the *Georgics* which is again used to describe local people. Describing a roadside scene in the Peloponnese, Miller writes:

> Great numbers of shepherds with huge flocks of sheep and goats met us on the way, and at times completely blocked the path. Few sights of country life are more picturesque than this exodus of the herdsmen from the low-lying winter-pastures round Sparta in the valley of the Eurotas to the higher feeding grounds near Tripolis. The shepherds had their families and their few chattels with them. Some of the women were carrying babies, slung in a sort of quiver on their backs; some of the men had lambs or puppies in their arms; others were transporting their possessions on donkeys. One was irresistibly reminded of the picture of pastoral life in the *Georgics*:
>
> Omnia secum
> Armentarius Afer agit, tectumque Laremque,
> Armaque, Amyclaeumque canem, Cressamque pharetram.[25]
> [The African herdsman takes everything with him, his shelter and his hearth, his weapons, his Amyclaean dog and his Cretan quiver.]

The rural people of the Peloponnese remind the author of nothing so much as the African herdsman in *Georgics* 3. Unlike that scene, and indeed unlike most sources examined in this and the following chapter, agricultural life here includes women and children, visible though relegated to the background. Miller's aestheticization of what he sees ('few sights of country life are more picturesque') is not matched by inquiry: description takes precedence over interaction. Any sense of the hardship of their lives is lost amid a highly literary act of imagination, as the traveller processes an unfamiliar experience by means of familiar text.

Ethiopia

In 1841 William Cornwallis Harris led a two-year mission from British India to the kingdom of Shoa (Shewa), in the area of what is now Addis Ababa, Ethiopia, which resulted in a formal treaty between Shoa and Britain.[26] It was almost certainly as a member of this mission that Captain Graham, an officer in the Bengal Native Infantry, compiled his 'Report on the Agricultural and Land Produce of Shoa' for the Asiatic Society of Bengal.[27] It takes the form of an ethnographical study which discusses the inhabitants, climate and landscape of the area, as well as its agriculture. Graham is clear about both Shoa's extraordinary fertility and the primitive state of its agriculture. 'Unburdened by over-population', he writes, 'and possessed of a fertile soil and favourable seasons, in the absence of all luxuries a sufficient abundance is produced for the mere maintenance of life. Yet the science of husbandry is little understood, the implements of culture are few, and of the rudest construction'.[28]

It is this combination of fertility and primitivism which Graham describes in Virgilian terms. He notes that the local practice of burning land to clear and to fertilize areas for cultivation is ancient, but is no longer considered effective in 'modern husbandry':

> This their only attempt to fatten the soil, is mentioned as being in use in the most ancient recorded system of agriculture –
> > saepe etiam sterilis incendere profuit agros
> > atque leuem stipulam crepitantibus urere flammis
> > [Often too it has been beneficial to scorch unproductive fields and to burn the light stubble with crackling flames]
> But the system in modern husbandry has been very nearly exploded as erroneous and inefficacious, except in obstinate bog lands.[29]

In bee-keeping, meanwhile, 'the same customs prevail in this country which have been generally practised since the days of Virgil; the whimsical one of making a confused clamour to induce the swarm to settle, and that of rubbing the interior of the hive with sweet-scented herbs to induce the bees to remain'.[30] Finally, the abnormal fertility of Shoa is compared to the idyllic picture of Italian agriculture given in the *laudes Italiae*:

Two harvests are yearly garnered in by the provident husbandman from the fat land, without its utter exhaustion and impoverishment. Whilst the ripe grain is being reaped from one field, the seed is but just deposited in the next adjacent one; the cattle employed in ploughing up the fertile soil in one location, whilst the muzzled oxen are trampling out its lately yielded treasures in the next; and all the various processes of husbandry, from the breaking up of the ground, to the winnowing of the grain, may be witnessed in one small locality simultaneously –

   hic uer adsiduum atque alienis mensibus aestas:
   bis grauidae pecudes, bis pomis utilis arbos.[31]
   [Here there is constant spring, and summer out of season; twice a year the animals produce new young, twice a year the tree has a fresh crop of fruit.]

Graham's report thus uses the *Georgics* to emphasize the fertility of Shoa – a place where the climate of *G.* 2. 149–50 becomes a reality – but also the timelessness of its people and their way of life, who still keep bees and prepare their fields in the ways which Virgil prescribes. Such a picture serves to aestheticize, as well as to depoliticize, the local people and so contributes to the ideology of imperial rule. This imperial context is clear when, for instance, Graham states that 'unless some European power interferes for good with a strong hand, a great length of time must inevitably elapse before the habits and prejudices of this uncivilised nation be overcome for its own benefit'.[32] The same sentiment was expressed by Cornwallis Harris: 'There is, perhaps, no portion of the whole continent to which European civilisation might be applied with better ultimate results.'[33]

While Abyssinia (as Ethiopia was then known) was never subject to official British rule, in 1868 an expedition led by Robert Napier and staffed by the Indian Army invaded the country.[34] The official objective was to rescue European missionaries held hostage by Tewodros II; once this had been accomplished and Tewodros had committed suicide, Napier's force, before departure, stole hundreds of precious items, including over one thousand Geʿez and Amharic manuscripts, many of which were destined for the British Museum.[35] And in the 1930s Abyssinia felt the full force of European imperialism, in the guise of invasion and occupation by fascist Italy, its people subjected to chemical attacks.[36] It should be said that as of 2019 those stolen Ethiopian treasures, of great historical, religious and cultural value, still reside in British institutions, and official calls for their restitution have been ignored. Until they are answered, it seems to me that the book of British imperial power in and over Ethiopia remains open: 'Stealing them was a gesture of power, and keeping them still is a gesture of power.'[37]

'The Georgics of Algeria'

Algeria endured French colonial occupation between 1830 and 1962, while the extent to which the Roman Empire has shaped the historiography of Algeria, and North Africa more generally, cannot be overestimated. 'As for the native inhabitants', writes Laroui, 'we sense their presence, working in the fields, paying the *annona*, confined to the Aurès Mountains or driven beyond the *limes*, but we never see them. We should doubtless be grateful that a shadow of their presence endures, but let us not be dazzled by false riches: Roman history is not the history of the Maghrib.'[38] The extent to which this Roman past influenced colonial ideology in North Africa in the nineteenth and twentieth centuries is also important, as Mattingly notes:

> Both French and Italians in North Africa presented themselves as the direct and natural inheritors of the Romans and actively sought to ape and emulate the achievements of the earlier imperial regime. The role of indigenous people was relegated to one of being passive receptors of the fruits of civilization or characterized as anarchic barbarians, incapable of proper self-government or socioeconomic advancement without outside (European) intervention.[39]

Here we can see the political contexts behind descriptions of African people as primitive or picturesque, their ways of life ancient and timeless. This rhetoric of primitivism directly supports, that is, the ideology of colonization and imperialism: people who are seen to be apolitical are ideal candidates for beneficent and paternal European rule, for the progress and development implied by the word 'civilization'.

In 1925 *The Times* published a series of three articles on Algeria. A correspondent tours the country by car and highlights places of potential interest to the British tourist. A distinction is made between the 'civilization' of the colonial centres and the timeless, primitive lives of the rural inhabitants.

'Along the coast is South Europe', we are told, where there is 'the most modern civilization, with all the apparatus of comfort and convenience in the great cities and towns.'[40] It is clear that the writer views French rule as unproblematic, at one point querying whether or not Algeria will, in the future, be 'able to compete with the Riviera as a resort for European hibernators'.[41] The civilization of colonial society is contrasted with rural Algeria and its Roman archaeological sites, in which little has changed over time. Jemila, now the UNESCO World Heritage Site of Djémila, is 'as the Romans left it', but has now 'been brought into direct communication with the well-beaten track of French civilization'.[42] Yet, the writer continues, 'with all its strategic strength and the power of legions to which it points, Jemila . . . is almost wholly lacking in anything that can be called history'.[43]

For this correspondent, civilization and history are distinctly European, not African, things. The history which ended with the Roman Empire has been revived only by French rule; what happened in between is of no concern. Algeria is, in fact, presented in entirely classical terms: a reference to Sallust,[44] a quotation in Greek from Aeschylus's *Suppliants*,[45] Virgil's *sunt lacrimae rerum* (which, we are told, 'was first said in Africa'[46]) and reports of a Roman inscription recently uncovered in a hotel garden.[47] Such classical comparisons serve to strengthen the colonial Roman inheritance, and important here is Mattingly's awareness of the twin processes at work in the depiction of North Africa in Roman terms. 'If the European claim to be the rightful inheritors of North Africa was to carry weight', he argues, 'it was necessary to disinherit the native peoples. An important corollary, then, to making a close identification between the modern imperial power and Rome was to reinforce the feeling of inferiority and separateness of the indigenous population.'[48]

This act of disinheritance is seen both in the denial of non-colonial history and in the descriptions of Algerian rural life. It is this latter aspect which involves the *Georgics*. The people of Africa are simple and rustic, their way of life ancient, their country a timeless place reminiscent of the classical past. The main produce in the area of Bishkra (modern Biskra) is dates, '*hinc anni labor*', we are told, while in October it is still warm enough 'for *nudus ara* to be appropriate'.[49] The pruning of vines still happens 'according to Virgilian precept', while the people of Kabylia, a mountainous region east of Algiers, still use Virgil's *trapetum* for pressing olives.[50] They are 'the purest remnant of the ancient race whom the Romans had to conquer', and a people whom the writer cannot help but admire, 'the last to be tamed by all the successive conquerors of this beautiful land'.[51]

The most prominent example comes when the antiquity of Algerian life is juxtaposed with the modernity of the motor car:

> One's car, as it purrs along at 60 kilometres or so an hour, over distances which took horses long and weary days to accomplish, affords glimpses of rude health on all sides. This country is the home of Virgil's Libyan shepherd – his *armentarius Afer* – who still, as in that magic time, drives his all before him – flock, gear, roof, and hound; and when one has seen some of the mighty evidence of Roman power one understands why Virgil added his patriotic simile: –
>
> As when in arms our own keen Roman soldiery marcheth
> Under a load ill at ease, and where he is unsuspected
> There hath arrived, his camp ready pitched, his station in order.
>
> As one speeds south one overtakes caravans yet more picturesque: herds moving with the camels, which bear women and children and bedding and even poultry, on their backs. . .[52]

The sense of identification with Rome is evident in the phrase 'that magic time', and also in the introduction – not in the Latin – of 'our own' to the translation of *G*. 3. 346–8. The militarism of the simile is, for the writer, patriotic, not problematic. 'Picturesque' Algerian rural life is little changed since Roman days, in contrast to the 'civilization' of French colonial society.

In these three articles, then, use of the *Georgics* serves to aestheticize, and so to depoliticize, the life of the Algerian colonial subject. Algerians are labelled and described in literary terms, not interviewed or sought out for meaningful discourse. Any sense of the realities of colonial rule is lost within an image of a simple way of life little changed since antiquity. If the Roman comparison serves to support colonial ideology by emphasizing, in the case of the colonizer, development, inheritance and civilization, in the case of the native population it emphasizes the opposite: stasis, underdevelopment, the absence of history. This Algerian context offers a prime example of the way a text like the *Georgics* is implicated in the facilitation and legitimation of imperial power. The three articles are designed to whet the appetite of the tourist, intrigued by a land of Roman ruins, but little interested in the problems of the colonial subject, or, it should be said, the brutality of French colonial rule. As Laroui points out, it was precisely the Arab and Berber populations of the plains and plateaux who suffered most from colonization, through land appropriations and heavy taxation, and through an inherently unjust legal system weighted in favour of those in sympathy with the colonial power.[53] It is this political context which makes the depiction of Algerians in terms of the *Georgics* most problematic. The question for readers of the *Georgics* is this: to what extent are Virgil's own descriptions of the world implicated in the realities of Roman imperialism?

7

'Happy Farmers'

The *Georgics* was implicated in the cultural politics of the British Empire as tourists, journalists, soldiers and politicians quoted the poem in their descriptions of foreign peoples and places. The poem was used to aestheticize peoples and places in ways which served to depoliticize those described, to portray their ways of life as simple, carefree and timeless. Nothing has changed, the argument goes, since Virgil's day. More than representing the condescension of the tourist – the inability or unwillingness of travellers to see the larger political contexts behind the situations in which they find themselves – this depoliticization can, at times, be seen as part of an apologetic imperialist rhetoric. People whose ways of life are deemed primitive are considered either to lack, or to be in need of, the benefits of European 'civilization'. In its strongest form, a line from the poem was consistently used to construct the experience of the colonial subject. That line opens a famous passage in praise of country life, one based on devotion to the land and freedom from conflict:

> O fortunatos nimium, sua si bona norint,
> agricolas! quibus ipsa procul discordibus armis
> fundit humo facilem uictum iustissima tellus.
>
> G. 2. 458–60

O farmers, happy beyond measure, could they but know their blessings! For them, far from the clash of arms, most righteous Earth, unbidden, pours forth from her soil an easy sustenance.[1]

Virgil's original does not specify the identity or status of the farmers in question, something which, coupled with the contrast between this section of the poem and its darker moments, invites different readings (the exclamation mark in Mynors's text is a modern editorial decision, not Virgil's own). Do these lines celebrate the rural life of ordinary Italian farmers? Or do they condescend to those farmers by depicting a countryside of primeval and conflict-free bliss? Are the lines in fact meant, as Thibodeau argues, as an encouragement to elite Roman landlords to cultivate their estates?[2] The decision rests with each reader. What is relevant here is that the ambiguity of the lines was lost in British contexts, as they became a simplistic hymn to an idealized and elite vision of the countryside.[3] The receptions which follow are meant to politicize this trend, by demonstrating the deeply political nature of the lines' reception in different colonial contexts. Those receptions then feed back into Virgil's text, prompting renewed questioning of the poem's attitude to its happy farmers.

J. A. Froude's *Oceana*

In 1886 James Anthony Froude (1818–94) published *Oceana, or England and Her Colonies*, an account of his visit to Australia and New Zealand the previous year. Froude had graduated from Oxford in 1842, and after a scandal over his novel *The Nemesis of Faith* (1849) had resigned his fellowship at Exeter College, Oxford and embarked on a career as an historian and literary editor.[4] In 1892, aged 74, he was appointed Regius Professor of History at Oxford. Froude wrote in many different fields, and *Oceana* is one of two pieces of travel literature he published in the early 1880s.[5] It takes its title from a seventeenth-century work of political theory by James Harrington (1611–77) and is concerned with the political future of the British colonies in Australia and New Zealand, whether they will remain within the Empire as part of a broad commonwealth (the *Oceana* of the title) or seek to gain independence from Britain. It is this question that Froude tasks himself with investigating in the book.

He adopts the tone of a genial narrator, full of pride that Harrington's dream of a worldwide British Empire has become a reality and, like many of his contemporaries, firmly convinced of the Empire's civilizing mission. Rome is a constant reference point throughout the book – Froude takes as his epigraph a line from Ennius – and it is clear that classical literature is a major interest for Froude himself, who discusses the relative merits of Lucretius, Virgil, Ovid and Horace, and who never travels on expeditions, we are told, without 'a few volumes of pocket classics'.[6] The time spent at sea gives Froude the opportunity to reflect on modernity, reflections which appear to be based on Froude's reading of the first book of the *Georgics*.[7] As Brady argues, such quotation serves as a kind of moral anchor amid the flux of late-Victorian moral struggle, loss of faith and advancing modernity.[8]

Froude quotes the *Georgics* on two further occasions. Describing his lunch by Sydney Harbour, he uses a detail from Book 1 to aestheticize the colony:

> Here we had luncheon – one of those luncheons which linger on in memory, set in landscapes of lake or river-side or mountain glen; where food becomes poetical, and is no longer vulgar nutriment; and old friends, now 'gone to the majority,' show their pleasant faces to us as figures in a dream. Instead of wine we had our grape-basket – great bunches like those which Virgil's countrymen gathered wild to mix with the waters of Achelous.[9]

Froude picks up on three lines which recount the invention of wine through the beneficence of Bacchus. Here 'food becomes poetical', as we picture a location full of mystery and novelty. This sort of mythologizing of the colony can be seen in political terms, emphasizing an image of Australia as a primeval land. 'In the conquest of this continent', argue Denoon and Wyndham, 'no treaties were made: colonists elaborated a doctrine of *terra nullius* [no one's land] which asserted that British settlement extinguished native rights to land.'[10] Hand in hand with this pernicious doctrine went racial views of British superiority. In his best-selling 1883 work *The Expansion of England*, the Regius Professor of Modern History at Cambridge, J. R. Seeley, wrote that 'the native Australian race is so low in the ethnological scale that it can never give the least trouble.'[11]

Oceana received favourable reviews in the British press. *The Edinburgh Review* discussed at length the book's implications for imperial policy, while *The Observer* remarked that 'the story of a delightful holiday has never been more delightfully told'.[12] But we can begin to see the idealizing tendency in Froude's account by noting the criticisms of Edward Wakefield, a member of the New Zealand House of Representatives. Wakefield attacked Froude for his 'almost incredible inaccuracy' about life in the colonies, particularly when he had been lavishly received and hosted by local dignitaries at almost every stop.[13] Wakefield is scornful of Froude's description of South Australia, and of

Adelaide in particular. Froude had described it as 'a city of a hundred and fifty thousand inhabitants, not one of whom has ever known, or will know, a moment's anxiety as to the recurring regularity of his three meals a day'.[14] This account of a bountiful and thriving colonial city was in reality far from the truth, as there was severe economic depression at the time of Froude's visit. 'The population of Adelaide with all its suburbs', countered Wakefield, 'never exceeded seventy-five thousand, and when Mr. Froude was there great numbers of them were leaving daily, starved out by the failure of the harvest, the drought, and the commercial depression.'[15] Quite apart from obscuring the political context of Australia's indigenous population, therefore, Froude also obscures the hardships of life among the colonial population.

This idealizing attitude to colonial Australia is twinned with assertive political rhetoric. Reflecting on the possibility of Australia and New Zealand gaining political independence from Britain, Froude foresees the dangers of external invasion and internal strife on the path to nationhood: 'it has always been so from the Greek democracies to the Italian republics or the Spanish states in modern South America'.[16] He is clear that the best future for the colonies is within the British Empire, within the commonwealth of *Oceana*:

> Out of such struggles great men have risen and great nations, and, so far as we know, greatness cannot be purchased at any lower price. For the English colonies there is no such school yet opened, nor while they remain attached to us on the present terms can such a school ever be opened.
>
> Fortunati nimium sua si bona norint.
>
> We must ourselves be a broken power before a stranger can invade Australia or New Zealand. Revolutions and wars are not permitted to them as long as they are British dependencies. They have no foreign policy, no diplomatists, no intercourse with the political circles in other parts of the world, to call out their intellect or extend their interests beyond their own shores.[17]

Froude imagines the colonies of Australia and New Zealand as naïve and helpless subjects ('no foreign policy, no diplomatists'), as being utterly dependent on Britain for their political institutions and directions. They, like the farmers in *Georgics* 2, are unaware of the advantages of their position; their life is imagined to be carefree and apolitical. Virgil's lines become, in effect, a thinly veiled threat about the dangers of political autonomy – part of the condescension in Froude's account which so annoyed Edward Wakefield.[18]

The Irish People and the Irish Land

Nineteenth-century Ireland was ruled by Britain, and Irish MPs had sat in Westminster since the Act of Union's abolition of the Irish Parliament in Dublin in 1801. The Famine of 1845–51 had had a catastrophic effect on the country's rural, agricultural populations: the number of those killed by starvation and disease is estimated at between 1 and 1. 1 million, while mortality combined with massive emigration led to a decline of over 2 million in the national population.[19] In the following decades, demands for national independence and land reform increased, culminating in the 1870s and 1880s with Michael Davitt's Land League and Charles Stewart Parnell's leadership of the Irish Parliamentary Party. Tenants fought for what have traditionally been known as the '3 Fs' – fair rent, fixity of tenure and free sale – demands which were partially granted by Gladstone's Land Act of 1870. Landlords incurred criticism for unfair evictions and absenteeism, but were in turn faced with protecting their property and livestock from the agrarian violence which recurred sporadically in this period.[20]

Without entering into a detailed analysis of particular issues, it is nevertheless true to say that land in Ireland in the middle and late nineteenth century was a source of profound political conflict – evictions, boycotts, agrarian violence, mass movements for tenant rights – exacerbated at times by the actions (or inactions) of British rule from Westminster. Agriculture for some and in some parts of the country was no doubt a generally prosperous and profitable occupation, but for others in other parts it was a matter of bare subsistence. It is this latter aspect which gives these Irish receptions of G. 2. 458–9 their irony, coupled with the failure of the tourist or the politician to appreciate local realities and their relation to colonial rule.

In an Irish context the lines are consistently used to argue that the Irish are either unappreciative of British rule or unaware of the comparatively prosperous state of Irish agriculture. In 1851 an anonymously published book, *The Saxon in Ireland*, recounted the travels of an Englishman, John Hervey Ashworth, in the west of Ireland during the Famine. His account combines appreciation of the landscapes of Mayo and Galway with accounts of meetings with desolate people. 'Strange it is', he writes of his stop at Leenaun in Co. Mayo, 'that, where nature is so lovely, man should be so degraded and so wretched.

The maimed, the blind, the naked, the widow and the orphan crowded around me as I alighted from the car.'[21] In spite of his direct experience of areas affected by famine, Ashworth nevertheless argues that agriculture is more advantageous in Ireland than in England:

> Upon my English property the taxation, or rather the outgoings, are fearful … Add to these the many calls upon private charity, the public subscriptions, which a man cannot put aside without odium, the relatively high scale of wages, which nevertheless ought not to be reduced, the continual wear and tear of implements, the long blacksmiths' bill, and the various prerequisites to servants and labourers, which, allowed in more prosperous days, cannot now be discontinued without murmurs and dissatisfaction. From the great portion of this ruinous pressure Ireland is free, while her labour is fifty percent cheaper, and her soil equally, if not more fertile.
> 'O fortunatos nimium, sua si bona norint,
> Agricolas!'[22]

In August 1869 a man describing himself as a North Lincolnshire tenant farmer wrote to *The Times*, expressing his surprise on reading the newspaper's report on Irish agriculture and at the seemingly benign conditions farmers enjoyed in Tipperary.[23] A week later an editorial in the paper took up the correspondent's point and expressed surprise at the apparent contradiction between the conditions for farming in Ireland and the political unrest it occasioned:

> Over here a man has to rise early and go to bed late, he has to economize every rood of land to crowd as much flesh on every sort of animal as its frame will bear, if he is even to hold his head above water, not to speak of continuous advances. What would he not give for a chance in a country where fences are gigantic and ditches gulfs, and there is an opportunity of adding some five or six per cent, to the available land on his farm? 'O *fortunatos nimium sua si bona norint*', might, it seems, be said with abundant reason of Irish agriculturalists.[24]

Ashworth and *The Times* thus both quote the *Georgics* to question the perceived grievances of Irish farmers. This Virgilian rhetoric also reached the House of Commons, where it was again used to question the state of Irish agriculture, but it was also taken up by Irish MPs as part of an ironic and assertive political strategy.

In June 1863, a motion calling for a select committee to investigate agricultural depression in Ireland was proposed by Irish MPs and debated in the House of Commons.[25] Colonel Dunne, MP for Laois (then known as Queen's County), argued that severe population decline, exacerbated by the Famine, had led to a drop in agricultural production and thus in exports, while 'the only thing which had increased in Ireland', Dunne challenged the Chancellor of the Exchequer, 'was taxation'.[26] W. H. Gregory, MP for Galway, spoke in support of John Francis Maguire, MP for Dungarvan,[27] criticizing the reaction Irish MPs received when they brought forward grievances:

> When the Irish Members represented that state of things, they were told that they were exaggerating, and bringing forward fictitious cases of distress. The hon. Member for Dungarvan (Mr. Maguire) was told that his facts and figures were quite fallacious, and his complaints were dismissed with uncommonly little ceremony. In fact, the Irish people might have been addressed in this way –
>
> 'O fortunatos nimium, sua si bona norint,
> Agricolas!'
>
> But they did not know their happiness and were exaggerating the evils of their condition.[28]

Two weeks later, as the debate continued, Robert Peel (1822–95)[29] spoke against Maguire's speech advocating a royal commission, and he referenced Gregory's Virgil quotation. Maguire had raised the problem of emigration, and Peel countered:

> There can be no doubt there has been a vast diminution of the population by means of emigration, which still continues to a great amount; but I am not one who regards that diminution of the population with unmixed regret. I believe that the persons who leave Ireland for the Colonies, or America, acquire there for themselves a position which they would never have obtained in their own country, owing to its enormous over-population, and have been able, in a period of twelve years to send a vast amount of money to Ireland. For these reasons, I do not think the Government would be acting fairly towards owners and occupiers if they acceded to the Motion of the hon. Member . . . The debate the other night conclusively showed, that taking

the population per head, the Irish are more leniently treated in regard to taxation than the rest of the Empire. Well might the hon. Member for Galway exclaim –

'O fortunatos nimium, sua si bona norint,
Agricolas.'

The fact is, that such a discussion might tend to induce a Chancellor of the Exchequer to consider whether he could not do away with exceptional taxation in favour of Ireland, and place the people of both countries on the same footing.[30]

Peel's remarks allude to the Famine and also to the context of the prevailing laissez-faire economic theory of the time. Peel's father had been prime minister from 1841 to 1846, and his measures to combat famine in Ireland were proactive yet insufficient. But Peel's government lost power after its repeal of the Corn Laws, and John Russell's administration pursued a policy of minimal state intervention, with disastrous consequences for the Irish population.[31] Irish policy was also influenced by stereotypes about the Irish character and a Malthusian theory of population control[32] – stereotypes which should be seen in the context of a racist element often present in discourse about Ireland and the Irish in the nineteenth century.[33] Whereas Gregory appropriated *G.* 2. 458–9 ironically, Peel uses the lines to downplay perceived injustices, problems and suffering in Ireland and in Irish agriculture, further demonstrating how the *Georgics* was implicated in colonial discourse.

Irish politicians' combative appropriation of Virgil is further found in the writing of Isaac Butt (1813–79),[34] the Donegal-born politician and barrister who was leader of the Home Rule League from 1873. This organization sought restoration of the Irish parliament in Dublin, something Daniel O'Connell had failed to achieve in the 1830s and 1840s. Under later leaders Charles Stewart Parnell and John Redmond, Home Rule would continue to be a major issue in British politics until the outbreak of the First World War. Butt was educated at Trinity College, Dublin and graduated in 1835. Throughout his early career as a barrister and Professor of Political Economy at Trinity, Butt's political views were Conservative and unionist, but the distress he observed in Ireland during the Famine led him to criticize British policy and, in the following decades, make renewed calls for land reform in Ireland.[35]

In 1866 Butt published *Land Tenure in Ireland* and then, a year later and in response to criticisms his arguments had received, *The Irish People and the Irish Land*.[36] In this latter book, Butt delivers a lengthy (298-page) riposte to three Irish land owners – Lord Lifford, Lord Dufferin and the Earl of Rosse – who had publicly criticized his scheme to solve the land question in Ireland. Lifford labelled Butt's idea to grant a fixed tenure of sixty-three years to every Irish occupier 'communistic' and 'subversive to the rights of property', while Dufferin wrote to *The Times* to suggest, as Peel had done in the House of Commons, that emigration was in fact a good thing for the Irish population.[37] The debate attracted the attention of Karl Marx, who included his own riposte to Dufferin in the first volume of *Capital*, published in 1867.[38] Butt, meanwhile, had no trouble defending his proposals, attacking the powers of arbitrary eviction exercised by Irish landlords and calling out the colonial ideology which underpinned the views of landowners and politicians on both sides of the Irish Sea. 'The perpetual origin of misery and degradation', he wrote, 'has been the fact that the great mass of the people have been treated as belonging to a conquered race.'[39]

Butt quotes the *Georgics* three times in *The Irish People and the Irish Land*. He compares the 'landlordism' afflicting Ireland to a shape-changing monster, which must be followed through every mutation until it can be grasped in its true form.[40] His footnote at this point quotes G. 4. 405–6[41] and 411–14,[42] thus making his allusion to Proteus explicit. In the book's final pages he quotes from Book 2 – 'immensum spatiis confecimus aequor' – to signal his conclusion.[43] Butt had translated the *Georgics* while at Trinity in 1834, a prose version with critical notes.[44] The reason for the poem's prominence in this book is, perhaps, that Butt knew the poem well from his university days, and knew also that, in a book about land reform, the subject of the poem made it an appropriate and desirable reference point. This is borne out by Butt's third quotation, when he makes it clear that he and his cause will not be silenced or put aside:

> But if I do not believe that parliamentary discussion can do much even to aid the advent of justice on the land question to the Irish people, I am quite sure that it is not possible for any number of vehement declarations on the part of the any number of Irish landowners, who have seats in either House of Parliament, to do anything to prevent it. Surely, my Lord, he knows nothing of the elements that are involved in the struggle of a people for the

right to live in their own land who can gravely express a hope that a few words from a Prime Minister, in reply to an appeal from an Irish peer, will put an end to the demand for tenant right, or even extinguish my poor *Plea for the Celtic Race.*

'Hi motus animorum atque haec certamina tanta,
Pulveris exigui jactu, compressa quiescent.'[45]
[These popular disturbances and these great contests will quieten, once suppressed with a little throw of dust.]

At the climax of his argument, Butt ironically quotes Virgil's lines about the suppression of a swarm of bees. His quotation is particularly effective because the lines contain no explicit reference to the apian context, and because *motus animorum* is well suited to a popular political movement such as Home Rule. Butt's quotation of Virgil thus lends weight to an authoritative and pugnacious rejoinder to his critics, implying that his demands will not easily be ignored.

India

British involvement in South Asia had increased steadily from 1757, when the Battle of Plassey gave the East India Company political primacy in Bengal. Until 1858 the East India Company was the official agent of British power, with a monopoly on British trade to and from South Asia until 1833. Throughout the nineteenth century Britain annexed increasing amounts of territory – Assam in the north-east (1826), Sindh (1843) and Punjab (1849) in the north-west and Burma (1852) – although it should be remembered that British rule in South Asia was never total, but was reliant on a series of alliances with local rulers, as well as on direct Company or Crown rule. The major shock to British imperial confidence in the region was the Rebellion of 1857, precipitated by an uprising of Indian troops in the British Army at Meerut.[46] Throughout the summer of 1857 the situation escalated to threaten the centres of British power in North India – Delhi, Agra and Lucknow. There were atrocities on both sides, but the Rebellion sparked a wave of frenzied, racialized violence on the part of British troops wholly incommensurate with military suppression of rebels and the restoration of order.[47] In political terms, the Rebellion precipitated the handover of British rule from the East India Company to the Crown, a process which culminated in the crowning of Queen Victoria as Empress of India in 1876.

In January 1885 the *Leamington Spa Courier* reported the speech of the Reverend W. C. Furneaux to the Leamington Institute, entitled 'Life in the East', in which the speaker entertained his audience with anecdotes from his time in India.[48] Furneaux illustrates his descriptions of life in Bombay with biblical and classical allusions. Women stand around wells gathering water like Rebecca, while outside the city:

> one might see an old plough, such as Virgil might have looked upon when he described the plough of the bucolics of the 'Georgics'. Just such a one might be seen to-day in India, while overhead were the great line of telegraph wires by which Mr. Gladstone would flash in a few minutes a message from London to the Viceroy, and with equal speed receive another message in return – a wonderful contrast to the old condition of things when it occupied a year-and-a-half to inquire of a friend 'How's your fever?' and to get the answer, 'That now it's all right.' (Laughter).[49]

Following a pattern we have seen before, Furneaux contrasts the modernity of British civilization, here represented by telegraphic communication, with the supposed backwardness of Indian agriculture, which seems as ancient as the *Georgics*. As in Graham's account of Ethiopia, this can be seen as rhetoric offering an implicit apology for British rule in India. This image of primitivism is combined with racism and allied to a belief in Britain's civilizing mission.[50]

In 1859 a series of riots and protests broke out among indigo cultivators in Bengal.[51] Indigo was an important and valuable British export, used as the principal source of blue dye in European textiles and uniforms.[52] Production in Bengal was controlled by European planters, who entered into direct commercial relationships with the ryots who cultivated the crop.[53] Various expenses deducted from the price paid to cultivators meant that they relied on a series of advances provided by planters, and debt often accumulated to the point where repayment became impossible and was transferred from one generation to the next.[54] In this way arose 'a marketing and production mechanism that efficiently and relentlessly attached unpaid labour to indigo cultivation'.[55]

Under the contract, the peasant was to bear the entire cost of production, be responsible for the loss of the plant, permit factory servants to measure his land before cultivation, and deliver the harvested plant to the factory – all at a rate fixed by the planter. The advance system could be so manipulated that the question of payment might not arise: 'Of 33,200 indigo raiyats, who cultivated for the Bengal Indigo Company's concerns in 1858–9, only 2448 were shown by Mr. Larmour to have received any payment.'[56]

This exploitative system and the coercion used to enforce it, coupled with the discrepancy between cultivators' desire to plant more profitable or useful crops like rice or jute, and the commercial pressures on planters to make use of two short, seasonal windows for indigo growing, led to tensions which contributed to the riots of 1859–62.

These events feature in *The Competition Wallah*, G. O. Trevelyan's best-selling, fictional account of the life of an Indian civil servant, as told through a series of letters between Henry Broughton, a recent Indian Civil Service recruit, and his school friend Charles Simkins back in England.[57] Trevelyan's account was criticized in *The Calcutta Review*, where it was argued that Trevelyan had been too harsh on the planter community and their desire to have breaches of contract over non-production of indigo treated as criminal, rather than civil, cases.[58] Of importance here is the fact that this review quotes Virgil in its dissection of the controversy. Both Trevelyan's character and the review, it should be noted, admit the unscrupulousness of planter behaviour. The review admits that 'the whole root of the difficulty is the insufficiency of price offered for Indigo in comparison with other crops'.[59] But discussing (and dismissing) the charge that planter policy is to have indigo sown on lands meant for rice, the reviewer denies that this is the case, and states that:

> [T]he ryots will learn with no less surprise than gratifaction, that in the selection of land for Indigo, the factory servants are scrupulously enjoined to see that rice land is not taken, and that only such portion of their land is to have Indigo sown in it, as would otherwise in the regular rotation of crops have had to be fallow.
>
> O fortunatos nimium sua si bona norint
>
> Agricolas ...
>
> only unfortunately the ryots know nothing of this as theory, and are hopelessly ignorant, not to say incredulous, of it as practice.[60]

Here again there is paternalistic language, used of farmers who will be surprised to learn how simple the situation is and how benevolent to them is official British policy and practice. In ways similar to the Australian and Irish examples discussed above, lines 458–9 from *Georgics* 2 are used to assuage allegations of misconduct and neglect. The tensions inherent in the colonial economy of nineteenth-century Bengal, between the profit-driven motives of European planters and the resistance of local cultivators – on whom the industry was reliant – to exploitative and unfair treatment, find ironic expression in the *Georgics'* depiction of unknowingly happy farmers.

Over one million Indian troops served in the First World War as part of the British Army, in East Africa, in Mesopotamia and on the Western Front, and yet India's loyalty served to highlight the hypocrisies and complacencies of British rule.[61] The sacrifice of Indians was lauded in Britain, while repressive measures like the Defence of India Act (1915) curtailed civil liberties and sought to stave off the growing and multifaceted movement for greater independence.[62] In 1919 the Rowlatt Acts extended the extrajudicial wartime powers established by the Defence of India Act. In April of that year General Dyer ordered his men to fire on a peaceful crowd in Amritsar, Punjab, killing hundreds and injuring over a thousand. The lionization of Dyer in the British press only served to heighten the shock and anger of many Indians, all the while reinforcing the hypocrisy of 'benevolent' British rule.[63]

In response to wartime agitation for political reform in India, the secretary of state for India, Edwin Montagu, declared the goal of 'responsible government' for India.[64] In 1918 he travelled to India and met with the Viceroy Lord Chelmsford; together the two men drafted and published what became known as the Montagu-Chelmsford Report in 1918. The language of the report is a stark example of what one might call the self-justifying rhetoric of British imperialism. The proposed reforms are presented not as pragmatic wartime politics, but rather as the final push of a benevolent father: European education has naturally resulted in a desire among Indians for European institutions; it is the duty of Britain to honour its commitment now that some, but not all, Indians, are 'ready' for self-government.[65] This manifest condescension reveals the supposed *raison d'être* for British rule in India: imperialism as a kind of benevolent tutelage.

Thirteen days after the massacre at Amritsar, and one year after the publication of the Montagu-Chelmsford Report, a one-line article in London's *The Saturday Review* quoted the report under the title 'O fortunatos nimium': 'The placid, pathetic contentment of the masses is not the soil on which Indian nationhood will grow.'[66] This line comes from a section of the report arguing that the 'sheltered existence' in which Britain has left the Indian population to date should be brought to an end:

> We believe profoundly that the time has now come when the sheltered existence which we have given India cannot be prolonged without damage to her national life; that we have a richer gift for her people than any that we have yet bestowed on them; that nationhood within the Empire represents something better than anything India has hitherto attained; that the placid, pathetic contentment of the masses is not the soil on which such Indian nationhood will grow, and that in deliberately disturbing it, we are working for her highest good.[67]

The Virgilian title neatly links the attitude of the Report with the end of *Georgics* 2. For the reader acquainted with the poem, the Indian population become happy farmers, unaware of how blessed their passive and disenfranchised existence within the British Empire has really been. Yet the article can be read ironically, satirizing this very complacency in the language of the Report at a time when nationalist politics in India were anything but placid or tame. Just below the article a six-verse poem is printed which appears to satirize the position of Montagu and Chelmsford. The first verse I quote here:

> A Statesman, landed from the West,
> Found India steeped in calm –
> With secular indifference blest,
> She lay beneath the palm.
> 'Tis surely very sad, said he,
> That folk so poor content should be.[68]

Thus the lines from *Georgics* 2 become politicized in the context of the Montagu-Chelmsford Report. The complacent and paternalistic tone of the report suggested to the author of *The Saturday Review* piece G. 2. 458, whereby the Indian colonial subject is imagined as a happy farmer. But the piece and the accompanying poem can be seen not only to report but to satirize this attitude as patently hypocritical given the contemporary political context.

The Second South African War (1899–1902)

European settlement in southern Africa was dominated by British and Dutch-Afrikaner populations, with the latter outnumbering the former 3:2 at the end of the nineteenth century.[69] Two British colonies along the coast, the Cape Colony and Natal, coexisted with two Afrikaner republics, the South African Republic (Transvaal) and the Orange Free State, whose origins lay in the Great Trek of the 1830s, when Dutch settlers had migrated north to establish their independence from British rule. The discovery of gold reserves on the Witwatersrand in 1886 meant that by 1898 the Transvaal had become the largest single producer of gold in the world, and this economic context was a major factor in relations between Britain and the Boer Republics.[70]

The first phase of the second South African War of 1899–1902, between Britain and the two republics, witnessed a series of British defeats which caused shock and embarrassment among Britain's political class. By September 1900 the Transvaal and the Orange Free State had been annexed by the British Crown, at which point a further and more entrenched phase of the war began. In order to counteract the guerrilla tactics adopted by their enemy, the British government adopted a scorched-earth policy, involving the construction of 8,000 blockhouses and a vast network of wire fencing, the destruction of some 30,000 farms and the incarceration of Afrikaner civilians in what were called 'concentration camps', in which some 28,000 civilians died, mainly from disease.[71] Many in Britain were outraged by such a policy.[72] The Treaty of Vereeniging, signed 31 May 1902, ceded control of the two Afrikaner republics to Britain in exchange for promises of eventual self-government (and agreed that any discussion of political rights for the native African population would be indefinitely postponed).[73]

In November 1902 the colonial secretary, Joseph Chamberlain, toured South Africa in order to assess the post-war situation.[74] British policy was one of conciliation, emphasizing the need for the two major settler populations in South Africa to work together, conscious both of British economic and trading interests and the numerical superiority of the Dutch-Afrikaner population. The Treaty of Vereeniging had allotted the sum of £3 million in aid for the defeated republics, designed to compensate farmers who could prove their losses and to speed up the process of post-war reconstruction.[75] Before his departure for South Africa, Chamberlain was called before a committee of MPs to clarify confusion as to the source of this money. British MPs had assumed the money would come from a loan advanced by Britain, but the Boer representatives were adamant that the money should be a free gift of aid from the imperial treasury. Chamberlain's remarks are recorded in Hansard. 'You cannot make war without suffering on both sides,'[76] he stated, but he took issue with the notion that the material devastation was as bad as had been reported:

> One thing is certain. The property of the ordinary Boer consisted in his farm, in his farmhouse and buildings, and in his cattle and stock. No doubt in very many cases his farmhouse has suffered or been actually destroyed and his cattle have been taken . . . But the land, which, after all, is his principal capital asset, has increased in value since the war, and I am informed – I speak only from information – that the average value of land in the Transvaal and the Orange River Colony at the present time is very much greater than it was before the war.[77]

An article in London's *The Speaker* took issue with Chamberlain's responses:

> 'O fortunatos, sua si bona norint, agricolas.' This remark was once, I believe, made by one Virgil, and was very literally paraphrased the other night by Mr. Chamberlain, since Boer is certainly the Dutch for *agricola*. The Colonial Secretary urged that the Boers are much better off, if only they knew it, as the result of the war. He admitted that 'in very many cases' their farmhouses had suffered or been destroyed and their cattle had been taken. But the land, their 'principal capital asset,' had increased in value! Which must be very consoling to the Boers, who have lost house, cattle, and agricultural implements, and so cannot farm the land . . .[78]

This piece highlights the paradox of a British government seeking to assist in the reconstruction of a warzone they themselves had been in large part responsible for creating. 'Boer' *is* the Afrikaans word for 'farmer', and the writer is acutely aware of the relevance of Virgil's line. The idea that the Afrikaner population are still happier than they realize, that despite the patent devastation caused to their property by the war they have something to be grateful for, fits the same pattern observed in examples from Australia, Ireland and India: colonial subjects are unaware of their luck in being subjects of the British Empire, and their complaints are consequently dismissed as less justified than they appear. Seymour writes:

Liberal imperialism constructed the colonial subjects at best as passive victims, needful of tutelage, capable of self-government only after a spell of European supremacy, and at worst as fanatics and murderers, racially degenerate peoples given to tyranny and unnatural practises, fit only for subordination. The imposition of highly exploitative systems on the colonized was seen not only as advantageous to them, but as natural – a logical step en route to civilization.[79]

The hypocrisy of this imperial ideology is succinctly satirized in *The Speaker* by reference to Virgil's happy farmers.

The *Georgics* at Home

Here I move from Britain's empire to Britain itself, in order to demonstrate two things. Firstly, that during the First World War the *Georgics* gained sudden and immediate relevance for some of its readers, in the context of the social changes, food shortages and drives to increase production occasioned by the conflict. This georgic moment reveals a living text which, for all its erudition, could still speak to twentieth-century agricultural concerns, and shows that the *Georgics'* reception history has a previously unknown political aspect in domestic as well as international contexts. But secondly, it also demonstrates the imperial implications of that moment. Amid talk of 'back to the land' and 'a land fit for heroes', the *Georgics* was appropriated to champion Britain's post-war reconstruction at home and abroad, in ways which further complicate the notion that it is simply a poem of peace. Geography and empire, therefore, are themes relevant not only to the periphery, but to the imperial centre.

Land reform

The Liberal Unionist MP Jesse Collings had notable successes in the 1880s in expanding and securing the access of working people to allotments across Britain, guiding two bills into law.[1] In 1906 he published *Land Reform*, which went further in advocating for a system whereby tenants could receive loans for the purchase of their holdings. This time, however, his attempts to get the required legislation passed were unsuccessful.[2] *Land Reform* is in part a history of rural England, covering the history of the peasant revolts and the enclosures, and in part a political pamphlet calling for changes to rural education and the law. Collings is keenly aware of the historical contexts of land in Britain, arguing that any assessment of land tenure in England must recall 'the historic processes by which it was created – processes by which the yeoman farmer was reduced to the position of a dependent tenant, and the peasant proprietor to that of a landless man'.[3] The radicalness of this idea is underlined by Readman, who notes that:

> [Collings's] basic aim was to transform the British land system, which since the enclosure movement … had been squarely based on the tripartite structure of landlord, tenant farmer and labourer. Instead of this, or alongside it if it could not be completely replaced, he sought to institute a system based on occupying ownership: tenant would become yeoman, wage labourer would become peasant proprietor, 'landlordism' would disappear.[4]

Land Reform is premised on fears about national health and self-sufficiency of a kind conspicuous in Edwardian discourse: the prosperity of agriculture is, for Collings, inextricably linked to the prosperity of the nation. But more than this, self-sufficiency in agricultural production is an urgent necessity in case of war. 'We are every year becoming more dependent for our daily bread on foreign imports', Collings writes, 'the stoppage of which, from any cause, even for a few months, would cause a famine in the land.'[5] 'In the case of a war with a great Power or combination of Powers (themselves self-feeding) it would not be difficult … for our opponents … to place this country in a perilous position.'[6]

He begins by comparing British agriculture to that of ancient Greece and Rome: 'The ancients regarded that industry as the basis of civilization. They had their goddesses of agriculture, to whom temples were built and splendid offerings made. Our harvest festivals, feasts, and other rural festivals, so real even up to recent times, were also offerings of gratitude for the fruits of the earth on which human life and welfare depend.'[7] 'Amongst the ancient writings which exalt agriculture', he writes, 'the Pastorals and Georgics of Virgil may be said to take the first place. Though written about two thousand years ago they are still fresh and living to-day.'[8] What is more, 'they are wonderfully applicable to the agricultural industry of the present time. The advice given to cultivators has never been bettered.'[9] The *Georgics* is seen as evocative of a vanishing rural past, 'so real even up to recent times', and as a still-relevant guide to agricultural life.

Collings then proceeds to quote at length, in English, several passages from the *Georgics*,[10] and ends by linking the idealized image of agriculture portrayed in *Georgics* 2 with his hopes for national self-sufficiency and prosperity. The most commonly quoted part of the poem in British reception, the second half of Book 2, is put by Collings to political use in his calls for land reform:

> the leading ideas through these charming pages [of the *Georgics*] are that agriculture is a divine calling, and that on it and on nothing else the strength and glory of nations depend:
> 'This life of yore the ancient Sabines led,
> This Remus and his brother. So in strength
> Etruria grew. So Rome herself became
> The beauty and the glory of the world.'[11]

Thus, for Collings, the *Georgics* provides the perfect means of concluding his call for land reform as a means to national prosperity. A comparison between Rome and the British Empire is implicit: by following Collings's advice, Britain can retain (or recover) its status as 'the beauty and the glory of the world'. He invokes an authority he can expect a certain audience – that is, the audience of politicians necessary to the success of his bill – to understand and appreciate. Rhetorical appropriation of the poem's vision of rural prosperity is put to political use, in an effort to counter what Collings sees as the social inequality engendered by industrial modernity: 'There is not another civilized country in Europe in which the contrast between penury and wealth is so marked as it is in England.'[12]

DORA

When war did come, it put great pressure on British agriculture and food production, creating situations which brought Virgil's agricultural advice to the minds of certain readers. In particular, the allotments which Collings had championed gained sudden importance. The powers given to the government by the 1914 Defence of the Realm Act (DORA) allowed it to appropriate land for use as allotments, which then led to a public campaign to encourage their use.[13] An Allotment and Smallholdings Department was set up to help plot-holders, and by the end of the war there were 400 affiliated allotment societies with a membership of 60,000, the number of allotments having tripled in eighteen months from half a million to 1.5 million.[14] With the effort to produce food during wartime now encompassing rural and urban communities and individuals, the *Georgics* came to be of relevance for some of its readers.

In May 1917, the *North Devon Journal* published a column giving expert advice to allotment gardeners for the summer ahead. Amid the range of tasks prescribed – sowing, watering, monitoring growth – the column turns to Virgil for inspiration. 'An old saying of 2,000 years ago from Virgil's *Georgics* I., 121, "Pater ipse colendi haud facilem esse viam voluit" (God so ordained that there should be no short cuts in gardening) is still true. When the crops are in soil, watering, weeding and watching will be the chief work of the season.'[15] The writer's idiosyncratic translation neatly shows how adaptable to different contexts a quotation from the poem could be, and his or her familiarity with the *Georgics* can perhaps be further gleaned from the military language used a few lines later: 'The hoe must be the weapon continually in use, warring destruction on all weeds.'[16] This military metaphor fits the wartime context of Britain in 1917, but it is also reminiscent of the martial language used to describe agriculture in the *Georgics*.[17]

In the same month the *Gloucestershire Chronicle* reported a speech given by Ms F. M. Priday concerning local measures, planned by the Agricultural Sub-Committee of the County Council, to encourage cheese production in the area. She was introduced by Col. W. F. N. Noel, Chair of the Gloucestershire Chamber of Agriculture, who began by offering some historical remarks. 'Virgil, the poet of agriculture for all time', he told the audience, 'does not tell us how to make cheese, but he implies in the fourth Georgic that the Roman farmer made cheese from the morning milk, and took the evening milk to market the next day.'[18] The passage in question is G. 3. 400–3:

> quod surgente die mulsere horisque diurnis,
> nocte premunt; quod iam tenebris et sole cadente,
> sub lucem: exportant calathis (adit oppida pastor),
> aut parco sale contingunt hiemique reponunt.[19]

G. 3. 400–3

The milk they've milked at dawn and during the day they press at night; that which they've milked in the evenings and at dusk, at dawn: they send the cheese out in baskets (the shepherd heads out to the towns), or else they sprinkle a little salt on it and store it away for the winter.

While Noel does not employ the *Georgics'* instructions directly, the poem's image of bustling rural production is used to inspire similar local support of a wartime initiative. As Noel does not quote the actual lines, however, the effect would have been partly reliant on the audience's (or, subsequently, readers') awareness of the passage described.

An article of March 1918, again from the *North Devon Journal*, relates the *Georgics* to wartime production more explicitly. 'Certainly, to borrow some words from Mr. Micawber', the author notes, 'universal applicability distinguishes many precepts contained in the Georgics. Look, for instance, at the lines that enforce the need of studying local conditions of weather and soil.'[20] The relevant passage is from *Georgics* 1, the lines just before the description of foreign produce examined in Chapter 2:

> ac prius ignotum ferro quam scindimus aequor,
> uentos et uarium caeli praediscere morem
> cura sit ac patrios cultusque habitusque locorum,
> et quid quaeque ferat regio et quid quaeque recuset.
> hic segetes, illic ueniunt felicius uuae,
> arborei fetus alibi atque iniussa uirescunt
> gramina. nonne uides, croceos ut Tmolus odores
> India mittit ebur

G. 1. 50–7

But before we cleave the untested plain with the plough, we should take care to learn beforehand the winds and the changeable habit of the sky, native methods of cultivation and the character of different places, and what each land produces and each land refuses to produce. In one place a crop of corn grows better, in another, grapes, in another place plantations of trees and unbidden grasses thrive. Don't you see how Tmolus exports fragrant saffron, India ivory

The particular issue at hand is apple-growing in Devonshire, and how the potential of the area in this regard has not, it is argued, been sufficiently exploited. The reader is informed of an old study which noted the suitability of the local soil and climate for apples, and a report demonstrating that 'a very palatable jelly' could be made from cider apples, without the need for added sugar. 'The Food Production Department', we are told, 'is at least anxious that the greatest possible amount of food should be extracted from North Devon orchards.'[21] The article concludes by invoking Virgil's lines for support:

> That brings me back to Virgil's advice referred to above. Local conditions are the things of paramount importance. Local conditions, which may be classed as permanent, make the apple producing capacity of North Devon great. Local conditions, which may be classed as transient, cripple that capacity ... The country wanted potatoes. It got them. The country will want apples. North Devon can help it get them.[22]

The war thus brought Virgil's agricultural advice to the minds of certain readers, but for some such advice was of limited applicability. A letter to *The Times* in early 1917 took issue with the opinion of Cecil Harmsworth, who had written to suggest that boys from the upper forms of public schools should be exempted from class and deployed to help on farms.[23] Lionel James wrote in reply from the School House, Monmouth that enough work could be done by boys in their free time and in the time allotted for games, without interfering directly with their schoolwork: 'it is not at our discretion to substitute the spade for the pen, or practical farming for the Georgics, however desirable we may think it to do so'.[24]

The *Georgics* in wartime

Charles William Brodribb (1878–1945) joined the staff of *The Times* in April 1904, having graduated in Classics from Trinity College, Oxford in 1901.[25] Throughout his long career Brodribb combined his work as a journalist with classical scholarship, penning several contributions to the *Classical Review* and publishing, in 1928, an experimental translation of the *Georgics* in English hexameters.[26] An obituary in *The Times* in 1945 noted Brodribb's patriotism, something evident in those other poems of Brodribb's which take inspiration from the *Georgics*.[27] 'Among the Lakes', an undated poem, imagines a Roman in Roman Britain reading Virgil in the Lake District,[28] while the 1943 poem 'Praises of Wiltshire' adapts the *laudes Italiae* to an English context: 'But let not the forests of Scotland, harbour of horned deer, / Nor Cornwall's coastline nor green Shakespearean Arden / Muster against Wiltshire's praises'.[29]

In March 1917 Brodribb wrote to *The Times Literary Supplement*, again with reference to the *Georgics*, this time noting its appropriateness in the light of a recent speech by the prime minister, Lloyd George. I quote the letter here in full:

> Sir, – Mr. Lloyd George's great speech may have sent others besides myself to the end of the second Georgic: –
>
> Agricola incurvo terram dimovit aratro:
> Hinc anni labor, hinc patriam parvosque nepotes
> Sustinet ...
> [The farmer has cleaved the earth with curved plough, from this the year's
> work, from this he sustains his country and his little grandchildren.]
>
> Why *nepotes*? Why his grandchildren, and not his children? The war (and the war also which Virgil had in mind) will explain. The farmer's sons are of military age and have joined the army; Agricola, being elderly, remains at home. This should give the death-blow to the inferior rival reading *penates*. Later on we read: –
>
> Casta pudicitiam servat domus.
> [The blameless household preserves its virtue.]
>
> Agricola's household is patriarchal, and includes his sons' wives as well, whose husbands are away. But 'domus = "familia," in this case the wife,' says Conington with less imagination. The war gives *domus* a more comprehensive meaning, such as Virgil must have intended it to bear. Thus do our present experiences enrich our interpretation of Virgil, which tends to become diluted in more easy-going times.[30]

Beginning at the end of Brodribb's letter, we find a bold statement as to the impact the war had on reading Virgil: it is only in wartime, he argues, that a full appreciation of the poet is possible.

By exploring precisely this context we can begin to see how the theme of agriculture in wartime brought the *Georgics* to mind. 1 February 1917 marked the beginning of a second phase of unrestricted submarine warfare by Germany, which meant that all shipping bound for the United Kingdom, allied or neutral, could be sunk without warning.[31] This precipitated concerted efforts on the part of the British government to ensure both the nation's food supply and the levels of domestic production required for the war effort. This process had begun before 1917, but the renewal of unrestricted submarine warfare meant that it now demanded top priority. Indeed, the war from the outset had had a definite impact on British agriculture. It is estimated that 15 per cent of men employed in agriculture had left for service by July 1915, while in the first months of the war there was widespread requisitioning of horses, hay, oats and straw for the military.[32]

In December 1916 Lloyd George succeeded Herbert Asquith as prime minister, and by January 1917 a Ministry of Food and a Food Production Department had been set up, with Lord Davenport appointed food controller.[33] The drive to increase the area of arable land was legislated for by the Corn Production Act of 1917, which guaranteed minimum prices for wheat and oats.[34] Conscription had been introduced in 1916, which increased the demand for women in what were seen as male jobs: in munitions factories, in transport and also in agriculture, with organizations like the Women's Land Army set up to counter shortfalls in labour on farms.[35] So Brodribb's reading of Virgil is influenced by the contemporary context: farms and families with absent men, and women managing households in their stead. The lines he quotes speak of the virtue of agricultural life specifically in time of war; the image is one of steady continuity, in marked contrast to the lives of those 'who delight in their brothers' blood'.[36]

The speech of Lloyd George referred to by Brodribb was given in the House of Commons on 23 February 1917, when the new prime minister informed the nation about the 'alarmingly low' state of food stocks and the new measures introduced to increase production.[37] To counter the German submarine threat, a new (and ultimately successful) strategy was announced: increased shipbuilding, incentives for farmers to switch from pasture to arable farming, increased domestic production of timber and iron ore and the rationing of all 'non-essential commodities' (apples and tomatoes were to be prohibited; oranges, bananas, grapes and almonds restricted).[38] In an effort to convince his audience of the necessity for this strategy, Lloyd George deployed his rhetorical skills. 'Women are working now on the land', he declared, 'the country is alive now as it has never been before to the essential value of agriculture to the community.'[39] Reviewing a history of government indifference to agricultural production, he alluded to the years of agricultural depression and to the nervousness of farmers:

There is no memory as tenacious as that of the tiller of the soil, and the furrows are still in the agricultural mind. Those years have given the British farmer a fright of the plough, and it is no use arguing with him. You must give him confidence, otherwise he will refuse to go between the shafts. Now the plough is our hope. You must cure the farmer of his plough fright, otherwise you will not get crops.[40]

One can see how this rhetorical emphasis on agriculture, reference to the 'tiller of the soil' and slogans like 'the plough is our hope' might suggest the *Georgics* to those acquainted with Virgil, as it did to Brodribb. The modest recognition of the value of women's labour which the war occasioned in Britain can furthermore be used to critique the *Georgics'* own reticence about that labour: in a patriarchal society the 'blameless household' (*G*. 2. 524) is typically an engine room of productive, essential and undervalued work.[41]

That Brodribb uses this context to support a particular textual reading serves to emphasize the strength of his response. *Nepotes* (grandchildren) is printed by Mynors (1969), Geymonat (1973) and Hirtzel ((1900); the Oxford Classical Text at the time Brodribb was writing).[42] *Penates*, referring to the Roman household gods known by that name, is the reading of M, the Codex Mediceus, one of the most important witnesses to Virgil's text, and was argued for by Markland in the eighteenth century and printed by Ribbeck in the nineteenth.[43] What might seem like a modern consensus for *nepotes*, however, has been disrupted by Conte's printing (in his 2013 edition) of *penates*, in line with his stated preference for M.[44] The arguments for either reading are subjective, and the final decision remains with each individual reader: *nepotes* stresses the intergenerational continuity and resilience of agricultural life, but, as Markland objected,[45] not every farmer has grandchildren; *penates* is something common to all and is the reading of M, and yet it can been judged, as it is by Geymonat and Mynors, to be an inference from *Aeneid* 8. 543. For Brodribb, it was the experience of war which carried the argument decisively in favour of *nepotes*.

'The Empire and the Land'

Herbert Warren was president of Magdalen College, Oxford, 1885–1928, as well as vice-chancellor of the university (1906–10) and professor of poetry

(1911–16).[46] In September 1916, Warren wrote a review of an American translation of the *Georgics* for *The Spectator*, entitled 'The Empire and the Land', which he uses to assert the contemporary relevance of Virgil's poem.[47] 'If the *Eclogues* are partly mirage', Warren writes, 'the *Georgics* very largely "mean business." "After the war", "back to the land", exactly describes their history and their philosophy.'[48] He reads the lines at *G*. 2. 442–53, which discuss different timbers, as advocating 'afforestation' and argues that Virgil endorses a settlement policy for veterans, 'whole-heartedly' advocating the policy of 'back to the land … in a most glorious and most successful manner'.[49] By the end of the review, it is clear that Warren sees in this history a lesson for the British Empire after the war, and sees the *Georgics* as perfect reading for a post-war world:

> Virgil, in truth, like Tennyson, and like Kipling, did much not only to bless and blazon, but to build, an Empire. And those who have to-day the leisure to think forward, and dream of the future of their land, and of its soldier sons, may do worse than read the *Georgics* again, whether here or in Canada or in South Africa, in Australia or New Zealand, whether in Latin or in English.[50]

Before critiquing Warren's reception, it is necessary to examine briefly the contemporary context, in order to note that Warren's pronouncements were in fact to be borne out by government policy. The Hobhouse Committee had reported in early 1916 and had recommended that a plan be put in place for the settlement of veterans, while the Selborne Committee, whose report was published in March 1917, recommended government help towards the revival of forestry in Britain.[51] In a campaign speech at Wolverhampton in advance of the 1918 general election (which the ruling coalition was to win by a landslide), Lloyd George used language which was strikingly similar to Warren's. Britain was to be made a land 'fit for heroes to live in'.[52] This entailed learning the lessons of the war and striving for national self-sufficiency, reducing waste and increasing the yields of British agriculture. 'A systematic effort must be made', Lloyd George told the assembled crowd, 'to bring the population back to the land.'[53]

Like Warren, he called for afforestation[54] and then drew a direct comparison with ancient Rome. *The Times*' report reads:

Now I come to the next point. There must be a scheme for settling gallant soldiers and sailors on the land. (Cheers.) Those of you who have read the history of Rome know that this was a problem that always came up after every war, and how the soldiers who had been settled on the land, through lack of balance in tackling the problem, brought about a general failure at the end of every war in achieving the purposes and redeeming the promises that were given. You will recollect that the great Emperor Augustus finally settled the soldiers on the land, and it was only then that you had really peace and prosperity in the Roman Empire. Now, that is a lesson. I do not say that all the soldiers will go back to the land. The vast majority will return to their old occupations. But I am told that a good many of them who have been living an open-air life do not want to return to the close atmosphere of the workshop and factory. If that is the case they ought to have the opportunity of living on the land, but they ought to be trained for the purpose.[55]

Such promises were ostensibly kept when the coalition was returned to power. The Forestry Act of 1919 allocated £3.5 million over ten years to plant 150,000 acres of forest trees.[56] The Land Settlement (Facilities) Act, meanwhile, allocated £20 million to fund county councils in providing smallholdings for ex-servicemen.[57] 250,000 acres were bought and some 17,000 tenants were settled as part of the scheme, which ran into difficulties amid the slump of 1921, but continued until 1925.[58]

Amid planning for post-war life in Britain, the example of Octavian's Rome, and of the *Georgics*, attained sudden relevance in national politics. Yet Warren's review should also been seen within an international – which is to say, imperial – context. He identifies strongly with the poem's Italian passages, which he calls 'the most splendid and lasting ornament which the "purple Caesars" ever wore'.[59] This identification is one of the most consistent features in the British reception of the *Georgics* and, as for Jesse Collings, one which incorporates a comparison between Rome and Britain. While this comparison is often implicit, here it is strikingly obvious, in lines ostensibly referring to the composition of the poem:

To refresh the love of Italy, her land and story, to multiply her population and military power by planting a sturdy peasantry and restoring family life, to develop the economic resources of the Empire, to distribute wealth more widely, to strengthen public spirit and private virtue, and bring back faith and justice – these were the ideals set before Rome by the legislation of Augustus and the truly laureate lays of Virgil and Horace.[60]

The blurring of 'Empires' is clear: Virgil's poem, implies Warren, applies equally to Britain in 1916. More than this, Warren sees aspects of continuity in the history of European imperial power. Referring to Virgil, Horace and Octavian, he asks, 'Did they fail or did they succeed, these idealists? They made a system which lasted almost intact nearly half a thousand years, in some senses a thousand more, and whose effects are living yet.'[61]

Warren's identification with Italy is premised, however, on a binary worldview. If Italy is a familiar land, the 'East' is its antithesis – something also found in Thomson's description of indigenous people in South America, quoted in Chapter 5, and in Sellar's contrast between 'the beauties and riches of Italy' and 'the prodigal luxuriance in the forests and jungles of the East'.[62] Such descriptions are part of the construction of difference, racial or climatic, that underpins imperial ideology. By making the victims of European rule seem foreign or other, their subjugation and suffering could be more easily defended or ignored. Here again a reader reproduces, rather than critiques, the imperial rhetoric of the *Georgics* itself, both the political and climatic supremacy of Italy in Book 2, and the representation of vague and threatening Eastern forces on the doors of the temple in Book 3:

> In Virgil's lifetime, as in our own, the whole known world was involved in wars, culminating in one general convulsion of Europe, Asia, and Africa. Fighting during those years of struggle went on upon the Thames and the Seine, the Aisne, the Marne, the Rhine, the Danube, the Nile, the Euphrates, in Mesopotamia and Spain, in Belgium and Switzerland, in Tunis and Egypt and Arabia.
>
>   'Hinc movet Euphrates, illinc Germania bellum.'
>
>   [From here the Euphrates, from there Germany incites war.]
>
> And again: –
>
>   'Aut conjurato descendens Dacus ab Istro.'
>
>   [Or a Dacian coming down from the conspiratorial Danube.]
>
> How up to date and natural these lines sound! The sea-war was decided not far from Corfu, and the land-war between Salonika and Kavala. The contest, it is true, was a civil one; but it became a struggle of East and West, in which Germania and the East, as the lines just quoted remind us, made common

cause, and of conflicting ideals of free citizenship, though under a monarch, and Oriental tyranny.[63]

Warren maps the battlefields of the First World War onto the battlefields of late-Republican Rome, referencing in particular the Battles of Philippi ('between Salonika and Kavala') and Actium ('not far from Corfu'). But by following the poem's rhetorical portrayal of civil conflict as 'a struggle of East and West', Warren repeats the most vague and simplistic of cultural clichés. The alliance between Germany and the Ottoman Empire in the First World War allows him to link the *Georgics'* reference to *Germania* with its orientalizing depiction of the 'East'. The civilized forces of Britain and its allies, so the argument runs, are forced to defend themselves against an 'Oriental tyranny'.

Warren's patriotic (even jingoistic) appropriation echoes the way in which many academics in belligerent countries rushed to endorse the war and used their public position to advocate for its legitimacy and even its necessity, rather than to voice independent criticisms of government policy, or to question the political basis of the conflict.[64] This is despite the fact that Warren was in a prime position to gauge the human cost of the war, as he received frequent news throughout the conflict of Magdalen men killed or injured.[65] The image of European political leaders as 'sleepwalkers', as the title of a recent history characterizes them, should not obscure the fact that the war met with the general assent of the business and political classes in Britain, and that it was, at least in part, the result of a network of competitive European imperialisms.[66] The conflict was a 'world' war because it mobilized and threatened European empires (war is 'global' at *G.* 1. 505 too, and for the same reason); it cannot be understood without understanding the desire of British diplomats and politicians to maintain and advance Britain's global influence both during and after and conflict.[67]

Warren's narrow metropolitan viewpoint can thus also be found in Virgil's poem. The *Georgics'* focus on civil war serves to obscure the persistent belligerence of Roman foreign policy, in much the same way as Warren's view of the poem obscures the imperial contexts both of the First World War and the violence of the settlements which followed it. As it was for Mackail, the central assumption of the review is one which is pervasive yet problematic: that the *Georgics* is 'a poem of peace'. In a certain sense this is no doubt true, as one can read Virgil's poem as a hymn to the staying power of the natural world amid human chaos. But while it might celebrate peace, it also celebrates victories over civil and foreign enemies, both real and imagined, champions a divisive and autocratic victor, and depicts peoples and places caught up in the history of Roman imperialism. Warren's reception is thus one further example of the imperial contexts which are fundamental to the British reception of the *Georgics*.

Conclusion: Towards a Decolonizing Pedagogy of Latin Literature

Why read the *Georgics*? What gives this poem its authority, its privileged position at the centre of a privileged canon? I have my own thoughts on these questions, as others will, and I don't intend to answer them here. But I think they should be first on the list in any pedagogy of Latin literature. To paraphrase Noam Chomsky, writing in a different context, the authority of these texts is not innate, but is granted in every generation by a new community of readers. And every reader has the right to read or to reject them according to his or her own judgement.[1] The great strengths of classical philology, its emphasis on grammar and close reading, its attention to detail and curatorial responsibility, also risk a loss of perspective. We go so close in that we can't see the wood for the trees, and famous texts become masterpieces to be venerated in the minutest detail. It is useful to distinguish here between personal and pedagogical reading. I make no claim over anyone's personal reading of Virgil: it is in an educational setting that this uncritical appreciation I am talking about is a significant limitation.[2]

The classical canon, unlike others, is fixed. No one is going to write Latin poetry of a kind that will join Virgil and his contemporaries as part of the Latin canon. These texts have been so studied for so many years that the risk of stasis, of a loss of perspective, is more acute than in other disciplines. And this is where I see the strength of reception: not as a supposedly disinterested cataloguing of influence, but as a politicizing and iconoclastic practice, one that offers some breathing space amid the claustrophobia of the canon, one that brings new and different perspectives to classical texts, emphasizing not the world as it was, but the world as it is now. By zooming out from the *Georgics* in 29 BCE, by introducing non-Roman, British imperial and modern angles on the poem, my hope is that it can now be seen more in 3D, its limitations as well as its achievements be better delineated and a critical appreciation more successfully fostered.

Here are four perspectives I've gained from my work on the poem.

1. **Post-colonial.** Empire is fundamental not only to the *Georgics* in its original, Roman context, but to at least one strand of its reception history as well. In the attention it gives to a single man (Octavian), its hyperbolic imagery of Roman power and its depiction of other peoples and enemies of state in threatening or supine terms, it has in embryonic form what reappears in the *Aeneid* and in contemporary Latin poetry's treatment of Cleopatra.[3] That Actian moment in turn became, as Quint has shown, a wellspring for a whole tradition in later European poetry.[4] And it is important to realize that there was nothing inevitable about the inclusion of such elements in this poetry; its achievement in general should not diminish the attention given to its particular and objectionable disfigurations. Such disfigurations have never been centre stage in the reception of the *Georgics*, a text that has always been studied more in imperial centres than in the places where the worst of empire has been revealed. It is worth trying to imagine Latin literature from the perspective of India, ancient and modern, or Ethiopia, ancient and modern, in order to deflate the 'Roman' perspective we are always getting, to trace certain continuities in the history of European imperial power, and to make connections that can inform the present. What I've tried to suggest in this book is that the *Georgics* itself invites and accommodates such perspectives.[5]

2. **Institutional.** The reception history of a text can fundamentally shape what that text is taken to be. The *Georgics* in Britain was interpreted and taught over many generations by a very narrow section of society, which is to say, with some exceptions, a class of privileged and conservative white men residing in elite institutions. The scholarship those men produced was, in my experience, consistently of a very high quality, but was inevitably limited in its perspective. It is not surprising that the *Georgics* became depoliticized, but the point is that institutional narrowness is still an issue. Virgilian bibliography before the final decade of the twentieth

century was still written by a remarkably circumscribed demographic, and despite a greater plurality of voices emerging in the meantime, the elite basis of academic institutions, and of the formal study of ancient Greece and Rome in particular, means that there remains an imbalance. This is not to essentialize the work of any scholar, but to reaffirm that a more diverse academy can generate a more diverse range of perspectives (which can only be a good thing), and that the narrowness of the scholarly tradition is relevant to the history and pedagogy of these texts.

3. **Pedagogical.** My abiding impression of the *Georgics* is the range of its utility as a teaching text. This is not news, of course, and incorporates the traditional strengths of classical education: philology, translation and literary history, as well as access to the big themes (and whatever else) that poetry gives its readers. But by taking the *Georgics* as a whole tradition of literature and reception, centred in the present, other themes present themselves. These include the universalizing pretensions of European knowledge and their relation to European conquest and global domination; the histories of racism, patriarchy and empire inextricably bound up with the study of ancient Greece and Rome; the limitations of academic discourse, the politics of (classical) tourism in the modern world; ecology and capitalism in an age of climate crisis and diminishing biodiversity; the long-standing denial of value or visibility to women's labour – agricultural, domestic, emotional, reproductive – in a predominantly male academy. Others will have their own ideas, but I think that there is much to be gained from broadening what is expected pedagogically from a poem like the *Georgics*.

4. **Literary-historical.** In the institutional study of the ancient Roman world, literature has always held a central place, but the highly accomplished, artful and allusive Latin of Virgil and his contemporaries is only one kind of Latin. It was invigorating for me, at any rate, to get away from Virgil and company and to read the *Georgics* in the light not just of Cato and Varro and Plautus and Terence, but of the kind of informal and often non-elite Latin that has been recently anthologized by J. N. Adams.[6] The Latin of ordinary people helped me to see the high literature in clearer, less intense and less exaggerated terms, as did my discovery of the histories of the

Italian Peninsula and the diverse range of languages spoken there which eventually lost out to Latin. This kind of perspective seems to me important in decolonizing the study of the literature. And as I've said above, what also seems important in this regard is to question the apparently ubiquitous use of the honorific and reverential title 'Augustus' for Octavian, as well as its companion adjective 'Augustan', however useful the latter may be as a chronological marker. The word and its connotations, to my mind, give undue deference to political power, in Octavian's case a kind of power that was autocratic, patriarchal and imperial, and that has inspired rulers of that kind ever since.[7]

I hope that these reflections, and the preceding study, will be of use to those with similar interests, and to readers of Virgil and students of Latin more generally. I have deliberately tried to avoid putting forward definitive statements about the poem, preferring to emphasize its complexity and the independence of the reader. The *Georgics* arguably does the same thing that many of its receptions do, aestheticizing places and peoples in ways which obscure and even facilitate the workings of imperial power; the poem and its tradition thus raise questions about the role of the artist (as well as the scholar and the journalist) in society. But there is plenty, too, in the *Georgics*, of a poet's love of the world, and Virgil's map can be read in ways which undermine, as well as promote, its depiction of the world in Roman terms. It is a question of, in bell hooks' words, remembering the past and imagining the future, if only to realize the possibility of change.[8]

Appendix: The Geography of the *Georgics*

At Appendix 1A I've listed every word in the poem which denotes a geographical location in the *orbis terrarum* (as the inhabited world was known in Latin) including rivers, lakes, seas and mountains, but excluding winds, celestial bodies, non-specific literary locations (like the 'the woods of Alcinous' at G. 2. 87), metaphysical locations (like the Elysian fields at G. 1. 38) and the underworld, except in three instances where the toponyms concerned also denote physical locations: Mt. Olympus, Taenarus and Lake Avernus. Rivers, mountains, lakes and periphrases are indicated by (R), (M), (L) and (P) respectively. At Appendix 1B I've listed every word which denotes a people, including literary examples like the Hyperboreans, but excluding named individuals and figures mythical, historical or divine (Camillus, Jupiter, Hercules, *Cyclopes*, etc.). References to the poem are given according to Mynors's edition (1969) and I've translated all the Latin and given the modern names of rivers and mountains where they are clearly identifiable. Studies of different aspects of the poem's geography include Fischer (1968), McKay (1970), Goodfellow (1981), Thomas (1982) 35–92, Horsfall (1997) and Harrison (2008); for more general studies see Thomson (1965), Nicolet (1991), Romm (1992) and Jones (2005), and for a comprehensive atlas of the ancient Greek and Roman worlds see Talbert (2000).

1A Toponyms in the *Georgics* listed alphabetically by location

Aegean, The

Carpathian Sea	4.387	*Carpathio . . . gurgite*	'in the Carpathian swell'
Crete	3.345	*Cressamque pharetram*	'and a Cretan quiver'
Delos	3.6	*Latonia Delos*	'Latona's Delos'[1]
Dicte (M) (on Crete)	2.536	*sceptrum Dictaei regis* (sc. *Iouis*)	'the sceptre of a Dictean king' (i.e. Jupiter)
	4.152	*Dictaeo . . . sub antro*	'within a Dictean cave'
Ceos	1.14	*pinguia Ceae / . . . dumeta*	'the dense thorn bushes of Ceos'
Cnossos (on Crete)	1.222	*Cnosiaque ardentis . . . stella Coronae*	'and the Cretan star of the blazing Crown'
Cynthus (M) (on Delos)	3.36	*Troiae Cynthius auctor*	'the Cynthian founder of Troy' (i.e. Apollo)
Lesbos	2.90	*Lesbos*	'Lesbos'
Methymna (on Lesbos)	2.90	*Methymnaeo . . . de palmite*	'from the Methymnian vine'
Paphos	2.64	*solido Paphiae de robore myrtus*	'Paphian myrtles [propagate best] from the solid stem'[2]
Paros	3.34	*Parii lapides*	'Parian stones'
Phanae (on Chios)	2.98	*rex ipse Phanaeus*	'the Phanaean, king of vines'
Rhodes	2.102	*Rhodia* (sc. *uitis*)	'the Rhodian vine'
Thasos	2.91	*Thasiae uites*	'vines from Thasos'

Asia

'Asia' in the Georgics (*and in modern usage*) *is an inherently vague toponym. Places listed here include mainly those in what is now Turkey, but also locations in Central and South Asia.*

Abydos (in the Hellespont)	1.207	*ostriferi fauces . . . Abydi*	'the straits of oyster-producing Abydos'
Ascanius (R)	3.270	*transque sonantem / Ascanium*	'and across the sounding Ascanius'
Asia	1.383	*Asia . . . / . . . prata Caystri*	'Asian meadows by the river Cayster'
	2.171	*extremis Asiae . . . uictor in oris*	'a victor on the farthest shores of Asia'

	3.30	*urbes Asiae domitas*	'the conquered cities of Asia'
	4.343	*Asia Deiopea* (sc. *nympha*)	'Asian Deiopea' (a nymph)
Assyria	2.465	*alba neque Assyrio fucatur lana ueneno*	'nor white wool be soaked in Assyrian dye'[3]
Bactra (mod. Balkh)	2.138	*Bactra*	'Bactra'
Caicus (R) (mod. Bakırçay)	4.370	*Mysusque Caicus*	'and the Mysian Caicus'
Caucasus Mountains	2.440	*ipsae Caucasio steriles in uertice siluae*	'even the barren woods of the high Caucasus'
Cayster (R) (mod. Küçükmenderes)	1.384	*Asia . . . / . . . prata Caystri*	'Asian meadows by the river Cayster'
Corycus	4.127	*Corycium . . . senem*	'an old man from Corycus'
Cytorus (M)	2.437	*undantem buxo . . . Cytorum*	'Cytorus teeming with boxwood'
Euphrates (R)	1.509	*Euphrates*	'Euphrates'
	4.561	*ad altum / . . . Euphraten*	'to deep Euphrates'
Ganges (R)	2.137	*pulcher Ganges*	'beautiful Ganges'
Gargara (M)	1.103	*ipsa . . . Gargara*	'Gargara itself'
	3.269	*trans Gargara*	'across Gargara'
Hellespont, the	4.111	*Hellespontiaci . . . tutela Priapi*	'[as] guardian [of the hive] Priapus of the Hellespont'[4]
Hermus (R) (mod. Gediz)	2.137	*auro turbidus Hermus*	'the Hermus cloudy with gold'
Hydaspes (R) (mod. Jhelum)	4.211	*Medus Hydaspes*	'the Median Hydaspes'
Ida (M)	2.84	*Idaeis cyparissis*	'cypresses on Ida'
	3.450	*Idaeasque pices*	'and the pitch pines of Ida'
	4.41	*Phrygiae . . . pice lentius Idae*	'stickier than the pitch of Phrygian Ida'
India	1.57	*India mittit ebur*	'India exports ivory'
	2.116	*sola India nigrum / fert hebenum*	'only India yields black ebony'
Lycus (R)	4.367	*Lycumque*	'and the Lycus'[5]
Lydia	4.211	*ingens / Lydia*	'great Lydia'
Maeonia (in Lydia)	4.380	*Maeonii carchesia Bacchi*	'cups of Maeonian wine'
Media	2.126	*Media*	'Media'[6]
	4.211	*Medus Hydaspes*	'the Median Hydaspes' (mod. Jhelum)
Miletus	3.306	*Milesia . . . / uellera*	'Milesian fleeces'

	4.334	*Milesia uellera*	'Milesian fleeces'
Mysia	1.102	*Mysia*	'Mysia'
	4.370	*Mysusque Caicus*	'and the Mysian Caicus'
Niphates (M)	3.30	*pulsumque Niphaten*	'and Mt. Niphates driven back'
Panchaia	2.139	*totaque . . . Panchaia*	'and all Panchaia'[7]
	4.379	*Panchaeis adolescunt ignibus arae*	'altars burn with Panchaian fires'
Phrygia	4.41	*Phrygiae . . . pice lentius Idae*	'stickier than the pitch of Phrygian Ida'
Pontus (region in mod. n. Turkey)	1.58	*Pontus*	'Pontus'
Pontus (Black Sea)	1.207	*Pontus*	'Pontus'
Thymbra	4.323	*Thymbraeus Apollo*	'Thymbraean Apollo'[8]
Tmolus (M)	1.56	*Tmolus*	'Tmolus'
	2.98	*Tmolius* (sc. *uitis*)	'the vine from Tmolus'
Troy	1.502	*Laomedonteae luimus periuria Troiae*	'we've paid for the deceits of Laomedon's Troy'
	2.385	*Ausonii, Troia gens missa, coloni*	'Ausonian farmers, a people sent out from Troy'[9]
	3.36	*Troiae Cynthius auctor*	'the Cynthian founder of Troy' (i.e. Apollo)

Africa

The area comprising what is now Egypt and Libya. Modern and ancient usages of 'Egypt' and 'Libya' differ considerably.

Canopus	4.287	*Pellaei gens fortunata Canopi*	'the happy people of Pellean Canopus'
Cinyps (R) (mod. Wadi Ka'am)	3.312	*Cinyphii . . . hirci*	'[the beard] of a Cinyphian he-goat'
Cyrene	4.321	*Cyrene mater*	'mother Cyrene'
	4.354	*Cyrene soror*	'sister Cyrene'[10]
Egypt	3.5	*inlaudati . . . Busiridis aras* (P)[11]	'the altars of unpraised Busiris'
	4.210	*Aegyptus*	'Egypt'
	4.291	*uiridem Aegyptum*	'green Egypt'
Libya	2.105	*Libyci . . . aequoris*	'[sand] of the Libyan plain'

	3.249	*Libyae solis . . . in agris*	'in the deserted fields of Libya'
	3.339	*pastores Libyae*	'Libyan shepherds'
Mareotis (L, at Alexandria)	2.91	*Mareotides albae* (sc. *uites*)	'the white vines of Lake Mareotis'
Nile (R)	3.29	*undantem bello magnumque fluentum / Nilum*	'the Nile in spate and surging with war'
	4.288	*effuso stagnantem flumine Nilum*	'the pools of the flooded Nile'
Pelusium	1.228	*Pelusiacae curam . . . lentis*	'cultivation of the Pelusian lentil'

Europe

These locations are in the Mediterranean and Alpine region, with the exception of Thule, the most northerly place named in the poem.

Alps, the	1.475	*insolitis tremuerunt motibus Alpes*	'the Alps shook with strange disturbances'
	3.474	*aërias Alpis*	'the lofty Alps'
Balearic Islands, the	1.309	*stuppea . . . Balearis uerbera fundae*	'the hempen thongs of a Balearic sling'[12]
Germania	1.474	*armorum sonitum . . . Germania . . . / audiit*	'*Germania* heard the sound of arms'
	1.509	*Germania*	'*Germania*'
Ionian Sea (w. of Greece)	2.108	*Ionii . . . ad litora fluctus*	'to the shores of the Ionian Sea'
Noricum	3.474	*Norica . . . / castella in tumulis*	'the hilltop garrisons of Noricum'
Raetia	2.96	*Rhaetica* (sc. *uitis*)	'the Raetian vine'[13]
Thule	1.30	*ultima Thule*	'furthest Thule'[14]
Timauus (R) (mod. Timavo)	3.475	*Iapydis arua Timaui*	'the Iapydian fields of the Timavus'
Tyrrhenian Sea (w. of Italy)	2.164	*Tyrrhenusque . . . aestus*	'and the Tyrrhenian tide'

Greece

The area comprising the modern Greek mainland and some of southern Albania, ranging from Epirus and Pella in the north to Taenarus in the southern Peloponnese, with multiple references to Olympia, Sparta, Arcadia, Thessaly and Delphi.

Achelous (R)	1.9	*poculaque . . . Acheloia*	'and cups [of water] from the river Achelous'
Alpheus (R) (mod. Alfeios)	3.19	*Alpheum*	'Alpheus'
	3.180	*Alphea . . . flumina Pisae*	'the Alphean streams of Pisa'
Amphrysus (R)	3.2	*pastor ab Amphryso* (sc. *Apollo*)	'the shepherd from the Amyphrysus' (i.e. Apollo)
Amyclae	3.89	*Amyclaei . . . Pollucis habenis*	'by the reins of Amyclaean Pollux'
	3.345	*Amyclaeumque canem*	'and an Amyclaean dog'
Arcadia	3.392	*Pan deus Arcadiae*	'Pan, god of Arcadia'
	4.283	*Arcadii memoranda inuenta magistri*	'the famous discoveries of an Arcadian beekeeper' (i.e. Aristaeus)
Ascra	2.176	*Ascraeumque cano . . . carmen*	'and I sing an Ascraean song'
Athos (M) (mod. Athos)	1.332	*Atho*	'Athos'
Attica	4.463	*Actias Orithyia*	'Attic Orithyia'
Beroea	4.341	*Beroe soror* (sc. *nympha*)	'sister Beroe' (a nymph)
Ceraunian Mountains	1.332	*alta Ceraunia*	'high Ceraunia'
Chaonia	1.8	*Chaoniam . . . glandem*	'Chaonia's acorn'
	2.67	*Chaoniique patris glandes* (sc. *Iouis*)	'and acorns of the Chaonian father' (i.e. Jupiter)
Cithaeron (M) (mod. Kithairon)	3.43	*uocat ingenti clamore Cithaeron*	'Cithaeron calls with a great shout'
Corinth	2.464	*Ephyreiaque aera*	'and Corinthian bronze'
	4.343	*Ephyre* (sc. *nympha*)	'Ephyre' (a nymph)

Delphi	3.293	*Castaliam*	'Castalia' (i.e. the fountain on Mt. Parnassus).
Dodona	1.149	*Dodona*	'Dodona'
Eleusis	1.163	*Eleusinae matris*	'[the wagons] of the Eleusinian mother' (i.e. Ceres)
Elis	1.59	*Eliadum . . . palmas equarum*	'the palms for Elean mares'
	3.202	*ad Elei metas*	'to the turning posts at Elis'
Emathia	1.492	*Emathiam*	'Emathia'
	4.390	*Emathiae portus*	'the harbours of Emathia'
Enipeus (R)	4.368	*altus . . . Enipeus*	'deep Enipeus'
Epidauros	3.44	*domitrixque Epidaurus equorum*	'and Epidaurus, tamer of horses'
Epirus	1.59	*Epiros*	'Epirus'
	3.121	*Epirum*	'Epirus'
	3.405	*acremque Molossum* (sc. *canem*)	'and a fierce Molossian' (a breed of dog)
Graecia	1.38	*Graecia*	'Greece'
	3.20	*cuncta . . . / . . . Graecia*	'all Greece'
Helicon (M)	3.11	*Aonio . . . uertice*	'from Helicon's peak'
Hymettus (M)	4.177	*Cecropias . . . apes* (P)[15]	'Cecrops's bees'
	4.270	*Cecropiumque thymum* (P)	'and Cecrops's thyme'
Lycaeus (M) (mod. Lykaion)	1.16	*saltusque Lycaei*	'and the woodlands of Lycaeus'
	3.2	*siluae amnesque Lycaei*	'the woods and streams of Lycaeus'
	3.314	*siluas et summa Lycaei*	'the woods and heights of Lycaeus'
	4.539	*uiridis . . . summa Lycaei*	'the heights of green Lycaeus'
Maenalus (M) (mod. Mainalo)	1.17	*tua Maenala*	'your Maenalus'
Mycenae	3.121	*fortisque Mycenas*	'and strong Mycenae'
Nemea	3.19	*lucosque Molorchi* (P)	'and the groves of Molorchus'[16]
Olympia	3.49	*Olympiacae . . . praemia palmae*	'the rewards of an Olympic palm'
	3.181	*Iouis in luco* (P)	'in Jupiter's grove'[17]
Olympus (M) (mod. Olympos)	1.96	*alto . . . Olympo*	'from high Olympus'
	1.282	*frondosum . . . Olympum*	'leafy Olympus'
	1.450	*emenso . . . Olympo*	'from the sky [the sun] has passed through'[18]

	3.223	*longus Olympus*	'the whole sky'
	4.562	*uiamque adfectat Olympo*	'while [Caesar] sought a path to Olympus'
Ossa (M) (mod. Ossa)	1.281	*ter sunt conati imponere Pelio Ossam*	'three times [the giants] tried to put Ossa atop Pelion'
	1.282	*atque Ossae frondosum inuoluere Olympum*	'and [they tried] to roll leafy Olympus onto Ossa'
Pallene	4.391	*patriamque reuisit / Pallenen* (sc. *Proteus*)	'and he returns to his homeland of Pallene'
Parnassus (M) (mod. Parnassos)	2.18	*Parnasia laurus / parua*	'the little laurel of Parnassus'
	3.291	*Parnasi deserta per ardua*	'through the lonely heights of Parnassus'
Pelethronius	3.115	*Pelethronii Lapithae*	'Pelethronian Lapiths'[19]
	1.281	*ter sunt conati imponere Pelio Ossam*	'three times [the giants] tried to put Ossa atop Pelion'
	3.94	*altum / Pelion*	'high Pelion'
Pella	4.287	*Pellaei gens fortunata Canopi*	'the happy people of Pellean Canopus'
Peneus (R) (mod. Peneios)	4.317	*Peneia Tempe*	'Tempe, the valley of the Peneus'
	4.355	*Penei genitoris ad undam*	'to the waters of his father Peneus'
Philippi	1.490	*Philippi*	'Philippi'
Pisa	3.180	*Alphea . . . flumina Pisae*	'the Alphean streams of Pisa'
Sicyon	2.519	*teritur Sicyonia baca trapetis*	'the Sicyonian olive is pressed in mills'
Sparta	2.487	*uirginibus bacchata Lacaenis / Taygeta*	'Taygetus witness to the revels of Spartan girls'
	3.405	*uelocis Spartae catulos*	'swift Spartan pups'
Spercheus (R) (mod. Spercheios)	2.487	*campi / Spercheosque*	'and the plains of the Spercheus'
Taenarus (mod. Cape Matapan)	4.467	*Taenarias . . . fauces*	'the jaws of Taenarus' (i.e. the underworld)
Taygetus (M) (mod. Taygetos)	2.488	*uirginibus bacchata Lacaenis / Taygeta*	'Taygetus witness to the revels of Spartan girls'
	3.44	*Taygetique canes*	'and dogs of the Taygetus'
Tegea	1.18	*o Tegeaee* (sc. *Pan*)	'o Tegean one' (i.e. Pan)
Tempe	2.469	*frigida tempe*	'a cool valley'[20]
	4.317	*Peneia Tempe*	'Tempe, the valley of the Peneus'

Italy

Italian locations in the poem encompass the whole peninsula from Como to Locri (plus Sicily's Mt. Etna), with numerous references to the areas around Mantua and Campania in particular. See especially Book 2, lines 136–76.

Acerrae	2.225	*uacuis . . . Acerris*	'empty Acerrae'
Alburnus (M) (mod. M. Panormo)	3.147	*ilicibusque uirentem / . . . Alburnum*	'and Alburnus green with its holm oaks'
Ameria	1.265	*Amerina . . . lentae retinacula uiti*	'Amerian ties for the pliant vine'
Anio (R) (mod. Aniene)	4.369	*Aniena fluenta*	'Anio's streams'
Avernus (L)	2.164	*fretis . . . Auernis*	'the channels of Avernus'
	4.493	*ter fragor stagnis auditus Auernis*	'the crash was heard three times in the pools of Avernus'
Benacus (L) (mod. Garda)	2.160	*Benace*	'Benacus'
Calabria	3.425	*ille malus Calabris in saltibus anguis*	'that harmful snake found in Calabrian woodlands'[21]
Capua	2.224	*diues . . . Capua*	'wealthy Capua'
Clanius (R) (mod. Clanio)	2.225	*Clanius non aequus*	'the unfair Clanius'
Clitumnus (R) (mod. Clitunno)	2.146	*Clitumne*	'Clitumnus'
Crustumerium	2.88	*Crustumiis . . . piris*	'pears from Crustumerium'
Eridanus / Padus (R) (mod. Po)[22]	1.482	*fluuiorum rex Eridanus*	'Eridanus, king of rivers'
	2.452	*leuis innatat alnus / missa Pado*	'a light alder boat swims down the Po'
	4.372	*et gemina auratus taurino cornua uultu / Eridanus*	'and Eridanus, with both horns of his bull's brow gilded'[23]
Etna (M) (mod. Etna)	1.472	*undantem ruptis fornacibus Aetnam*	'Etna overflowing, its furnaces broken'
	4.173	*gemit impositis incudis Aetna*	'Etna groans when the anvils are set in place'[24]
Etruria	1.499	*Tuscum Tiberim*	'the Etruscan Tiber'
	2.533	*fortis Eturia*	'strong Etruria'
Falernus, ager	2.96	*cellis Falernis*	'Falernian cellars'
	2.97	*Aminneae uites*	'Aminean vines'[25]
Galaesus (R) (mod. Galeso)	4.126	*niger . . . Galaesus*	'the dark Galaesus'
Herculaneum	2.225	*uicina Vesaeuo / ora iugo* (P)	'the shore close to Vesuvius's slope'[26]

Italia	2.138	*laudibus Italiae*	'the praises of Italy'
	2.173	*Saturnia tellus*	'Saturn's land'[27]
Larus (L) (mod. Como)	2.159	*Lari maxime*	'Larus, greatest of all'
Locri Epizephyrii (mod. Locri)	2.438	*Naryciaeque picis lucos* (P)	'and groves of Narycian pitch pine'[28]
Lucrinus (L)	2.161	*Lucrinoque addita claustra*	'and barriers added to the Lucrine'
Mantua (mod. Mantova)	2.198	*infelix . . . Mantua*	'unhappy Mantua'
	3 .12	*Mantua*	'Mantua'
Massicus (M) (mod. M. Massico)	2.143	*Bacchi Massicus umor*	'the liquor of Massic wine'
	3.526	*Massica Bacchi / munera*	'Bacchus's gifts from Massicus'
Mella (R) (mod. Mella)	4.278	*curua . . . flumina Mellae*	'Mella's meandering streams'
Mincius (R) (mod. Mincio)	3.15	*ingens . . . / Mincius*	'the great Mincio'
Naples	4.564	*dulcis . . . / Parthenope*	'sweet Naples'[29]
Paestum	4.119	*biferique rosaria Paesti*	'and the rose beds of Paestum that flower twice a year'
Palatine Hill	1.499	*Romana Palatia*	'Roman Palatine'
Rome	1.466	*Romam*	'Rome'
	1.499	*Romana Palatia*	'Roman Palatine'
	2.148	*Romanos . . . triumphos*	'Roman triumphs'
	2.176	*Romana per oppida*	'through Roman towns'
	2.498	*res Romanae*	'Roman affairs'
	2.534	*rerum . . . pulcherrima Roma*	'Rome the fairest place on earth'
Sila, la	3.219	*in magna Sila*	'on great Sila'
Silarus (R) (mod. Sele)	3.146	*lucos Silari circa*	'by the groves of the Silarus'
Syracuse (Ortigia)	4.344	*velox Arethusa* (sc. *nympha*)	'swift Arethusa' (a nymph)[30]
Taburnus (M) (mod. M. Taburno)	2.38	*magnum . . . Taburnum*	'great Taburnus'
Tanager (R) (mod. Tanagro)	3.151	*sicci ripa Tanagri*	'the bank of the dried-up Tanager'
Tarentum	2.197	*saturi . . . Tarenti*	'[the woods] of rich Tarentum'
	4.125	*sub Oebaliae . . . turribus arcis* (P)	'under the towers of an Oebalian citadel'[31]
Tiber (R) (mod. Tevere)	1.499	*Tuscum Tiberim*	'the Etruscan Tiber'
	4.369	*pater Tiberinus*	'Father Tiber'
Vesuvius (M) (mod. Vesuvio)	2.224	*uicina Vesaeuo / ora iugo*	'the shore close to Vesuvius's slope'

Levant, the

Idumaea	3.12	*Idumaeas . . . palmas*	'Idumean palms'
Syria	2.88	*Syriisque piris*	'and Syrian pears'[32]
Tyre	2.506	*Sarrano . . . ostro*	'in Sarrian purple'[33]
	3.17	*Tyrio . . . in ostro*	'in Tyrian purple'
	3.307	*Tyrios . . . rubores*	'Tyrian purple'

orbis terrarum **(the world)**[34]

Oceanus	1.246	*Oceani . . . aequore*	'by Ocean's sea'
	2.122	*quos Oceano propior gerit India lucos*	'those groves of India close to Ocean'
	2.481	*Oceano*	'in Ocean'
	3.359	*Oceani rubro . . . aequore*	'in Ocean's red sea'
	4.233	*Oceani spretos . . . amnis*	'the spurned streams of Ocean'
	4.341	*Oceanitides ambae*	'both daughters of Ocean' (i.e. the nymphs Cleo and Beroe)
	4.381	*Oceano libemus*	'Let us offer a libation to Ocean'
	4.382	*Oceanumque patrem rerum*	'and Ocean, father of all things'
orbis (*terrarum*)	1.26	*maximus orbis*	'the great world'
	1.62	*uacuum . . . in orbem*	'into an empty world'
	1.505	*tot bella per orbem*	'so many wars across the world'
	1.511	*saeuit toto Mars impius orbe*	'unholy Mars rages across the entire world'
	2.114	*extremis domitum cultoribus orbem*	'the world conquered by far-off farmers'
	2.123	*extremi sinus orbis*	'a bay at the world's edge' (of Indian groves)

Scythia

An area not strictly defined in Greek and Roman sources, corresponding roughly to the area extending from the north-western, northern and north-eastern shores of the Black Sea. See especially Book 3, lines 349–83.

Hypanis (R)[35]	4.370	*saxosusque sonans Hypanis*	'and sounding, stony Hypanis'
Maeotian Lake (mod. Sea of Azov)	3.349	*Maeotiaque unda*	'and the waters of Maeotia'
Phasis (R) (mod. Rioni)	4.367	*Phasimque*	'and the Phasis'
Riphaean Mountains	1.240	*ad Scythiam Riphaeasque … arces*	'to Scythian and Riphaean towns'
	3.382	*gens … Riphaeo tunditur Euro*	'a people buffeted by a Rhipaean wind'
	4.518	*aruaque Riphaeis numquam uiduata pruinis*	'and fields never without Riphaean hoar frosts'
Scythia	1.240	*ad Scythiam Riphaeasque … arces*	'to Scythia and Riphaean towns'
	3.197	*Scythiaeque hiemes*	'and Scythian winters'
	3.349	*Scythiae gentes*	'Scythian peoples'
Tanaïs (R) (mod. Don)	4.517	*Tanaimque niualem*	'and the snowy Don'

Thrace

An area not strictly defined in Greek and Roman sources, corresponding roughly to modern Bulgaria, southern Romania, north-east Greece and Turkey west of the Bosporus. See especially Book 4, lines 460–3 and 516–27.

Haemus Mountains	1.492	*latos Haemi … campos*	'the broad plains of Haemus'
Hebrus (R) (mod. Maritsa/Evros)	4.463	*Hebrus*	'Hebrus'
	4.524	*Oeagrius Hebrus*	'King Oeagrus's Hebrus'
Hister (R) (mod. Danube)	2.497	*coniurato descendens Dacus ab Histro*	'a Dacian coming down from the conspiratorial Danube'
	3.350	*turbidus et torquens flauentis Hister harenas*	'the cloudy Danube churning its yellow sands'

Ismarus (M)	2. 37	*iuuat Ismara Baccho / conserere*	'it's a joy to plant vines on Ismarus'
Pangaeum (M) (mod. Pangaion)	4. 462	*altaque Pangaea*	'and high Pangaeum'
Rhodope Mountains	1. 332	*Rhodopen*	'Rhodope'
	3. 351	*quaque redit medium Rhodope porrecta sub axem*	'and where Rhodope bends back, stretching up to the central pole'[36]
	3. 462	*cum fugit in Rhodopen* (sc. Gelonus)	'when a Gelonian flees into Rhodope'
	4. 461	*Rhodopeiae arces*	'Rhodopian towns'
Strymon (R) (mod. Struma)	1. 120	*Strymoniaeque grues*	'and cranes from the river Styrmon'
	4. 508	*deserti ad Strymonis undam*	'to the waters of the lonely Styrmon'
Thrace	4. 462	*Rhesi Mauortia tellus* (P)	'the warlike land of Rhesus'[37]

1B Ethnonyms in the *Georgics* listed alphabetically

Aethiopes	2. 120	*nemora Aethiopum molli canentia lana*	'groves of the Ethiopians, white with soft wool'
Afer	3. 344	*armentarius Afer*	'an African herdsman'
Arabes	2. 115	*Eoasque domos Arabum*	'and the eastern homes of Arabs'
Ausonii	2. 385	*Ausonii, Troia gens missa, coloni*	'Ausonian farmers, a people sent out from Troy'
Belgae	3. 204	*Belgica . . . esseda*	'Belgic chariots'
Bisaltae	3. 461	*Bisaltae*	'Bisaltae'
Britanni	3. 25	*intexti . . . Britanni*	'embroidered Britons'
Chalybes[38]	1. 58	*Chalybes nudi*	'the naked Chalybes'
Cicones[39]	4. 520	*Ciconum . . . matres*	'Ciconian women'
Curetes[40]	4. 151	*canoros / Curetum sonitus crepitantiaque aera*	'the tuneful sounds and noisy cymbals of the Curetes'
Dacus	2. 497	*coniurato descendens Dacus ab Histro*	'a Dacian coming down from the conspiratorial Danube'
Gangaridae	3. 27	*pugnam . . . / Gangaridum*	'the battle of the Gangaridae'[41]
Geloni	2. 115	*pictosque Gelonos*	'and painted Gelonians'
	3. 461	*acerque Gelonus*	'and a fierce Gelonian'
Getae	3. 462	*in deserta Getarum*	'into the deserts of the Getae'

	4.463	*Getae*	'Getae'
Grai	2.16	*habitae Grais oracula quercus*	'oaks considered oracles by the Greeks'
	3.90	*Grai . . . poetae*	'Greek poets'
	3.148	*Grai*	'Greeks'
Hiberi	3.408	*impacatos . . . Hiberos*	'unsubdued Iberians'
Hyperborei	3.196	*Hyperboreis . . . ab oris*	'from Hyperborean shores'
	3.381	*Hyperboreo Septem subiecta trioni / gens effrena uirum*	'an unbridled people, living under the seven stars of the northern plough'[42]
Iapydes	3.475	*Iapydis arua Timaui*	'Iapydian fields by the river Timavus'
Indi	2.138	*Indi*	'Indians'
	2.172	*imbellem . . . Indum*	'the unwarlike Indian'
	4.293	*coloratis . . . ab Indis*	'from coloured Indians'
	4.425	*sitientis . . . Indos*	'thirsty Indians'
Ituraei	2.448	*Ituraeos taxi torquentur in arcos*	'yews are shaped into Ituraean bows'
Ligures	2.168	*adsuetumque malo Ligurem*	'and the Ligurian accustomed to trouble'
Marsi	2.167	*Marsos*	'Marsi'
Medi	2.136	*Medorum silvae*	'the forests of the Medes'
	2.134	*animas et olentia / Medi ora*	'a Mede's bad breath'
Parthi	3.31	*fidentemque fuga Parthum*	'and a Parthian trusting in flight'
	4.211	*populi Parthorum*	'Parthian peoples'
	4.314	*leues . . . Parthi*	'the swift Parthians'[43]
Pellaei gens fortunata Canopi	4.287	*Pellaei gens fortunata Canopi* (P)	'the happy people of Pellean Canopus'
Persis[44]	4.290	*pharetratae uicina Persidis*	'the proximity of the quivered Persian'
Quirites[45]	4.201	*paruosque Quirites* (sc. *apes*)	'and little Quirites' (i.e. the bees)
Romanus	3.346	*acer Romanus*	'a fierce Roman'
Sabaei	1.57	*molles . . . Sabaei*	'soft Sabaeans'
	2.117	*solis est turea uirga Sabaeis*	'the sprig of frankincense is the Sabaeans' alone'
Sabellus	2.167	*pubemque Sabellam*	'and the Sabellian youth'

	3. 255	*Sabellicus . . . sus*	'a Sabellian boar'
Sabini	2. 532	*ueteres . . . Sabini*	'the old Sabines'
Scythiae gentes	3. 349	*Scythiae gentes*	'Scythian peoples'
Seres	2. 121	*Seres*	'Silk people'
Thesidae	2. 383	*Thesidae*	'sons of Theseus' (i.e. Athenians)
Tyrrhenus	2. 193	*pinguis . . . Tyrrhenus*	'a fat Etruscan'
Volsci	2. 168	*Volscosque uerutos*	'and the spear-wielding Volsci'

Notes

Introduction

1 In this approach I have been influenced by Edward Said's idea of 'contrapuntal reading' (Said 1994: 59) and, in particular, by Walter Benjamin, who speaks of the historian's task as being to 'brush history against the grain' (see Benjamin (1999) 248).

2 The metaphor was initially suggested by Jacob's discussion of the map of Eratosthenes as being symbolic of the 'centripetal dynamic' of the intellectual culture of Ptolemaic Alexandria (Jacob 1999: 33). For Agrippa's map in the *Porticus Vipsania* see Zanker (1988) 143; for other maps referenced in contemporary Roman literature see Varro *Rust.* 1. 2. 1 and Livy 41. 28. 10.

3 This phrase is taken from Louis MacNeice's poem 'Snow': see MacNeice (1966) 30.

4 A recent survey of scholarship on the poem can be found in the introduction to Xinyue and Freer (2019); for a comprehensive bibliography up to 2015 see Holzberg (2015). Political scholarship on the *Georgics* has tended to focus, understandably, on the relationship between Virgil and Octavian, and on the Roman civil wars. For a representative sample see Lyne (1974), Boyle (1979), Nadeau (1984), Griffin (1985), Tarrant (1997) 176–7, Morgan (1999), Thomas (2001a) 25–54, Kaster (2002), Hardie (2004) 106–11, Nappa (2005), Formicola (2008), Willis (2011), Nelis (2013), Foulon (2014), Weeda (2015), Whitcomb (2018). Parker (2011) examines the representation of India, Egypt and Parthia in Augustan poetry within the framework of Said's *Orientalism*, but includes only brief discussion of the *Georgics*. Spencer (2010) 38–41 discusses the imperial landscape of *G.* 3. 1–48 and Harrison (2008) emphasizes the orientalist material in the *laudes Italiae*, while O'Rourke (2011) and Wyke (1992) include the *Aeneid* (but not the *Georgics*) in their discussions. For an Italian focus see Ando (2002), Powell (2008) and Dominik (2009); Lowrie (2015) and Geue (2018) discuss Egypt, and Giusti (2019) discusses Britons.

5 Martindale (2013) 171–2: 'Reception … makes it more difficult to fall into one of two opposed illusions common in literary interpretation, which we may call vulgar historicism (the view that we can know the past as it really was, untainted by what came after) and an equally vulgar presentism (the view that everything is

wholly adapted to what we think in the present).' Cf. Martindale (1993) 28: 'Reception theory will allow us to steer a course around both the radical and conservative positions.' For introductions to reception and classics see Hardwick (2003) and Hardwick and Stray (2008); for edited volumes see Martindale and Thomas (2006) and Butler (2016).

6   See Benjamin (1999), Said (1994) and Rich (2001); in classical terms I have found Haley (1993) and (2009), Rabinowitz (1993) and Richlin (2014) particularly useful. On comparisons between the British and Roman Empires see Vance (2000), Vasunia (2005) and Butler (2012); on classics and colonialism see the collections edited by Goff (2005), Hardwick and Gillespie (2007), Bradley (2010) and Stephens and Vasunia (2010), as well as Vasunia (2009a), (2009b), (2013) and Hagerman (2013). I would like also to record here my debt to Thompson (2013).

7   hooks (1992) 4–5.

8   On Virgil's farmers see Spurr (1986) and Geue (2018). On the slave economy of Roman Italy see Hopkins (1978) and Bradley (1994), who estimates (pp. 29–30) that the slave population of Italy at the end of the first century BCE was 2–3 million, i.e. between 33 and 40 per cent of the total population. For a picture of the sufferings endured by the people of Italy during the decades of civil conflict see App. *B Civ.* 5. 18, 27 and 77 with Brunt (1971) 285–93, esp. 290–1.

9   There are many mythological and divine female characters in the poem, as well as anthropomorphic treatments of animal life and the implied didactic subject/ reader, but in terms of explicitly human female characters I count only the wife (*G.* 1. 293–4) and the girls (*G.* 1. 390–2) weaving by night. On women in the poem and its tradition see Oliensis (1997) 310, Perkell (2014) 1391 and Braund (2019), who discusses Vita Sackville-West's Virgilian poem *The Land* (1926). On the invisibility of women's labour in Roman agricultural discourse see Scott (n.d.).

10 See Verg. *G.* 2. 170–2, 3. 25–33, 4. 559–62. In this the poem foreshadows the othering that occurs in the *Aeneid* and in contemporary Latin poetry's treatment of Cleopatra: see Quint (1993) 25 and Wyke (1992) respectively. On the ethnographic tradition in ancient Greek and Latin literature see Thomas (1982).

11 On Charlotte Guest (1812–95), Florence Nightingale and Mary Shelley, see Guest and John (1989) 9, McDonald (2003) 736 and Bennett (1980) 1: 85 respectively; on Victorian women writers and the classics see Hurst (2006).

12 Purvis (1991), Howarth (1994), McWilliams Tullberg (1998).

13 Symonds (1991), Stray (1998), Vasunia (2009a).

14 Haley (2009), McCoskey (2012), Mbembe (2017).

15 Mbembe (2017) 7.

Chapter 1: The World and Its Peoples

1 Horsfall (1997) is a brief survey of the poem's geography, focusing mainly on its Italian and Greek toponyms, which it classifies in an appendix. Fischer (1968) surveys the geography of the poem beyond Italy, while Goodfellow (1981) examines its North Italian geography. See also Thomson (1951), (1955). On geography and geographical knowledge in ancient Greece and Rome more generally see Thomson (1965), Rawson (1985) 205–67 and Romm (1992). All ancient dates are BCE except where otherwise stated.

2 On Pytheas, the Massiliot explorer who claimed to have circumnavigated Britain and reported information about Thule, see Cunliffe (2002) 130–1 and Thomson (1965) 143–51. Strabo 1.4.2 (= 63 C) records Pytheas's claim that Thule was six days' sail north of Britain.

3 What the title of Hinds (1998) calls the 'dynamics of appropriation in Roman poetry' is a much-discussed topic, as is the particular import of the different terms (allusion, reference, intertextuality) used. For an overview of the issue see Hinds (1998) 17–51. Thomas (1986) discusses the *Georgics*' 'art of reference'.

4 Hom. *Il.* 8. 47–8: (sc. Ζεύς)Ἴδην δ᾽ ἵκανεν πολυπίδακα μητέρα θηρῶν / Γάργαρον, ἔνθά τέ οἱ τέμενος βωμός τε θυήεις (To Ida he came, the many-fountained, mother of wild beasts, to Gargarus, where is his precinct and his fragrant altar.) Translation = Murray (1999). Cf. *Il.* 14. 283 and 15. 151.

5 Compare *G.* 2. 105–8 with Catull. 7. 3–4. Thomas's (1988) note to *G.* 2. 103–8 suggests further conflation with *Ap. Rhod.* 4. 214–15 and Theoc. *Id.* 16. 60–1.

6 Posidipp. 1. 1 = Austin and Bastianini (2002) 22, with their text and translation. The link with *G.* 4. 211 is made by Hutchinson (2008) 94.

7 Powell (1925) 62, reprinted with a translation in Mynors (1990) 325–6.

8 All Latin translations in this book are my own, except where otherwise stated. The text I use throughout is that of Mynors (1969).

9 Thomas (1982).

10 *G.* 4. 125: *sub Oebaliae . . . turribus arcis.* Cf. Serv. ad loc. and *OCD* s.v. 'Oebalus'.

11 Serv. ad loc. says Athenian, *Serv. Dan.*, Attic. A reference to the honey of Mt Hymettus is perhaps intended (see Appendix 1A, under 'Hymettus').

12 See [Probus] on *G.* 3. 19 (= Callim. *Aet.* fr. 60c Harder = fr. 54 Pfeiffer) in Thilo and Hagen (1986) 3: 321–90. On the spelling of *Molorc(h)i* see Morgan (1992).

13 Gigante (2004) 88–91, who also discusses the history of an alternative reading in these lines. Aulus Gellius claimed (6. 20. 1–2) that the text had originally read 'uicina Vesaeuo / Nola iugo' (Nola, close to Vesuvius's slope), but that the poet changed it after being slighted by the Nolans. Gigante, following Barchiesi (1979), regards this story as fictional and reads *ora*.

14 They are: *Seres*, 'silk people' (*G*. 2. 121), *Narycius*, 'Narycian' (*G*. 2. 438), *Idumaeus*, 'Idumaean', (*G*. 3. 12), *Cinyphius*, 'Cinyphian' (*G*. 3. 312), *Bisaltae*, a Thracian people, (*G*. 3. 461). On all of these words see the relevant entries in the *OLD*.

15 Virgil's appropriation of Arcadia is often firmly distinguished from its subsequent role in the European pastoral tradition. See Jenkyns (1989) and the comment of Clausen (1994) 289 n. 4: 'Arcadia conceived as an ideal or symbolic landscape, "la pastorale Arcadia", is the invention of Jacopo Sannazaro and Sir Philip Sidney – that is, a feature of the pastoral tradition, and should not be imposed retroactively on Virgil.' Nevertheless, I would argue that readers remain free to bring whatever associations they wish to the appearance of Arcadia in the *Eclogues*. For a history of pastoral poetry see Alpers (1996).

16 See, for instance, *G*. 3. 10–11 and Horace's boast at *Carm*. 3. 30. 10–14 with Braund (2017) 187, 196–7.

17 Polyb. 1. 1. 5–6 with Walbank (1957–79) ad loc.

18 Hor. *Epist*. 2. 1. 156–7: 'Graccia capta ferum victorem cepit et artis / intulit agresti Latio' (Captured Greece took its wild conqueror captive, and brought its arts to rustic Latium).

19 Varro, *Rust*. 1. 1. 4–6. Nelis and Nelis-Clément (2011) argue that *G*. 1. 1–42 recalls the *pompa circensis*, the procession of deities at the beginning of Roman circus games.

20 Nelis and Nelis-Clément (2011) 8.

21 Scholars continue to explore the significance of the temple. See Nelis (2004), Harrison (2005), Meban (2008) and Citroni (2015); for a recent political reading see Giusti (2019).

22 Wilkinson (1969) 167–9.

23 Spencer (2010) 41.

24 For the triumphal connotation see Hor. *Carm*. 1. 37. 30–2 (Cleopatra unbowed) and *TLL* 5. 1. 274. 51–62. For *deducere* and poetic composition cf. *G*. 3. 10–11, Hor. *Carm*. 3. 30. 14, Ov. *Met*. 1. 4. and *TLL* 5. 1. 282. 55–76.

25 Callim. fr. 384. 24 Pfeiffer.

26 [Scylax] 109 (see Müller (1882) 1: 85) and [Probus] on *G*. 3. 312 (see Thilo and Hagen (1986) 3: 321–90) refer to an *urbs* and an *oppidum*, respectively, called Cinyps. The river is also mentioned by Herodotus: Hdt. 4. 175, 198.

27 Acosta-Hughes and Stephens (2012) 204. For Callimachus's influence on Roman poetry see Fantuzzi and Hunter (2004) 461–7 and Hunter (2006) 1–41.

28 Acosta-Hughes and Stephens (2012) 239–40: both poems have four books and Hesiod as a primary model; both poems end with a *sphragis* and are 'fundamentally about homeland'.

29 Acosta-Hughes and Stephens (2012) 172. See in particular pp. 148–203 on Callimachean geography and geopolitics.

30 Cornell (1989b) 383.

31 For a comprehensive survey of Roman imperialism under Octavian, to which this section is much indebted, see Gruen (1996). For cursory evidence of Roman belligerence cf. the *Fasti Triumphales* published in Degrassi (1954) 90–110; Ehrenberg and Jones (1976) 32–43 conflates all extant epigraphic *Fasti* for the years 43 BCE–37 CE. For a critical discussion of the *Fasti* as historical sources see Beard (2007) 61–7, 72–80.

32 Verg. *Ecl.* 1. 66: 'toto diuisos orbe Britannos'.

33 Dio Cass. 49. 38. 2, 53. 22. 5, 53. 25. 2 with Gruen (1996) 189, and see also Giusti (2019). Octavian is called Octavian throughout this book because I want to question uncritical use of the reverential title 'Augustus', his traditional designation for dates in and after 27 BCE. See further *OLD* s.v. *augustus*[1]; *TLL* 2. 1379. 55–6, 1381. 34–6, and this book's conclusion.

34 Gruen (1996) 197.

35 Hom. *Il.* 10. 469–502; for Orithyia see Ap. Rhod. 1. 211–18 and Hdt. 7. 189. For the Hyperboreans cf. Verg. *G.* 3. 196, 381 and see *OCD* s.v., Hes. fr. 150 Merkelbach-West, Pind. *Pyth.* 10. 30 and Hdt. 4. 13, 32–6.

36 Dexter (2013). On the problem of the antecedent of *quo munere* at v. 520, see Egan (2001).

37 Livy, *Per.* 135.

38 Livy, *Per.* 140.

39 Dio Cass. 51. 23–7. For Crassus's triumph in 27 see Degrassi (1954) 110.

40 Vell. Pat. 2. 98. 1–2; Dio Cass. 54. 34. 5–7.

41 Conington and Nettleship (2007) 318 (on *G.* 3. 345).

42 See Thomas (1988) on *G.* 3. 345.

43 i.e. Nic. *Ther.* 670: σκυλάκεσσιν Ἀμυκλαίῃσι κελεύων, 'calling to his Amyclaean whelps', suggested by Richter (1957) 304 and noted by Thomas (1988) on *G.* 3. 345 (where the translation given here is also found).

44 For surveys of Roman political involvements in North Africa from 146 see Lintott (1994) 27–31 and Whittaker (1996).

45 *Fasti Triumphales* (Degrassi (1954) 110) for triumphs *ex Africa* in 34, 21 and 19; *Fasti Barberini* (= Degrassi (1947) 343, 345) for those in 33 and 28; all five are conflated at Ehrenberg and Jones (1976) 34–6. cf. Verg. *Aen.* 6. 794.

46 Cic. *Leg. Man.* 34, where Sicily, Sardinia and Africa are called *tria frumentaria subsidia rei publicae*.

47 *BAfr.* 97, with Whittaker (1996) 587.

48 *Aen.* 6. 794–5: 'super et Garamantas et Indos / proferet imperium' (He [sc. *Augustus Caesar*] will bring *imperium* beyond both the Garamantes and Indians.) On the Garamantes see Mattingly (2006).

49 Varro, *Rust.* 1. 16. 2: 'refert infesta regio sit necne. multos enim agros egregios colere non expedit propter latrocinia vicinorum, ut in Sardinia quosdam, qui sunt prope †Oeliem, et in Hispania prope Lusitaniam' (It matters whether or not the area is dangerous. For many fine lands are not worth farming because of the brigandage of the local people, as with certain lands in Sardinia that are near to †Oeliea, and in Spain close to Lusitania.).

50 Page (1898) 324.

51 Thomas (1988) on *G.* 3. 408.

52 Richter (1957) on *G.* 3. 406ff.: 'Dabei ist *Hiberi* ebenso charakterisierendes Einzelbeispiel für *homines* (als Räuber), wie v. 314 *summa Lycaei* für *saltibus* (Varro 2, 3, 6) eintritt; derartiges ist bei Verg. geläufig.' Fairclough (1999) 204 on the word *Hiberos* in line 408: 'Here equivalent to "brigands"'.

53 Serv. and *D. Serv.* (beginning at *et aliter*) on *G.* 3. 408.

54 There was another Iberia in what is now Georgia: the area was invaded by P. Canidius Crassus in *c.* 37, and Iberian kings, so the *Res Gestae* claims, sent ambassadors to Octavian (Cass. Dio 49. 24. 1–2, *RG* 31. 2, cf. Braund (1994) 205–17). Thus there is potentially an ambiguity here, but I read the line as referring to Spain because of the sustained nature of Rome's military involvement there during the years of the poem's composition; Varro *Rust.* 1. 16. 2 could be cited as evidence in this regard.

55 The main extant source for this history is App. *Hisp.*, with Cass. Dio 53–4 for the wars and rebellions of the 20s; for a succinct narrative account see Richardson (1996). Thomas (1988) 2: 118 and Erren (1985–2003) 2: 728 note Octavian's Spanish campaigns in passing, but only Page (1898) 324 gives a longer-term view: 'Spain was the first province entered by the Romans and the last subdued, the *Cantabri* especially in the north-west long maintaining a guerrilla warfare from their mountain fastnesses.'

56 Appian's account does not put Cato at Numantia; we have only a fragment of a speech (= fr. 17 Malcovati = Gell. 16. 1) apparently given by Cato *Numantiae apud equites* (at Numantia to the knights). For the actions of Nobilior, Marcellus, Pompeius and Mancinus see App. *Hisp.* 46, 50, 76–8 and 80 respectively. For Scipio's siege see App. *Hisp.* 84–98, and note the way Scipio's honorific military titles *Africanus* and *Numantinus* reflect another aspect of the relationship between Roman geography and imperial politics. For more on Appian's Iberian history see Richardson (2000).

57 App. *Hisp.* 98.

58 *Fasti Triumphales* (Degrassi (1954) 109–10) for triumphs in 36, 34 and 26; *Fasti Barberini* (= Degrassi (1947) 343, 345) for 33 (two triumphs to two separate commanders) and 28: all six are conflated at Ehrenberg and Jones (1976) 34–5.

59 See Dio Cass. 53. 25, Oros. 6. 21. 1 (the opening of the temple doors), Gruen
   (1996) 163–6 and Richardson (1996) 133–4.
60 Suet. *Aug.* 85. 1, with Gruen (1996) 164.
61 Dio Cass. 53. 29. 1–2, 54. 5. 1–3, 11. 2–5 and 20. 3.
62 Dio Cass. 53. 29. 1–2.
63 Foster (1988) 34.
64 App. *Ill.* 16–28, Dio Cass. 49. 36–7 (Octavian in Illyricum); Dio Cass. 51. 21. 5
   (Octavian's triumph). Dio (49. 36. 1) notes that Octavian's campaign in Illyricum
   was unpremeditated, and designed to keep his soldiers practised.
65 App. *Ill.* 17. 49 (the translation = White (1912) 81).
66 *G.* 1. 475: 'insolitis tremuerunt motibus Alpes'. Mynors (1990) on this line assumes
   it refers to earthquakes, but the word *motus* can mean an outbreak of violence or
   rebellion (see *OLD* s.v.).
67 On the *Salassi* see Strabo 2. 6. 7. (= 205–6 C) and *OCD*, s.v.
68 App. *Ill.* 17. 50–1 (Vetus and Messalla Corvinus), Dio Cass. 53. 25. 1–5. For a brief
   summary of Roman military activity in the Alps in this period see Cooley (2009)
   222–3.
69 Dio Cass. 53. 25. 1–5.
70 Dio Cass. 54. 22. 1–5, Strabo 4. 6. 9 (= 206 C).
71 Plin. *HN* 3. 136–7.

Chapter 2: Provincializing Rome

1 Nicolet (1994) 600.
2 Harris (2011) 257–87.
3 On the late-Republican Roman economy see Harris (2011), with Potter (1987)
   94–171 and Nicolet (1994), who focus on Italy.
4 Plut. *Vit. Aem.* 38. 1, Plin. *HN* 33. 56, Cic. *Off.* 2. 76 and cf. Badian (1972) 62–3.
5 Badian (1968) 47–9, (1972) 62–3. The *publicani* were private individuals to whom
   the Roman state sold contracts for the collection of taxes (see *OCD* s.v.).
   Gracchus's measure, only indirectly attested at Cic. 2 *Verr.* 3. 12 (cf. Badian (1968)
   49 n. 13), greatly increased the role of the *publicani* and the opportunities for
   profit available to them.
6 Potter (1987) 157, with Lomas (2014) on the villa economy of Roman Italy and
   Mediterranean business.
7 Harris (2011) 259. See Roussel and Launey (1937) nos. 1683–9 for Italians on
   Delos; Roussel and Launey (1937) no. 1699 (= *ILLRP* 343) and *ILS* 7273 (= *CIL* 10.
   1797) for Italians at Alexandria.

8   Strabo 14. 5. 2 (668 C), Nicolet (1994) 638.

9   On this slave economy see Hopkins (1978) 1–98, but in particular Bradley (1994), who estimates (29–30) that the slave population of Italy at the end of the first century BCE was 2–3 million, i.e. between 33 and 40 per cent of the total population.

10 On Rome's trade with Asia in the late Republic and early Empire see Thorley (1969), Raschke (1978), Fitzpatrick (2011) and McLaughlin (2014), (2016). Casson (1989) provides much useful introductory material; for the trade between China and Rome specifically see Ferguson (1978) and, in particular, Chuanxi (2012a) 58–78, (2012b) 184–91.

11 Strabo 2. 3. 4 (= 98–9 C) on the pioneering voyages of Eudoxus of Cyzicus to India from Egypt. See Casson (1989) 283–4 for further discussion of these monsoon winds.

12 Strabo 2. 5. 12 (118 C); what Casson (1989: 96) assumes was an annual voyage, whereas previously the number had been not more than twenty (Strabo 17. 13 (798 C)).

13 Casson (1989) 11, 17–18.

14 Ferguson (1978), McLaughlin (2016).

15 Chuanxi (2012a) 63–5.

16 Fitzpatrick (2011) 47–8, 54.

17 Van Minnen (1991) notes that, as well as lentils, beer, linen, salt and fish are all called 'Pelusian' by various classical Latin authors. He argues (pp. 168–9) that Pelusium's status as a major export hub for Egyptian products lies behind this.

18 Or perhaps Tarentum. *Syrius* can mean 'Syrian' (*OLD* s.v. *Syrius*), but cf. Columella, *Rust.* 5. 10. 18 for a possible Tarentine provenance: '[pira] Tarentina, quae Syria dicuntur' (Tarentine pears, which are called 'Syrian').

19 *OLD* 2 s.v. *Chaonius* with Clausen (1994) on Verg. *Ecl.* 9. 13.

20 See Plin. *HN* 34. 6–12 and *HN* 36. 14 respectively.

21 Aratus, *Phaen.* 733, Lucr. 2. 196, 2. 207, 2. 263, etc.

22 Aesch. *PV* 714–15, Hdt. 1. 28, Ap. Rhod. 2. 1001–8, Callim. *Aet.* fr. 110. 48 Harder.

23 Elis is associated with horses in Homer (*Od.* 4. 635, 21. 347), but Mynors (1990) on *G.* 1. 59 reads the phrase as an enallage (transferred epithet) for *Eliadas equarum palmas*, 'prizes to be won by mares at Olympia in Elis'.

24 On the role of commodities in Roman attitudes to, and depictions of, India see Parker (2008) 147–202; on the sea trade between Rome and India see Begley and De Puma (1991).

25 Plin. *HN* 12. 55: 'nec arboris ipsius quae sit facies constat. res in Arabia gessimus et Romana arma in magnam partem eius penetrauere, Gaius etiam Caesar Augusti filius inde gloriam petiit, nec tamen ab ullo, quod equidem sciam, Latino arborum earum tradita est facies' (Nor is it known what the tree itself looks like. We have had dealings in Arabia and Roman arms have penetrated a great part of it. Gaius

Caesar, the son of Augustus, even sought distinction there, and still, as far as I know, the appearance of these trees has not been related by any Latin writer.) For discussion see Murphy (2004) 99–105.

26 Gruen (1996) 148–51. C. Caesar's expedition = Plin. *HN* 2. 168; Aelius Gallus' = Strabo 16. 4. 22–4 (780–1 C), *RG* 26. 5 (with Cooley (2009) ad loc.), Dio Cass. 53. 29. 3.

27 Cooley (2009) 227: 'It may have been motivated by simple imperialism, or by the wish to gain control of a region noted for its wealth derived from trade in spices, and believed to contain quantities of gems, gold, and silver ... Alternatively, it may have been part of a larger strategy, whereby Augustus desired to influence the Parthian succession.'

28 Stereotypes examined by Said (1978).

29 On the citron tree (*Citrus medica*): see Theophr. *Hist. pl.* 4. 1. 5–4. 11. 13 with Thomas (1988) 1: 178–9, Mynors (1990) 116–18.

30 Plin. *HN* 12. 111, Joseph. *BJ* 1. 138. On balsam, the sap resin of the eponymous shrub highly valued in antiquity, see McLaughlin (2014) 42–9.

31 Plin. *HN* 12. 111–13. *Arborum* is a textual crux: the major manuscripts have *arbutum*, which is printed but obelized in Ernout's edition (see Ernout (1949)); *arborum* is Mayhoff's conjecture (marked *ego* in his critical apparatus; see Mayhoff (1875) 307). In spite of this difficulty, it is clear from the context of the passage that it is balsam to which Pliny refers. The text used here is found in Rackham (1968) 78–81; the translation is my own.

32 Plin. *HN* 12. 118, with McLaughlin (2014) 46–9.

33 Joseph. *BJ* 1. 138, 1. 148–9.

34 Joseph. *BJ* 1. 179.

35 *BAfr.* 20; Cic. *Phil.* 2. 112 with Ramsey (2003) 190: [Cicero to Antony] 'cur homines omnium gentium maxime barbaros, Ituraeos, cum sagittis deducis in forum?' (Why do you bring Ituraeans, the most barbaric of all peoples, with arrows into the forum?).

36 *ILS* 2683, of which I quote an extract: 'idem [sc. Q. Aemilius] missu Quirini adversus Ituraeos in Libano monte castellum eorum cepi' (I [Quintus Aemilius], dispatched by Quirinius against the Ituraeans, captured their fortress on Mount Lebanon).

37 Plin. *HN* 13. 26: 'Cetero terrarum omnium Aegyptus accommodatissima unguentis, ab ea Campania est copia rosae. Iudaea vero incluta est vel magis palmis, quarum natura nunc dicetur' (In other ways Egypt is the most suited of all lands to the production of unguents, next to it is Campania and its abundance of roses. But Judaea is even more famous for its palms, the nature of which will now be discussed.).

38 Joseph. *BJ* 1. 386–97 with Syme (1939) 300–1 for context. On Herod see *OCD* s.v. 'Herod (1)', Grant (1971) and Vermes (2014).

39 sc. *palmam dedit*. See Degrassi (1947) 338–47 (= Ehrenberg and Jones (1976) 34–5) with Beard (2007) 250, 304.

40 Hom. *Od.* 1. 22–3, where the Ethiopians are ἔσχατοι ἀνδρῶν (farthest of men), a
   literary conceit discussed by Romm (1992) 49–60.

41 *ILS* 8995 = *CIL* 3. 14147, Strabo 17. 1. 53 (819 C); Gruen (1996) 148. Note that
   Gallus (*RE* 164 s.v. 'Cornelius' and *OCD* s.v. 'Cornelius, Gallus') is a figure
   associated with Virgil, and that the dating of the *stele* is contemporary with the
   completion of the *Georgics*.

42 Strabo 17. 1. 54 (820–1 C), *RG* 26. 5, Dio Cass. 54. 5. 4; Gruen (1996) 149–50.

43 *RE* 2 A. 2 (1923) 1678, Ferguson (1978) 582.

44 *Sericus* (adj.), 'silken' (*OLD* s.v. 1b, 2) = Hor. *Epod.* 8. 15, Prop. 1. 14. 22, 4. 8. 23;
   Seres = Hor. *Carm.* 1. 12. 56, 3. 29. 27, 4. 15. 23, Ov. *Am.* 1. 14. 6.

45 Ferguson (1978) 583.

46 Beard (2007) 160.

47 Murphy (2004) 155, and see also p. 23: 'The Roman triumph, which is usually thought
   of in ceremonial and religious terms as a way of marking the return to the city of
   Rome of a victorious commander and his army, was also an instrument for educating
   the Roman people about the lands and nations newly added to its dominion. In the
   triumph, the fringes of the Roman world were exhibited to the centre, not just
   plundered as coin, works of art, and other treasures, but also as river-gods from the
   conquered territory, great maps on placards, images of mountains and cities, trains of
   handsome captives, exotic animals and plants never seen before in Italy.'

48 Plin. *HN* 12. 111.

49 Joseph. *BJ* 7. 132–62, esp. 138–49 on the floats which showed the crowds scenes
   from the war. Cf. Murphy (2004) 156. For an overview of the Arch, see Claridge
   (2010) 121–3.

50 See Murphy (2004) 138–54 for the 'ideological weight' rivers and mountains could
   bear in Roman literature.

51 See Dio Cass. 51. 22. 6 with *G.* 2. 497: 'aut coniurato descendens Dacus ab Histro'
   (Or a Dacian coming down from the conspiring Danube). For the date of the
   poem see Donat. *Vit. Verg.* 25, 27, followed by Thomas (1988) 1: 1.

52 Geue (2018) 3.

Chapter 3: Civil War

1 Nicolet (1991) 16. The most comprehensive treatment of this development is Vogt
   (1960) 156–62; Fischer (1968) 116–17 notes its role in the *Georgics*. For more
   condensed treatments see Brunt (1978) and Gruen (1984) 1: 274–87.

2 *Rhet. Her.* 4. 13. 21–4: 'imperium orbis terrae, cui imperio omnes gentes, reges,
   nationes partim ui, partim uoluntate consenserunt, cum aut armis aut liberalitate a

populo Romano superati essent' (power over the world, to which all peoples, kings and nations assented, either through force or voluntarily, when they had been conquered by the arms or the munificence of the Roman people). Cf. Cic. *Leg. Man.* 53 and *Mur.* 22, with further examples at Vogt (1960) 156 n. 13.

3　Vogt (1960) 157–9, Nicolet (1991) 35–7. For late-Republican examples see Crawford (1974) nos. 403, 426/4, 449/4, 480/3, 546/4.

4　See Beard (2007) 26–7 for discussion of this statue, which may in fact be authentic.

5　Vogt (1960) 159: 'Die Anschauung, daß das Imperium Romanum, wie vordem Machtbereich Alexanders, die gesamte bewohnte Erde, den ganzen orbis terrarum umfasse, war also in der ausgehenden Republik zu einem festen Bestandteil des nationalen Glaubens geworden.' See Nicolet (1991) 29–56 with Livy 1. 16. 7, 21. 30. 10, 34. 58. 8; Verg. *Aen.* 1. 279, Ov. *Am.* 1. 174, *Fast.* 2. 130, 683.

6　Green (1978) 1, 4–5.

7　Sall. *Hist.* 3. 88 (Maurenbrecher (1967) 145 for the Latin; for English translation see McGushin (1994) 39), Plut. *Vit. Pomp.* 13. 3–5 with Green (1978) 4–5.

8　Suet. *Iul.* 7. 1, Cass. Dio. 37. 52. 2, Plut. *Vit. Caes.* 11. 4–6, Green (1978) 6, Krebs (2006) 127–9.

9　See Spencer (2002) 24–6, and MacGóráin (2014) 3–9 on the Dionysiac aspect of Antony's self-fashioning as Alexander, and thus of the complex and potentially problematic nature of Octavian's subsequent self-fashioning.

10 Suet. *Aug.* 50 (Octavian's private seal with an image of Alexander), Plin *HN.* 35. 93 with Cooley (2009) 199 (the pictures of Alexander in the *Forum Augustum*). On the mausoleum see Nicolet (1991) 16–17 with Zanker (1988) 72–7.

11 *RG.* pr.: 'quibus orbem terrarum imperio populi Romani subiecit'. I have used the edition of Cooley (2009) throughout.

12 Cooley (2009) 219.

13 Nicolet (1991) 23.

14 Cooley (2009) 36–7, 211, 222. The extant historiographical tradition claims that Alexander had plans, before his death, to campaign in Western Europe as far as the Straits of Gibraltar (Arr. *Anab.* 7. 1. 1–4, Diod. Sic. 18. 4. 1–6, Curt. 10. 1. 17). According to Arrian (*Anab.* 7. 19. 2, 3. 16. 1), Alexander let the Greek ambassadors who met him at Babylon take back from that city the artworks stolen by Xerxes, and at Susa sent back to Greece the Greek artworks found there. For Alexander's reception of embassies from Western Europe while on campaign see Diod. Sic. 17. 113. 2 and Arr. *Anab.* 7. 15. 4.

15 For the translation of lines 24–5 I've followed the note of Mynors (1990) 8 on *G.* 1. 25.

16 On Pytheas see Chapter 1 n. 2.

17 An idea explored by Romm (1992) 157–71.

18 Harrison (2008) 233: 'These lines outlining the superiority of Italy to the East also present some echoes of the career of Alexander the Great. Bactria (138) had been a key part of Alexander's conquests, India (138) his final stopping-place, the river Ganges (137) his supposed ultimate destination, while the Hermus (137) as river of Sardis points to that city's surrender to Alexander in 334 BCE. This can be closely linked with the young Caesar's self-presentation as the new Alexander in the years 31–29.'

19 *G.* 3. 30, 'urbes Asiae domitas' (the conquered cities of Asia) and (more ambiguous) *G.* 2. 114–15, 'aspice et extremis domitum cultoribus orbem / Eoasque domos Arabum pictosque Gelonos' (Look too at the world conquered by far-off farmers, the eastern homes of Arabs and the painted *Geloni*).

20 On Octavian in Syria in 20 see Cass. Dio. 54. 7. 6 with Gruen (1996) 158–60.

21 Catull. 11. 10 (a link made by Krebs (2006) 128), Plut. *Vit. Pomp.* 13. 3–5. Plaut. *Mostell.* 775 is, at least, the earliest extant appearance of *Alexander Magnus* in Latin. I am grateful to Dr Shanc Wallace for letting me read his unpublished paper on the history of, and evidence for, Alexander's epithet in Greek and Latin. Fischer (1968) 28 links *G.* 4. 559–62 with *G.* 1. 24–31, suggesting that the poem begins and ends with an image of Octavian's world power, a pervasive theme: 'Immer, wenn Vergil in den Georgica auf Octavian anspielt, findet sich Ausseritalisches, das vorwiegend an den Grenzen des römischen Reiches, ja sogar der Welt gelegen ist.'

22 The Parthians appear three times in the *Georgics*, at *G.* 3. 31, 4. 211 and 4. 314. They had attacked Syria, Palestine and Asia Minor in 40; Roman losses were reversed by the campaign of Ventidius in 39. Antony's Parthian expedition in 36, ostensibly to reclaim the standards lost by Crassus at Carrhae in 53, ended in disaster (on all of which see Pelling (1996) 9–13, 21–36). *Germania* at *G.* 1. 509 is taken by Roddaz (1984) 68 n. 211 as an allusion to the campaigns of Marcus Agrippa in Gaul and along the Rhine between 40 and 37. But see also Gruen (1996) 179: 'Unrest persisted. The years 31 to 28 BC witnessed three uprisings requiring Roman military action: against the Morini, the Treviri and the Aquitani, each issuing in triumphs or imperial salutations for the victorious commanders.'

23 Cass. Dio 51. 20 (the closure in 29); Oros. 6. 21. 1 and Cass. Dio 53. 26. 3 for their reopening and closure in 27 and 25 respectively. The third closure mentioned at *RG* 14. 2 is debated: see Cooley (2009) ad loc.

24 But see Mynors (1990) 94–5, following Cartault (1899), for the idea that Virgil is referring to two separate engagements at Philippi.

25 App. *B Civ.* 2. 75 on the site of Pharsalus; 4. 105 on the site of Philippi.

26 App. *B Civ.* 4. 106, 136.

27 Keppie (1983) 59, 143–7 with App. *B Civ.* 4. 3.

28 *G*. 2. 198: 'qualem infelix amisit Mantua campum'. See Keppie (1981) 368: 70 per cent of Mantua's territory was covered by the new centuriation grid around Cremona.

29 On these works see Paget (1968) 162–6 with *Serv. Dan.* on *G*. 2. 162 and Cass. Dio 48. 50–1. Octavian's fleet had been wrecked in a storm off Sicily (App. *B Civ.* 5. 88–90, Cass. Dio 48. 48. 1–4); for Sextus's defeat at sea off Naulochus see App. *B Civ.* 5. 115–22.

30 App. *B Civ.* 5. 132.

31 The ultimate origin of the toponym 'India' is a Sanskrit word for river, specifically the Indus: *sindhu* (Keay (2000) 57–8). Knowledge of South Asia in the ancient Mediterranean world increased significantly in the wake of Alexander's campaign of 327–325, with works by Alexander's general Nearchus and the Seleucid ambassador Megasthenes becoming important sources for Diodorus, Strabo and Arrian: see Parker (2008) 11–65 for a survey of this tradition with the *OCD* s.v. 'India' and Bosworth (1996) on Megasthenes; ancient Greek and Latin accounts of India are collected and translated by Majumdar (1960). Note also that until 1947 'India' was used by the British government to designate what is now Pakistan, India, Sri Lanka, Bangladesh and Myanmar.

32 Arr. *Anab.* 5. 12–13.

33 Steinmayer (1997) 139: 'As for Virgil, I see him viewing the great rainforests of India in his imagination, tingling with a sense of the immensity, variety, and freshness of his world.'

34 *G*. 1. 57, 2. 116 (ivory and ebony), 2. 138 (*Indi*), 2. 172 (*imbellem . . . Indum*), 4. 425 (*sitientis . . . Indos*), 4. 293 (*coloratis . . . ab Indis*).

35 Thomas (1982).

36 On this point see Haley (2009).

37 Isaac (2004) 37–8 and 108–9. He defines 'proto-racism' as when (p. 38) 'Greek and Latin sources attribute to groups of people common characteristics considered to be unalterable because they are determined by external factors or heredity'. Thomas (1988) on *G*. 2. 170–2, contra the note of Servius to the same lines, reads the 'unwarlike' characteristic as ethnographical, i.e. innate, rather than a result of defeat at the hands of Octavian.

38 See *Verg.* Aen. 8. 678–728, Hor. *Epod.* 9. 11–16 and *Carm.* 1. 37, Prop. 3. 11. 39–46 and 4. 6. 65–6 with Wyke (1992) and Quint (1993).

39 Pieri (2011) 36.

40 Plut. *Vit. Alex.* 62. 3–4 (οἱ Γανδαριτῶν καὶ Πραισίων βασιλεῖς), Curt. 9. 2. 2–3 (*gentes Gangaridas et Prasios*), Diod. Sic. 2. 37. 2 (τὸ ἔθνος τὸ τῶν Γανδαριδῶν), 17. 93. 2 (τό τε τῶν Ταβραισίων καὶ Γανδαριδῶν ἔθνος).

41 Diod. Sic. 2. 37. 3, 17. 93–4.

42 Bosworth (1988) 131–3. cf. Strabo 15. 1. 35 (702 C) for the letter of Craterus alleging that Alexander had reached the Ganges, and the *Periplus Maris Erythraei* 47 (with Casson 1989 ad loc.) for the same assertion.

43 Plin. *HN.* 6. 65–6, Ptol. *Geog.* 7. 1. 81. See also *Serv. Dan.* ad *G.* 3. 27: 'Gangaridum: Indorum a Gange fluvio' (*Gangaridae*: Indians, from the river Ganges).

44 Strabo 15. 1. 4 (686 C).

45 On *Gandaris* see *RE* 7. 1 (1910) 695–6 and Strabo 15. 1. 30 (699 C); on *Gandaritis/Gandhara* see *RE* 7. 1 (1910) 696–702 and Asheri, Lloyd and Corcella (2007) on Hdt. 3. 91. 4.

46 On which see, for instance, Behrendt (2004) and Nadiem (2008).

47 *RE* 7. 1 (1910) 695. Kiessling's article here provides the best introduction to *Gandaridai/Gangaridae*.

48 See Valerius Maximus, *Argonautica* 6. 66–7, for the *acies … Martia … / … Gangaridum*, 'the warlike battle-line of the *Gangaridae*'.

49 For the 'Eastern' forces of Antony at Actium see Plut. *Vit. Ant.* 61. 1–4 with Pelling (1988) ad loc.

50 Verg. *Aen.* 8. 675–728; Quint (1993) 21–48.

51 Syme (1939) 270–1.

52 Note that to at least one reader, Octavian's conquest of the *Gangaridae* was factual. Serv. on *G.* 3. 27 has: 'Gangaridae populi sunt inter Indos et Assyrios, habitantes circa Gangen fluvium … hos vicit Augustus, unde est [*G.* 2. 172] inbellem avertis Romanis arcibus Indum' (The Gangaridae peoples are between the Indians and Assyrians, living along the river Ganges … Augustus conquered them, whence the line [*G.* 2. 172] 'You turn back the unwarlike Indian from the hills of Rome.').

53 Verg. *Aen.* 8. 714–28, esp. 722–3: 'incedunt uictae longo ordine gentes, / quam uariae linguis, habitu tam uestis et armis' (Conquered peoples proceed in a long line, as different in their languages as in their style of dress and weaponry).

54 The classic study of this tradition is Said (1978); for orientalism and the *Georgics*, see Lowrie (2015).

55 Callim. *Aet.* fr. 44 Harder (= fr. 44 Pfeiffer), with Harder 2: 369–70 for background: 'Busiris, an Egyptian king who killed strangers in order to put an end to a nine-year draught and was eventually killed by Hercules.'

56 I follow Mynors's text (1969) here: Conte (Ottaviano and Conte (2013)) prints 291, in italics, between 290 and 292, arguing that Virgil intended it as a replacement for line 292 that was left in the text by later editors. On this see the review of Heyworth (2014).

57 For Octavian in Egypt see Bowman (1996) 676–9 and Herklotz (2012); on the politics of Egypt in Book 4 see Geue (2018).

58 Cass. Dio 51. 21. 7–9.

59 See the silver denarius, minted *c.* 28, bearing an image of Octavian on the obverse
   and, on the reverse, a crocodile with the legend [*A*]*EGYPTO CAPTA* (= Grueber
   (1970) 2: 536).

60 Suet. *Aug.* 41, Cass. Dio 51. 21. 5.

61 Serv. on *G.* 3. 29: 'Augustus victor totius Aegypti . . . multa de navali certamine
   sustulit rostra, quibus conflatis quattuor effecit columnas, quae postea a
   Domitiano in Capitolio sunt locatae, quas hodieque conspicimus' (Augustus as the
   conqueror of all Egypt . . . took many prows from the naval battle, and combining
   them together made four columns, which later were placed on the Capitoline hill
   by Domitian, and which we see today).

62 Cass. Dio 51. 17. 4; on Gallus see *ILS* 8995 = *CIL* 3. 14147, Strabo 17. 1. 53 (819 C);
   Gruen (1996) 148.

63 See *OLD* 2 s.v. *fortunatus*, with *TLL* 6. 1196–7 and Gagliardi (2009) 94: 'considerato
   come participio perfetto, *fortunatus* dovrebbe infatti privilegiare il significato
   passivo di "chi è stato beneficato dalla fortuna", ma non è sempre così . . . poiché
   nell'uso sentito piuttosto come aggettivo, sinonimo di *felix* e di *beatus*, talora con
   un accento più forte sul rapporto con la ricchezza materiale (in linea con uno dei
   significati di *Fortuna*, quello concreto di "ricchezza")'.

64 Verg. *G.* 2. 458, 493.

Chapter 4: 'All Italy'

1 Thomas (1988) 1: 180, who gives a list of parallels. Cf. Serv. on *G.* 2. 136: 'iam
  incipit laus Italiae, quam exsequitur secundum praecepta rhetorica: nam dicit eam
  et habere bona omnia et carere malis uniuersis' (Now begins the praise of Italy,
  which proceeds according to rhetorical principles: for he says that it both has all
  good things and that it lacks every evil).

2 Thomas (1982) 36–51.

3 Most obviously the cattle plague at *G.* 3. 474–566, but also in the image of the boat
  carried downstream at *G.* 1. 199–203.

4 Ross (1987) 109–28, Thomas (1982) 35–69, (1988) 1: 179–80.

5 Thomas (1988) 1: 180.

6 For one aspect of this interest, the Sabellic etymological glosses in *Aeneid* 7, see
  Ferriss-Hill (2011).

7 Harrison (2008) 234: 'Both this episode and the whole of the *Georgics* are . . .
  presented as praise of Italy as superior to rival eastern attractions, mirroring the
  political confrontations of the 30's BC where Rome had faced first Parthia under
  Antony's leadership and then the East joined with Antony under the leadership of
  the young Caesar at Actium.'

8 For an introduction to the pre-Roman and pre-first-century history of the
peninsula see Cornell (1989a), (1995) and Lomas (2014). For a detailed study of
the history of Rome's relationship with Italy in the first century BCE see Bispham
(2007), esp. 436–46, who notes (p. 444) that any notion of Italian unity at the end
of the century is, despite increased political homogeneity and the propaganda of
Octavian, highly debatable.

9 Bispham (2007) 443–4.

10 Degrassi (1954) 90–100.

11 See Livy, *Per.* 12–14 and the six triumphs over *Bruttii* listed for the years 282–272
(= Degrassi (1954) 97–8), with Cornell (1995) 363–4. On the Bruttian revolt see
Livy 22. 61. 11–12 with Fronda (2010) 149–59.

12 Dion. Hal. *Ant. Rom.* 20. 15. 1–2 (= Toynbee (1965) 2: 545–6; I give his translation
here): 'The Bruttians submitted to Rome's hegemony voluntarily and ceded one
half of their highlands to the Roman state. This Bruttian highland country is called
the Sila. It is full of timber suitable for house-building, ship-building, and
construction-work of every kind. It contains an abundance of lofty fir, poplar,
sappy pine, beech, stone pine, oak with a wide spread of branches, and ash. This
forest of various species of timber is nourished by surface waters with which the
Sila oozes. This forest, which is not confined to these species, is so dense, and the
branches so closely interwoven, that there is continuous shade on the Sila at all
hours of the day. The timber that stands nearest to the sea and to the rivers is felled
at the root and is transported to the nearest harbours without having been sawn
up. There is enough of it to supply the demands of the whole of Italy for both
ship-building and house-building. The timber that stands at high altitudes and at a
distance from the sea and from the rivers is sawn up into logs that can be carried
by porters, and this material serves for the manufacture of oars, poles, arms and
tools of all kinds, and household utensils. The sappier timber, which is also the
most plentiful, is used for the extraction of pitch. This Bruttian pitch, to call it by
its trade-name, is the sweetest and most fragrant of any that I know. The leases of
the right to extract this pitch bring in a large annual revenue to the Roman
treasury.'

13 Brunt (1971) 281, Toynbee (1965) 2: 120.

14 *Ant. Rom.* 20. 15. 1–2.

15 Verg. *G.* 2. 438.

16 *G.* 2. 207–11: 'aut unde iratus siluam deuexit arator / et nemora euertit multos
ignaua per annos, / antiquasque domos auium cum stirpibus imis / eruit; illae
altum nidis petiere relictis, / at rudis enituit impulso uomere campus' (or land
from which an angry ploughman has carried off the timber, felling groves that
have been unproductive for many years, destroying root and branch the long-

standing homes of birds; they have fled skyward abandoning their nests, and now the cleared land shines under the ploughshare's blade).

17 Verg. *Aen.* 12. 715–24: 'ac uelut ingenti Sila summoue Taburno / cum duo conuersis inimica in proelia tauri / frontibus incurrunt, pauidi cessere magistri, / stat pecus omne metu mutum, mussantque iuuencae / quis nemori imperitet, quem tota armenta sequantur / illi inter sese multa ui uulnera miscent / cornuaque obnixi infigunt et sanguine largo / colla armosque lauant, gemitu nemus omne remugit: / non aliter Tros Aeneas et Daunius heros / concurrunt clipeis, ingens fragor aethera complet' (And just like on great Sila or on high Taburnus, when two bulls charge with horns bared in hateful battle; the terrified herders have retreated, all the animals stand dumb with fear, and the heifers murmur as to who will rule the wood, whom the whole herd will follow. They trade many blows between them with great strength, they lock opposing horns and bathe their necks and flanks with much blood, the whole wood resounds with groaning: not unlike this do Trojan Aeneas and the hero son of Daunus do battle with their shields, as a great crash fills the air.). Note also that a fragment of Sallust's *Histories*, preserved in Servius's note to *Aen.* 12. 715, appears to put Spartacus and his rebel army on La Sila during the war of 73–71 BCE: 'In silua Sila fuerunt' (They were in the forest of Sila). See McGushin (1994) 44 and 153 for translation and commentary.

18 Livy, *Per.* 11–14 and the seven triumphs over the Lucanians 282–272 (= Degrassi (1954) 97–8). For the Lucanian revolt during the Second Punic War see Livy 22. 61. 11–12 with Fronda (2010) 188–233. For recent historical and archaeological perspectives on ancient Lucania see Bispham (2014) and Isayev (2014) respectively.

19 There were foundations at Tempsa, Croton, Buxentum, Salernum and Sipontum in 194 (Livy 34. 45. 1–5), at Thurii in 193 (Livy 34. 53. 1–2) and at Vibo in 192 (Livy 35. 40. 3). See the map illustrating Roman colonial foundations in Italy at Lomas (2014) 208.

20 *ILLRP* 469–72. For discussion see Isayev (2007) 123–4, 176–7.

21 See Gabba (1989) 240.

22 *CIL* 1² 638 (= *ILS* 23) with Wiseman (1987a), (1987b) and Bernard, Damon and Grey (2014). Wiseman (1987a) 109 provides a useful map of the road's route; Bernard, Damon and Grey (2014) 956 provide a translation. The relevant extract is: 'VIAM FECEI AB REGIO AD CAPUAM ET / IN EA VIA PONTEIS OMNEIS MILIARIOS / TABELARIOSQUE POSEIVEI' (I made a road from Rhegium to Capua and on that road I placed bridges (all of them), milestones, and *tabelarii* (translation = Bernard, Damon and Grey (2014) 955)).

23 Wiseman (1987a: 108–15) argues that it was a *Via Annia*, and that the eponymous magistrate is T. Annius Rufus, *pr.* 131, *cos.* 128. Others have suggested P. Popilius

Laenas, *cos.* 132 and T. Annius Luscus, *cos.* 153 (Bernard, Damon and Grey (2014) 954 n. 2). The date is thus also uncertain, with both Isayev ((2007) 177 'the last decades of the second century BC') and Bernard, Damon and Grey ((2014) 954, second century BCE) exercising caution.

24 Bernard, Damon and Grey (2014) 975.

25 I'm thinking in particular of the 'Military Road' through the Wicklow Mountains, built in the aftermath of the rebellion of 1798, and of the memory of the loss of the trees as it survives in the song 'Cill Chais'. While the deforestation of Ireland was a complex process and not solely attributable to colonial rule, it is clear that that rule was its major impetus: see Ludlow and Crampsie 2018: 614–16.

26 Serv. on *G.* 2. 225: 'Acerrae ciuitas est Campaniae, haud longe a Neapoli, quam Clanius praeterfluit fluuius, cuius frequens inundatio eam exhaurit: unde ait 'uacuis', id est infrequentibus' (Acerrae is a town in Campania, not far from Naples, which the river Clanius flows past, and the regular flooding of the river empties it, whence he [sc. Virgil] says 'empty', which is to say 'depopulated').

27 Gigante (2004) 89–91.

28 Livy 23. 1–10, 26. 1 with Fronda (2010) 103–26.

29 Livy 23. 17. 1–7. *Serv. Dan.* on *G.* 2. 225 does mention this Hannibalic context: 'constat Acerranos ab Hannibale secundo bello Punico captos et necatos, unde ait uacuas Acerras' (It is known that people from Acerrae were captured and killed by Hannibal during the Second Punic War, which is why he says that Acerrae is empty).

30 i.e. Etruscans, Umbrians and perhaps men from Cisalpine Gaul. See Gabba (1994) 115.

31 On this conflict see Gabba (1994), App. *B Civ.* 1. 35–52 with Gabba (1958), and Diod. Sic. 37. 1. For a study of its ancient and modern historiography see Mouritsen (1998). 'Italica': Strabo 5. 4. 2 (241 C), Vell. Pat. 2. 16. 4; 'Italia': Diod. Sic. 37. 2. 7. Coins: Sydenham (1952) nos. 617–43.

32 See Degrassi (1954) 107 for Strabo's triumph *de Asculaneis Picentibus*.

33 Nicolet (1980) 23.

34 See App. *B Civ.* 1. 40 (Papius, one of the Italian commanders), 1. 42 (engagements around Acerrae), 1. 45–6 (relief of Acerrae, massacre of *Marsi* force) with Gabba (1994) 118–25.

35 Gabba (1994) 121.

36 App. *B Civ.* 1. 46.

37 But cf. *Serv. Dan.*'s reference (n. 29, above) to Acerrae's sack by Hannibal. McKay (1970) 230 discusses the Social War context of Acerrae, but does not press the ambiguity of *uacuis*.

38 Bourdin (2012) includes discussion of the *Volsci, Ligures, Marsi* and Samnites; see especially Dench (1995). For further reading on individual groups see Cornell

(1989a) 281–93 on the *Volsci*, Letta (1972) on the *Marsi* and Salmon (1967) on the Samnites. These should be supplemented with the more recent historiographical and archaeological perspectives found in Curti, Dench and Patterson (1996), Cornell and Lomas (1997), Bradley, Isayev and Riva (2007) and Aberson, Biella, Di Fazio and Wullschleger (2014).

39 Cornell (1989a) 282–4.

40 Cornell (1989a) 286–9.

41 Livy, 3. 8. 10 'ibi Volscum nomen prope deletum est' (There the Volscian name was almost destroyed (with Ogilvie ad loc.)); 9. 25. 9 'nullus modus caedibus fuit deletaque Ausonum gens' (There was no limit to the slaughter and the Ausonian people were destroyed); 9. 45. 17 'nomenque Aequorum prope ad internecionem deletum' (The Aequian name was destroyed almost to the point of extermination (with Oakley (1997–2005) ad loc)).

42 Hopkins (1978) 28–9.

43 For imperial conceptions of Roman power in Livy's work see Livy, *pr.* 7, 1. 16. 7.

44 Taking the *Georgics* as complete by 29 after seven years of work, and so underway from 36/35 (Donat. *Vit. Verg.* 25–9, followed by Thomas (1988) 1: 1), with Oakley's ((1997–2005) 1: 109–10) estimation that Livy began writing between 35 and 30 and that the second pentad of his history was published 'towards the beginning of the period 30–25'.

45 Bourdin (2012) 79–80. Plut. *Vit. Mar.* 19. 4–5 says that the Ligurians called themselves Ἄμβρωνες.

46 Bourdin (2012) 79–80, with Livy *Per.* 20 (the first campaign against the *Ligures* in 236) and the triumph of M. Claudius Marcellus in 155 (= Degrassi (1954) 105).

47 Livy 39. 1. 1–2: 'dum haec, si modo hoc anno acta sunt, Romae aguntur, consules ambo in Liguribus gerebant bellum. is hostis uelut natus ad continendam inter magnorum interualla bellorum Romanis militarem disciplinam erat; nec alia prouincia militem magis ad uirtutem acuebat' (While these things were happening at Rome, if indeed they happened in this year, both consuls were waging war against the *Ligures*. This enemy was almost born for the purpose of maintaining Roman military discipline during long periods without war, nor did any other territory rouse the soldiery more to valour.).

48 Livy 39. 1. 5–8.

49 Diod. Sic. 5. 39. 6.

50 Strabo 6. 6. 2 (202 C).

51 Serv. ad loc. glosses *malo* with the note 'id est labori' (that is, to toil).

52 See *OLD* s.v. *malum*. The word's meaning ranges from distress or hardship to misfortune, insult, damage and evildoing.

53 On this complex ethnonym see, in particular, *RE* 1A. 2 (1920) 1570–2, Salmon
(1967) 30–3, Dench (1995) 103–6 and *OCD* s.v. Dench (1995) 223–6 compiles all
extant occurrences in Latin and Greek.

54 Varro *Sat. Men.* fr. 17 Astbury = Serv. ad *G.* 2. 168. Diod. Sic. 37. 2. 12 refers to
Σάβελλοι in the context of the Social War, a fragment which Theiler (1982)
attributes to Posidonius. Such an attribution, however, is rejected by both Edelstein
and Kidd (1989) 20 and, most recently, Goukowsky (2014) 190–1. See Goukowsky
(2014) x–xx for a detailed discussion of the scholarly history on this question.

55 Philipp at *RE* 1A. 2 (1920) 1570–1 regards it as 'an invention of antiquarians' (eine
Erfindung der Antiquare) and a poetic variant of 'Samnites'; see also Dench (1995)
103–7.

56 Dench (1995) 106.

57 Livy 8. 1. 7, 10. 19. 20 (within the context of the narrative of the Samnite Wars). Cf.
Plin. *HN.* 3. 107 (beginning a list of Samnite settlements): 'Samnitium, quos
Sabellos Graeci et Saunitas dixere' (Among the Samnite territories, who were
called *Sabelli* and by the Greeks *Saunitae*). Further examples are collected by
Sonnenschein (1897).

58 Varro, *Ling.* 7. 29, Strabo 5. 4. 12 (250 C). The ethnic *safin, of which only oblique
forms are attested, is related to *Sabinus*, *Samnium* and the Oscan *safinim*, but
scholars are divided as to the import of this linguistic connection (Dench 1997:
45).

59 The easily assumed notion that *Sabellus* is a diminutive of *Sabinus* (Pallottino
(1991) 154), Salmon (1967) 32 refuted, arguing that the diminutive would be
Sabillus, not *Sabellus*. 'Sabine' is the translation of *Sabellus* given by Page (1898) on
G. 2. 168, the dictionaries of Lewis and Short (Lewis and Short (1969), s.v. *Sabelli*)
and Cassell (Simpson (1964), s.v. *Sabelli*), and by Mandelbaum (1981) and
Fitzgerald (1984) in their translations of *Aen.* 8. 510. Dench (1995) 104 argues that
Sabellus can refer to *both* Sabines *and* Samnites. I find this unconvincing given the
paucity of evidence (cf. Sonnenschein (1897)), particularly the two examples
Dench cites (104 n. 166) where she argues that *Sabellus* can only mean Sabine:
Hor. *Carm.* 3. 6. 38 (the youth 'taught by Sabellian mattocks' (Sabellis docta
ligonibus)) and Verg. *Aen.* 8. 510: Pallas's *mater Sabella*).

60 A point highlighted by Bourdin (2012) 79–80 on attested individual 'Ligurian'
peoples, and Cornell (2004) 127, who critiques the generalization inherent in
ancient and modern references to the 'Samnites'.

61 Salmon (1958) 166–7, Gabba (1994) 115.

62 Diod. Sic. 37. 2. 1. On the *Marsi* see Letta (1972) and Bourdin (2012) 137–40.

63 e.g. Cic. *Leg. agr.* 2. 90. 17, *Div.* 2. 54. 2, 2. 59. 4; Diod. Sic. 37. 1; Strabo 5. 4. 2 (= 241
C), Plin. *HN* 8. 221. 3.

64 See App. *B Civ.* 1. 87, 93, 94 with Seager (1994) 192–6.

65 Letta (1972) 26–7, 28 n. 17.

66 For more on wordplay in the *Georgics* see Katz (2008), (2016).

67 Barchiesi (2008) 251–2: 'È chiaro che dobbiamo immaginare scenari e localizzazioni diverse: i nonni di Ovidio, nel cuore del territorio peligno, non possono non essere stati coinvolti dal conflitto; Orazio era nato nell'unica colonia latina che si era schierata con gli insorti, Venusia, che per questo fu punita, e i fasti della città si aprono con l'annotazione "dopo la guerra marsica"; Properzio ci appare legato alle sue origine umbre, e quanto a Virgilio, semplicemente non sappiamo abbastanza delle sue ascendenze.'

68 See the *ueru Sabellum* at *Aen.* 7. 665, translated by Horsfall (2000) 35 as a 'Samnite rapier', and the extended scene featuring *fortissimus Umbro* at *Aen.* 7. 750–60. Horsfall (2000) provides useful commentary in both cases.

69 Barchiesi (2008) 253: 'Si è cercato di spiegare l'*escalation* virgiliana parlando di amplificazione epica, di competizione con Omero o di interesse per le tradizioni italiche, ma l'impatto emotivo di questa strategia è più chiaro se si ripensa al trauma collettivo del *bellum Italicum*.'

70 See Cooley on *RG* 25. 2 with Carter (1982) ad Suet. *Aug.* 17. 1–2. Bispham (2007) 443–4 argues that the oath 'manifestly represents a false claim for unity of sentiment, but also of culture and political outlook massed behind the young Caesar'.

71 Specifically because Bononia had to be exempted from taking the oath. See Syme (1939) 284 and Carter (1982) 108.

72 Verg. *Aen.* 8. 678–9: 'hinc Augustus agens Italos in proelia Caesar / cum patribus populoque, penatibus et magnis dis' (On this part [of the shield of Aeneas] is Augustus Caesar, leading Italians into battle with the senators, populace, Penates, and the great gods).

Chapter 5: An Aesthetic Trend

1 See, e.g., Røstvig (1962), Chalker (1969), Low (1985), O'Brien (1999), Pellicer (2012) and (2019), Cooper (2015) and Vance (2015) 51. On the poem's American reception see Sweet (2002).

2 See Chambers (1993) and Sayre (2002), Thomas (2001b) and De Bruyn (2004) on landscape gardening, georgic poetry and agricultural debates respectively. On the politics of landscape in the eighteenth century see Meiksins-Wood (2015) 111; for those of the georgic tradition see Crawford (1998) and, in particular, O'Brien (1999).

3   See Thomson's *The Seasons*, 'Summer', lines 875–85, edited by Sambrook (1981):
    'Ill-fated Race! the softening Arts of Peace, / Whate'er the humanizing Muses
    teach; / The godlike Wisdom of the temper'd Breast; / Progressive Truth, the
    patient Force of Thought; / Investigation calm, whose silent Powers / Command
    the World; the LIGHT that leads to HEAVEN; / Kind equal Rule, the Government
    of Laws, / And all-protecting FREEDOM, which alone / Sustains the Name and
    Dignity of Man: / These are not theirs. The Parent-Sun himself / Seems o'er this
    World of Slaves to tyrannize'. The most popular and influential of the eighteenth-
    century georgic poems, *The Seasons* first appeared in 1730, and in its final form in
    1746. For a history of European and US imperialism in Latin America see Galeano
    (2009).

4   'Then may we hope that even Africa, though last of all the quarters of the globe,
    shall enjoy at length, in the evening of her days, those blessings which have
    descended so plentifully upon us in a much earlier period of the world. Then also
    will Europe, participating in her improvement and prosperity, receive an ample
    recompense for the tardy kindness (if kindness it can be called), of no longer
    hindering that continent from extricating herself out of the darkness which, to
    other more fortunate regions, has been so much more speedily dispelled – *Nos
    primus equis oriens afflavit anhelis; illic sera rubens accendit lumina Vesper*'. Pitt
    (1792) col. 1157, quoting *G.* 1. 250–1 in Latin, which end Virgil's description of the
    celestial sphere by describing the movement of the sun through it: 'When the
    dawn has first breathed on us [i.e. in the northern temperate zone of the earth]
    with her panting horses, there [i.e. in the equivalent southern zone] red Evening
    has kindled its lingering light'. For more on the complexities of what is a difficult
    passage to understand see Page (1898) 211–12 and Mynors (1990) on *G.* 1. 233.

5   Dryden (1709) 1: 63.

6   Addison (1709) 85.

7   Addison (1709) 91: '[I] shall conclude this poem to be the most complete,
    elaborate, and finished piece of all antiquity. The *Aeneis* indeed is of a nobler kind,
    but the *Georgic* is more perfect in its kind'. In quoting this source, I have
    modernized the orthography and spelling.

8   Addison (1709) 92.

9   Addison (1709) 80 argues that didactic precepts require careful exposition, and
    should be 'so finely wrought together in the same piece, that no course seam may
    discover where they join; as in a curious breed of needlework, one colour falls
    away by such just degrees, and another rises so insensibly, that we see the variety,
    without being able to distinguish the total vanishing of the one from the first
    appearance of the other'.

10 Addison (1709) 83.

11 Addison (1709) 83: 'it is worthwhile to consider how admirably he has turned the course of his narration into its proper channel, and made his husbandman concerned even in what relates to the battle, in those inimitable lines, *Scilicet et tempus ueniet*' (quoting *G.* 1. 493).

12 Addison (1709) 89.

13 *Spectator* nos. 409 and 411–21, collected as 'Taste and the Pleasures of the Imagination' in Bond (1970) 172–209. No. 414 (25 June 1712) quotes *G.* 2. 467–70 (= Bond (1970) 184); no. 415 (26 June 1712) has as its epigraph *G.* 2. 155 (= Bond (1970) 186).

14 *Spectator* no. 409 (19 June 1712) = Bond (1970) 172: 'As this word [i.e. taste] arises very often in conversation, I shall endeavour to give some account of it, and to lay down rules how we may know whether we are possessed of it, and how we may acquire that fine taste of writing, which is so talked of among the polite world.'

15 *Spectator* no. 411 (21 June 1712) = Bond (1970) 177.

16 *Spectator* no. 414 (25 June 1712) = Bond (1970) 184: 'we always find the poet in love with a country life, where Nature appears in the greatest perfection, and furnishes out all those scenes that are most apt to delight the imagination [Addison then quotes Hor. *Epist* 2. 2. 77 and Verg. *G.* 2. 467–70]'.

17 *Spectator* no. 417 (28 June 1712) = Bond (1970) 195: 'the *Aeneid* is like a well-ordered garden, where it is impossible to find out any part unadorned, or to cast our eyes upon a single spot, that does not produce some beautiful plant or flower'.

18 *Spectator* no. 417 (28 June 1712) = Bond (1970) 196.

19 Addison (1709) 85: 'And herein consists Virgil's masterpiece, who had not only excelled all other poets, but even himself in the language of the *Georgics*; where we receive more strong and lively ideas of things from his words, than we could have done from the objects themselves: and find our imagination more affected by his descriptions, than they would have been by the very sight of what he describes.'

20 On British Grand Tourists in this period, and the influence of the classical past on their conceptions, see Black (1992), Ayres (1997), Chard (1999) and Sweet (2012).

21 Addison (1718).

22 'A Letter from Italy, to the Right Honourable Charles, Lord Halifax. In the Year MDCCI.' = Addison (1718) i–x. The epigraph to the letter is *G.* 2. 173–5: 'salue, magna parens frugum, Saturnia tellus, / magna uirum: tibi res antiquae laudis et artem / ingredior sanctos ausus recludere fontis' (Hail great giver of crops, Saturn's land, great giver of men: for you I embark on a subject and skill long-renowned, having dared to open up the hallowed springs).

23 Addison (1718) ii: 'Poetic fields encompass me around / And still I seem to tread on classic ground'.

24 Addison (1718) iv: 'Oh could the Muse my ravish'd Breast inspire / With Warmth like yours, and raise an equal Fire, / Unnumber'd Beauties in my Verse shou'd shine, / And *Virgil's Italy* shou'd yield to mine!' [emphasis original]

25 Addison (1718) 41, quoting *G.* 2. 159–60 with *adde* for Mynors's *anne* in line 159: 'Add to this its great lakes: you, Larus, greatest of all, and you, Benacus, swelling with waves and the sound of the sea.'

26 Letter dated 7 August 1701 (= Graham (1941) 29), partially quoting, and apparently slightly misremembering, *G.* 2. 488: 'o qui me gelidis conuallibus Haemi / sistat' (O if only there were someone who would place me in the icy enclosed valleys of Haemus).

27 Martyn (1741) ix.

28 Warton (1763) 294, 301; Mills (1780) v–vi.

29 Hoblyn (1825) i; Keightley (1846) xxi.

30 Merivale (1850–82) 4: 576, Wilkins (1874) v, Jerram (1892) 1: 3, Mackail (1895) 95, Sellar (1897) 278, Page (1898) iii and xxiii.

31 Sellar (1897) 231, with Addison (1709) 88: 'He [sc. Virgil] delivers the meanest of his precepts with a kind of grandeur, he breaks the clods and tosses the dung about with an air of gracefulness.'

32 Myers (1908) 115–16: '[Virgil] had discovered the hidden music which can give to every shade of feeling its distinction, its permanence, and its charm … his thoughts seem to come to us on the wings of melodies prepared for them from the foundation of the world.' This essay on Virgil was first published in 1883.

33 Jerram (1892) 1: 3.

34 Compare Addison (1709) 91: 'The *Aeneis* indeed is of a nobler kind, but the *Georgic* is more perfect in its kind.'

35 Turner (1993) 297: 'Roman literature in general remained on the aesthetic defensive for the entire nineteenth century. The difficulties Roman literature as literature confronted in the wake of the Greek revival and romantic aesthetics became clear in the most impressive effort to defend it.'

36 Myers (1908) 107: 'The set which the German criticism of this century has made against Virgil is perfectly explicable, and in one sense a perfectly justifiable thing. It is one among many results which have flowed from the application of the historical faculty, pure and simple, to the judgement of art.' For this rebuttal of German criticism of Virgil, see also Papillon (1882) xxii–xxiii and Sellar (1897) 60. For more on early-nineteenth-century disparagement of the poet, British as well as German, see Vasunia (2009b) 98–100, 109–10 and Turner (1993) 292–6.

37 Turner (1993) 294.

38 'Virgil', *Encyclopaedia Britannica*, 7th edn (1842), vol. 21, p. 655.

39 'Virgil', *Encyclopaedia Britannica*, 7th edn, p. 655.

40 Glover and Sellar (1911) 114. The entry on Virgil in the 11th edition is T. R. Glover's revision of W. S. Sellar's entry for the 9th edition of 1887.

41 Glover (1912) 39.

42 Martinengo-Cesaresco (1911) 139.

43 Gardner (1904) 5.

44 Berger (1972) 13.

45 Mackail (1895) 95.

46 Conington and Nettleship (2007) 155.

47 Keble (1912) 2: 369: 'He is to be ranked the poets who delight in country life, not in action. It is clear that he wrote the *Aeneid* somewhat against the grain: for, first, he is quite uninterested in the character of Aeneas himself: next he gladly catches at every opportunity of digressing into the quiet charms of Nature: finally, he makes it clear that he thoroughly detested war and warlike affairs.'

48 Royds (1914) xiii–xiv.

49 Glover and Sellar (1911) 114.

50 Martinengo-Cesaresco (1911) 139: 'The *Georgics* is one of the most faultless of poems; but perhaps a reader here and there has privately regretted that so much stress is laid upon the details of these animal plagues. But Virgil was resolved not to soften any of the lines of his picture, not to 'retouch' the photograph; it was a matter of conscience with him to be sincere.' See also Page (1898) xxv on the plague of Book 3 being 'less in accordance with modern than with ancient taste'.

51 Modern scholarship has balanced out this one-sided picture of the poem: see Thomas (1988) 1: 24 (on 'the complexity, ambivalence and ultimate darkness of the Virgilian world'), with Ross (1987) 241 (the *Georgics* as 'profoundly pessimistic') and Putnam (1979) 13 (the poem's 'pessimistic impression on the reader').

52 For a succinct view see Warde Fowler's introduction to Royds (1914) vii: 'No book of classical antiquity makes quite such a strong appeal to the Englishman as the *Georgics*.'

53 Jerram (1892) 1: 15.

54 Glover (1912) 163: 'Virgil ... found in Augustus a friend, a saviour of his country, and a heroic character.'

55 Sellar (1897) 236 (on the *laudes Italiae*): 'the great episode on the beauties and riches on Italy ... is introduced in immediate contrast to the account of the prodigal luxuriance of Nature in the jungles and forests of the East'. See also Merivale (1850–82) 4: 578 (on the 'pleasant indulgences of the East') and Mackail (1923) 18 (on 'the fatal lure of the East'). On East and West in the *laudes Italiae* see Harrison (2008).

56 Merivale (1850–82) 4: 577: 'To comprehend the moral grandeur of the Georgics, in point of style the most perfect piece, perhaps, of Roman literature, we must regard

it as the glorification of Labour.' The phrase is quoted approvingly by Conington and Nettleship (2007) 159 and Sellar (1897) 211. For the Roman labour context see Spurr (1986) and Geue (2018). In a British context, I'm thinking especially of the 1834 Poor Law, which criminalized poverty as a moral failing and prioritized the workhouse system over charitable relief: see Hollingsworth (1983) 107. In 1902 the historian J. A. Hobson's influential study of imperialism saw diligence in explicitly racist terms: 'the ease with which human life can be maintained in the tropics breeds indolence and torpor of character. The inhabitants of these countries are not "progressive" people.' (Hobson 1902: 239).

57 Sellar (1897) 266–8.

58 Glover (1912) 107: 'Just as to-day the significance of the British flag is best learned abroad, we may believe that the opening of the world of the East and the new world of Spain and Gaul to Italian commerce helped forward the detrition of old clan distinctions and made Marsian and Apulian conscious that they were both Italian in blood and Roman in fact, if not yet in the letter of the law. The Social War was essentially, like the American Civil War, a war for unity. The day of tribal independence was gone, and the Italian fought for Italy, and for a united Italy, against the Roman, who fought for a divided Italy.'

59 Mackail (1923) 70 and compare p. 69: 'perhaps no poetry has been written which combines in such perfection richness of colour with purity of line, which is so exquisite in its transitions and so suave in its modulations, so smoothly gliding and nobly sustained. All these qualities are reinforced or culminate in episodes, where the current of the poem spreads into large pools of beauty.'

60 Mackail (1923) 140 and 141. A forerunner of the United Nations, the League of Nations was founded 10 January 1920 to promote international peace and security in the aftermath of the First World War. See Ziolkowski (1993) 12–16 for further discussion of the 'Roman analogy' in European writing 1918–39.

61 On which see Morrow (2014), esp. 430: 'In January 1919 the British Empire reached its zenith, with more than a million additional square miles, primarily in former Ottoman domains, as [British Prime Minister] Lloyd George laid claim to dominance in the Middle East. In April 1920 the British and French agreed secretly to monopolise the oil supplies of the Middle East and in July the French took control of Syria and would later rule in Syria and Lebanon. After riots in Egypt and Egyptian demands for complete independence in 1919 and revolt in Iraq in 1920, an over-extended British government granted both limited autonomy in 1922. That same year, Britain assumed the League [of Nations] mandate over Palestine, west of the River Jordan, while Eastern Palestine became Jordan.'

62 Heitland (1921) 223, with p. 229, where the poem is called 'Virgil's most finished work'.

63 Heitland (1921) 3.

64 Heitland (1921) 1–2.

65 Heitland (1921) 222; see also 227–41. The Latin quotation is from *G.* 2. 468, 'leisure on large estates'.

66 Heitland (1921) 223 and 224, and see Spurr (1986) 174–5.

67 Heitland (1921) 229.

68 Heitland (1921) 237.

69 Wilkinson (1969) 11, and compare De Saint-Denis (1956) xl on translating the poem: 'l'affaire est plus périlleuse que jamais, quand le texte allie avec tant de souplesse et de virtuosité indications techniques et notations pittoresques, science et poésie, à l'intérieur d'une phrase, d'un vers, d'un groupe de mots. Cette conjonction de la précision et de la fantaisie fait peut-être des *Géorgiques* le chef-d'œuvre de Virgile.'

70 See Johnson (1981) 50 on the *Georgics* as 'Virgil's masterpiece, not only technically but emotionally and intellectually'.

71 Otis (1963) 151 (on the four books of the poem as movements in a Western classical symphony), Owen-Lee (1996), Johnson (1981) 53 (on the poem's 'lustrous harmonies'), Batstone (1997) 133 and Gale (2000) 11 (who both use the metaphor of polyphony to describe the poem's thematic complexity), Thibodeau (2011) 2.

72 For comprehensive bibliographies of scholarly work on the *Georgics* see Suerbaum (1981) and Holzberg (2015); for surveys of recent work see Volk (2008) 1–10 and the introduction to Xinyue and Freer (2019). A selective list of recent work focused on intertextuality and literary models would include Farrell (1991), Nelson (1998), Thomas (1999) and (2007), Gale (2000), Cadili (2001), Harrison (2004), Katz (2008), Heerink (2011), Henkel (2011), Dexter (2013) and Gardner (2014).

73 Thomas (2007) 73 with Batstone (1997). See also Thomas (2019).

74 Erren (1985–2003) 1: 12: 'daß speziell Vergils *Georgica* zu den schönsten und repräsentativsten Werken der römischen Literatur gehören'; Thibodeau (2011) 2: 'The passages of its four short books follow one another in a finely tempered ebb and flow that has aptly been likened to a symphony. The lyricism of its verse is such that any study of euphony in Latin verse risks turning into an anthology of lines from the poem.'

Chapter 6: The *Georgics* Abroad

1 Kincaid (1988) 24.

2 Broughall (2015) 129 argues that ancient Rome 'provided a crucial colonialist vocabulary for the British imperial project', but also shows (pp. 245–56) how

comparisons with Rome could critique or express anxiety about Britain's imperial power. For further studies in this area see Hagerman (2013), Bradley (2010) and Goff (2005).

3   Letter to Maria Gisborne, 22 January 1819 = Bennett (1980) 1: 85.

4   Bennett (1980) 1: 85.

5   Journal entry for 14 November 1838 = Thomas (2008) 1: 47.

6   Thomas (2008) 1: 47, quoting *G.* 2. 156–7.

7   'Italy at Work', *Dublin University Magazine*, September 1869, p. 273. Anonymous primary sources like this one are listed at the beginning of the References section at the end of the book; second and subsequent references to such articles in the notes are abbreviated for convenience.

8   'Italy at Work', p. 273, quoting in English from *G.* 2. 174: 'magna [parens] uirum'.

9   'Foreign Intelligence', *The London Evening Standard*, 25 July 1859, p. 5, quoting *G.* 2. 167–8.

10 Diary entry for 18 October 1838 = Foot (1968) 445.

11 i.e. *G.* 1. 171–2: 'huic a stirpe pedes temo protentus in octo, / binae aures, duplici aptantur dentalia dorso' (For this [the elm base of the plough] are prepared a pole extending eight feet from the base, two ears, and [?] double-ridged teeth to hold the share). On the intricacies and interpretative ambiguities of this passage see Mynors (1990) ad loc.

12 'Italy After the War', *The Aberdeen Daily Journal*, 13 May 1921, p. 4.

13 See Duggan (2008) 420–30 for context.

14 'Italy After the War', p. 4.

15 'Italy After the War', p. 4.

16 'Farming in Tuscany', *The Times*, 6 November 1935, p. 17.

17 'Farming in Tuscany', p. 17, quoting *G.* 2. 532–3, 539–40.

18 On the Abyssinian context see Hardie (1974) 101–12.

19 'Farming in Tuscany', p. 17.

20 For a brief biography of Miller see Runciman (2004).

21 Miller (1904) 639. The second part of the article, not quoted here, is Miller (1905).

22 Miller (1904) 641.

23 Miller (1904) 648.

24 Miller (1904) 640.

25 Miller (1904) 646–7, quoting *G.* 3. 343–5.

26 On the mission see Henze (2000) 127–32. For a brief biography of Cornwallis Harris see Chichester (2004).

27 Graham (1844). No first name is given for Graham in the source, but its date and title suggest the 1841–3 mission, and the list of mission members recorded by

Cornwallis Harris (Cornwallis Harris (1844) 1: vii) includes 'Captain Douglas Graham' as principal assistant.

28 Graham (1844) 254.

29 Graham (1844) 262, quoting *G.* 1. 84–5.

30 Graham (1844) 280. Graham then (p. 280) quotes *G.* 4. 62–5: 'huc tu iussos asperge sapores, / trita melisphylla et cerinthae ignobile gramen, / tinnitusque cie et Matris quate cymbala circum: / ipsae consident medicatis sedibus' (Here scatter the prescribed flavours, ground *melisphylla* and the lowly *cerintha* plant, and raise a din and shake Cybele's cymbals round the hive: they will settle of their own accord in their scented home).

31 Graham (1844) 279, quoting *G.* 2. 149–50.

32 Graham (1844) 255.

33 Cornwallis Harris (1844) 3: 185.

34 See Henze (2000) 137–42.

35 Henze (2000) 142 n. 39.

36 On the Italian invasion of Abyssinia, and the extensive use of mustard gas and other chemical weapons by the invaders, see Duggan (2008) 500–5.

37 Ethiopian-American author Maaza Mengiste, quoted in Trilling (2019), whose article details the history of the items' theft and current calls for their restitution.

38 Laroui (1977) 37.

39 Mattingly (2011) 43.

40 'Roman Africa: The Georgics of Algeria', *The Times*, 27 October 1925, p. 17.

41 'Roman Africa: The Georgics of Algeria', p. 17.

42 'Jemila: A Roman City in Algeria', *The Times*, 19 October 1925, p. 13.

43 'Jemila: A Roman City in Algeria', p. 13.

44 'Roman Africa: From Jemila to Timgad', *The Times*, 22 October 1925, p. 15, referring to Sall. *Iug.* 17. 5–6: 'All the same, Sallust, who knew Constantine well when it was Cirta, attests the healthiness of the country, where, he says, death comes only of old age or of the onslaught of wild beasts.'

45 'Roman Africa: From Jemila to Timgad', p. 15, quoting Aesch. *Supp.* 284–6 in (untranslated) Greek: 'Even Greek Aeschylus speaks of these nomad females, astraddle on their beasts, and his grandiloquent brevity hits them off perfectly. With his rather vague geography he has heard of them as Indians, and is the first European to use that name, but he puts them near the Aethiopians.'

46 'Jemila: A Roman City in Algeria', p. 13, quoting part of Verg. *Aen.* 1. 462 ('There are tears in human life') and referencing the fact that, in the poem, Aeneas speaks this line in Carthage.

47 'Roman Africa: From Jemila to Timgad', p. 15.

48 Mattingly (2011) 47–9.

49 'Roman Africa: The Georgics of Algeria', p. 17. The two quotations are from *G.* 2. 514 (where Mynors (1990) and Conte (Ottaviano and Conte (2013)) read *hic anni labor* for *hinc anni labor*), where ploughing is the basis of the farmer's year, 'hence the year's work'; and *G.* 1. 299, the instructions for fieldwork, 'plough and sow stripped'.

50 'Roman Africa: The Georgics of Algeria', p. 17: 'The olive they have, and the handmill – Virgil's *trapetum* – is still in use among them'. Cf. *G.* 2. 519: 'uenit hiems: teritur Sicyonia baca trapetis' (Winter comes: the Sicyonian olive is pressed in mills). Sicyon was a Peloponnesian town west of Corinth.

51 'Roman Africa: The Georgics of Algeria', p. 17.

52 'Roman Africa: From Jemila to Timgad', p. 15, quoting in English *G.* 3. 346–8: 'non secus ac patriis acer Romanus in armis / iniusto sub fasce uiam cum carpit, et hosti / ante exspectatum positis stat in agmine castris'.

53 Laroui (1977) 302–3 and 352–3 with Thomas (2005) 252: 'The colonial legal system undermined established patterns of Muslim land ownership and traditional farming practices. Land laws favoured the settler community, denying Muslim rights to common grazing and cultivable land unless written title could be produced. French colonization displaced Muslim cultivators from ancestral holdings . . . In 1917 settlers possessed 2.31 million hectares of farmland. By 1940 the figure stood at 2.7 million.'

Chapter 7: 'Happy Farmers'

1 I've used the Loeb translation here because I don't think I can better it: see Fairclough (1999).

2 For the poetic and philosophical contexts of *G.* 458–540 see Kronenberg (2000) and Gagliardi (2009) respectively; see also Wilkinson (1963), who notes (p. 83) the inconsistency between this passage and the rest of the poem. Thibodeau (2011) 108 reads lines 458–60 as referring to Roman landowners and thus to contemporary post-war elite Roman politics. For darker readings of the poem as a whole see Putnam (1979) 13 (the poem's 'pessimistic impression on the reader'), Ross (1987) 241 (the *Georgics* as 'profoundly pessimistic') and Thomas (1988) 1: 24 (on 'the complexity, ambivalence and ultimate darkness of the Virgilian world').

3 On this simplification see Thomas (2001b) 130 with O'Brien (1999) for historical context.

4 For a brief biography of Froude see Pollard (2004); for a detailed study see Brady (2013).

5 The other being *The English in the West Indies, or the Bow of Ulysses* (1888), on which see Brady (2013) 404–12.

6 Froude (1886) 21. The Ennian epigraph is 'moribus antiquis res stat Romana uirisque' (= Skutsch (1985) fr. 156: 'The Roman state depends upon its ancient customs and its men').

7 Froude (1886) 24: 'The sky to the Latin farmer was a dial-plate, on which the stars were pointers; and he read the hour of the night from their position on its face. The constellations were his monthly almanack, and as the sun moved from one into another he learned when to plough and when to sow, when to prune his vines, and clip the wool from his sheep.' The sky is prominent throughout *Georgics* 1, but in particular Froude's language appears to suggest *G.* 1. 1–4 ('when to plough and when to sow') and the farmer's calendar at *G.* 1. 204–30 ('the constellations were his monthly almanack').

8 Brady (2013) 400.

9 Froude (1886) 179, referencing *G.* 1. 7–9: 'Liber et alma Ceres, uestro si munere tellus / Chaoniam pingui glandem mutauit arista, / poculaque inuentis Acheloia miscuit uuis' (Bacchus and kindly Ceres, if by your gift the land has exchanged the acorns of Epirus for ears of plump corn, and has mixed cups of water from the river Achelous with new-found grapes).

10 Denoon and Wyndham (1999) 563.

11 Seeley (1971) 41.

12 'ART V: *Oceana; or England and Her Colonies*', *The Edinburgh Review*, April 1886, pp. 405–36; 'Literature: Oceana', *The Observer*, 21 February 1886, p. 6.

13 Wakefield (1886) 173. Wakefield had little time for Froude's seaborne classical musings: 'If there is a bore on this earth, it is a man who will talk about the details of life on board ship' (Wakefield (1886) 173).

14 Froude (1886) 86.

15 Wakefield (1886) 175. On Froude's misrepresentation *The Edinburgh Review* remarked, 'It is unfortunate that Mr. Froude could not make a longer stay at Adelaide' (= 'ART V: *Oceana; or England and Her Colonies*', p. 411).

16 Froude (1886) 167.

17 Froude (1886) 167, with *G.* 2. 458 slightly altered (nominative *fortunati* for exclamatory accusative *o fortunatos*).

18 For a recent study of further receptions and appropriations of classics in colonial Australia see White (2017).

19 Gray (2018) 664: 'Of the estimated population of 8.5 million in 1845, between 1 million and 1.1 million perished between then and 1851 of starvation and (more commonly) hunger-related disease. There were a further 0.4 million "averted births" due to the collapse of fertility during the crisis years. Another million

emigrated, reducing the island's population by over a quarter of an anticipated total of just over 9 million by the census of 1851.'

20 On agrarian violence in Ireland at this time see Townshend (1983) 1–50. For detailed histories of the period see Vaughan (1989) and Kelly (2018).

21 [Ashworth] (1851) 40.

22 [Ashworth] (1851) 217.

23 'The Irish Land Question', *The Times*, 25 August 1869, p. 8.

24 Editorial Article, *The Times*, 31 August 1869, p. 6.

25 Hansard, Parl. Debs. (series 3) vol. 171, cols. 817–62 (12 June 1863). The motion called for (col. 817) 'a Select Committee to inquire into the causes of such depression [in Ireland] and the effect of the taxation which it now bears'.

26 Hansard, Parl. Debs. (series 3) vol. 171, cols. 817–21 (12 June 1863). On the complicated question of how (un)fairly Ireland contributed to British and British imperial revenue in this period see Vaughan (1989) 784–94, esp. 786.

27 Maguire was MP successively for Dungarvan 1852–65 and Cork 1865–72. Jones (2009) notes that Maguire introduced a tenants' compensation bill (1858), proposed a select committee on landlord and tenant practice in Ireland (1863) and was appointed its chairman in 1865.

28 Hansard, Parl. Debs. (series 3) vol. 171, col. 839 (12 June 1863).

29 For a short biography of Peel (not to be confused with his father Robert Peel (1788–1850)) see Boase (2007).

30 Hansard, Parl. Debs. (series 3) vol. 171, cols. 1354–5 (23 June 1863).

31 Foster (1989) 327: 'Under the new dispensation, government intervention was to be strictly limited; private initiative must be relied on to provide food wherever possible, with the result that prices soared to levels that the wages paid by public works could not meet.' Irish poorhouses had 215,000 inmates by June 1849 (Foster (1989) 328).

32 Foster (1989) 325: 'Within both the government and the Treasury, humanitarian impulses came up against a violent disapproval of subsidized improvement schemes; there was also an attitude, often unconcealed, that Irish fecklessness and lack of economy were bringing a retribution that would work out for the best in the end.'

33 On which see Gibbons (2000).

34 For a brief biography of Butt see Bull (2009).

35 Butt (1847), (1866), (1867). Cf. Foster (1989) 329 (on the Famine): 'The government by and large adhered to the belief that private enterprise should provide the bulk of the food supply; hardly anyone supported the idea that the government *itself* should enter the market except, once again, the indomitable Butt' [emphasis original].

36 Butt (1866), (1867).

37 Lifford's comments are quoted in Butt (1867) 6; for Dufferin's letter on emigration
see Blackwood (1866). Dufferin doesn't name Butt explicitly in this letter, first
doing so in a subsequent letter dated the following January: see Blackwood (1867).

38 Marx and Engels (1996) 701: 'But the lion's share, which an inconceivably small
number of land magnates in England, Scotland and Ireland swallow up of the
yearly national rental, is so monstrous that the wisdom of the English state does
not think fit to offer the same statistical materials about the distribution of rents as
about the distribution of profits. Lord Dufferin is one of those land magnates. That
rent rolls and profits can ever be "excessive", or that their plethora is in any way
connected with plethora of the people's misery is, of course, an idea as
"disreputable" as "unsound". He keeps to the facts. The fact is that, as the Irish
population diminishes, the Irish rent rolls swell; that depopulation benefits the
landlords, therefore also benefits the soil, and, therefore, the people, that mere
accessory of the soil. He declares, therefore, that Ireland is still overpopulated, and
the stream of emigration still flows too lazily. To be perfectly happy, Ireland must
get rid of at least one-third of a million of labouring men.'

39 The quotation is found at Butt (1867) 91; on the landlords' powers of eviction see
Butt (1867) 8–9: 'The circumstances of Ireland are as such, that this power of
arbitrary eviction in the hands of the landlord gives him, over his tenant, a
dominion, compared with which the heaviest yoke of feudal vassalage was light.
To evict a tenant in Ireland is, in nine instances out of ten, to reduce him to
beggary – it is to deprive him of the means of living – to send him to the
workhouse – or to drive him from his native land.'

40 Butt (1867) 118.

41 'uerum ubi correptum manibus uinclisque tenebis / tum uariae eludent species
atque ora ferarum' (But when you have him bound by your hands and chains, then
his different forms and animal faces will deceive you'). The lines come from a
passage describing the magical transformations of Proteus to which, Cyrene tells
her son Aristaeus, he will resort to avoid capture.

42 'sed quanto ille magis formas se uertet in omnis / tam tu, nate, magis contende
tenacia uincla, / donec talis erit mutato corpore qualem / uideris incepto tegeret
cum lumina somno' (But the more he changes into every form, then you, child,
draw your strong bonds all the more tightly, until, after his transformations, he
takes the shape in which you saw him as he first fell asleep).

43 Butt (1867) 239. *G.* 2. 451 reads: 'Sed nos immensum spatiis confecimus aequor'
(But we have completed a course of great length). It is the penultimate line of the
book, and part of its concluding metaphor of finishing a horse race.

44 Butt (1834).

45 Butt (1867) 288, quoting *G.* 4. 86–7.

46 For a narrative of the Rebellion see James (1997) 233–98; for an introduction to its complex and contested historiography see Pati (2010) 1–15.

47 British opinion was particularly horrified by the massacre of 180 women and children on 15–16 July 1857 at Cawnpore (Kanpur), for which see James (1997) 251–3, 282–90. Reprisals carried out by British troops in North India, often sanctioned and instigated by senior officers, included mass hangings, lynchings, the strapping of prisoners to cannons and the religious defilement of Hindu and Muslim victims before execution. See Newsinger (2013) 84–9.

48 'Leamington Institute: The Rev. W. C. Furneaux on "Life in the East"', *Leamington Spa Courier*, 24 January 1885, p. 7.

49 'Leamington Institute', p. 7.

50 Furneaux describes the 'native character' as 'intelligent and intellectual, but lazy, untruthful, and given to petty thefts' ('Leamington Institute', p. 7). Of his high hopes for the conversion of India to Christianity, Furneaux finishes by saying: 'The duty of England in the present day was to sow the seed, and in God's good time his Kingdom would come' ('Leamington Institute', p. 7).

51 The most comprehensive account of these events and their context is Rao and Rao (1992); see also Bose (1993) 45–51, Bhattacharya (1977) and Kling (1966).

52 In 1859 there were approximately 500 planters managing 143 production facilities, which accounted for half the value of indigo imported into Britain at the time (Kling (1966) 26).

53 Roy (2011) 62. Ryot is the typical contemporary spelling in English sources of raiyat, a word derived from Urdu and Persian meaning a peasant or cultivating tenant.

54 Bose (1993) 48: 'Debts were reckoned to pass from father to son … Unpaid balances mounted over the generations to astronomical figures which no indigo peasant could hope to redeem.'

55 Bose (1993) 48. As Rao and Rao note (1992: 71), the system concealed further unpaid labour, namely the families of ryots who helped cultivate the crop.

56 Rao and Rao (1992) 70, quoting from the Minute of Governor-General Grant dated 17 December 1860 (= Buckland (1901) 1: 252).

57 See Trevelyan (2010) and, for the reception of Horace in the work, Harrison (2017) 102–4.

58 'ART VI: *The Competition Wallah*', *The Calcutta Review*, April 1864, pp. 329–30.

59 'ART VI: *The Competition Wallah*', p. 333.

60 'ART VI: *The Competition Wallah*', p. 334.

61 Morrow (2014) 429: 'The war had drawn some 1.5 million Indians into military service for the British Empire and brought heavy taxes, war loans, and requisitions

of grain and raw materials and inflation, but it did not bring independence or even autonomy. Instead, the British resorted to repression and violence during and after the war to maintain their power in India, culminating in the Amritsar massacre of 1919.'

62 See Keay (2000) 471–5. During the war two separate Home Rule Leagues were formed, and Gandhi, newly returned from South Africa, began to deploy his tactic of *satyagraha* in different parts of the country.

63 Keay (2000) 475–6.

64 The text of this declaration is printed in the Montagu-Chelmsford Report (= Montagu and Thesiger (1918) 6). For detail on the final reforms see Markowitz (2002) 368.

65 Montagu and Thesiger (1918) 138–9, 179.

66 'O, Fortunatos Nimium', *The Saturday Review of Politics, Literature, Science and Art*, 26 April 1919, p. 396.

67 Montagu and Thesiger (1918) 144.

68 'O, Fortunatos Nimium', p. 396.

69 Saunders and Smith (1999) 601.

70 Saunders and Smith (1999) 609.

71 Saunders and Smith (1999) 617–19; Crosby (2011) 153. For a history of Britain's use of concentration camps see Forth (2017).

72 Porter (2004) 177–8.

73 Saunders and Smith (1999) 620.

74 On Chamberlain and South Africa see Crosby (2011) 154 and Marsh (1994) 546–9.

75 Davenport and Saunders (2000) 238.

76 Hansard, Parl. Debs. (series 4) vol. 114, col. 236 (5 November 1902).

77 Hansard, Parl. Debs. (series 4) vol. 114, col. 237 (5 November 1902).

78 'Notes on Trade and Finance', *The Speaker: The Liberal Review*, 8 November 1902, p. 156.

79 Seymour (2012) 35.

Chapter 8: The *Georgics* at Home

1 These were the Allotments Extension Act (1882) and the Allotments Act (1887), on which see Foley (2014) 125–6. On Collings's political career see Readman (2008).

2 Readman (2008) 296.

3 Collings (1906) xv.

4 Readman (2008) 296.

5   Collings (1906) xiii–xiv.

6   Collings (1906) xv.

7   Collings (1906) 394.

8   Collings (1906) 395.

9   Collings (1906) 395.

10 Collings (1906) 396. These are *G*. 2. 212–13, 184–8, 458–60, 513–18 and 529–31.

11 Collings (1906) 396, quoting *G*. 2. 532–5: 'hanc olim ueteres uitam coluere Sabini, / hanc Remus et frater; sic fortis Etruria creuit / scilicet et rerum facta est pulcherrima Roma, / septemque una sibi muro circumdedit arces'.

12 Collings (1906) 410.

13 Foley (2014) 147.

14 Foley (2014) 147, 159.

15 'The Allotment Garden: Seasonable Notes of an Expert', *The Newcastle Daily Journal*, 18 May 1917, p. 3.

16 'The Allotment Garden', p. 3.

17 Discussed by Gale (1998) 116–18. Of several examples see in particular *G*. 1. 160–1: 'Dicendum et quae sint duris agrestibus arma, / quis sine nec potuere seri nec surgere messes' (The weapons of tough farmers should also be mentioned, without which it is impossible for crops to be sown or to grow) and *G*. 2. 369–70: 'tum denique dura / exerce imperia et ramos compesce fluentis' (Then at last carry out your harsh commands and check the overgrown [vine-]shoots).

18 'Cheese', *Gloucester Chronicle*, 5 May 1917, p. 2.

19 The inclusion of a colon in line 402 of Mynors's text implies that both the daytime and evening milk's cheese is sent out. But a colon is not printed by Hirtzel (1900) or Conte (Ottaviano and Conte (2013)), which implies either that only the evening milk's cheese, or else the unpressed evening milk, is sent. Col. Noel follows this latter interpretation.

20 'A Plea for Apples', *North Devon Journal*, 14 March 1918, p. 7.

21 'A Plea for Apples', p. 7.

22 'A Plea for Apples', p. 7.

23 Harmsworth (1916).

24 James (1917).

25 For a brief biography of Brodribb see Hudson (2004).

26 Brodribb (1913), (1922), (1928); Sargeaunt et al. (1917).

27 'Obituary: Mr. C. W. Brodribb', *The Times*, 22 June 1945, p. 7: 'Perhaps the deepest thing in Charles Brodribb was patriotism, solicitude for the *res publica*.'

28 Brodribb (1946) 32.

29 Brodribb (1946) 34–5. The posthumous collection *Poems* also includes 'Thoughts After Virgil', dated March 1943 and with *Aen*. 6. 806 (pp. 37–8) as its epigraph, and

'Praises of Italy' (pp. 81–2), an excerpt of *G*. 2. 136–76 from Brodribb's 1928 translation.

30 Brodribb (1917), quoting *G*. 2. 513–15 and 2. 524. Mynors (1990) and Conte (Ottaviano and Conte (2013)) print *hic* at the beginning of line 514, conjectured by Markland ad Stat. *Silv*. 1. 2. 144 (see Markland (1728) 26).

31 On which see Kramer (2014) 485–7.

32 Whetham (1978) 71–4.

33 Whetham (1978) 90.

34 Whetham (1978) 94–5.

35 The war revolutionized women's access to employment, although these gains were largely (but not entirely) reversed at the end of the war: see Grayzel (2002) 27–9, 106, and Storey and Housego (2010). A series of women's organizations played a role in agricultural production during the war: the largest of these, the Women's Land Army, had at its height about 23,000 members. For more see Storey and Housego (2010) 43–6 and Grayzel (2002) 42–3.

36 *G*. 2. 510: 'gaudent perfusi sanguine fratrum'.

37 Hansard, HC Deb. (series 5), vol. 90, cols. 1591–1614 (23 February 1917).

38 Hansard, HC Deb. (series 5), vol. 90, cols. 1608–10 (23 February 1917).

39 Hansard, HC Deb. (series 5), vol. 90, col. 1607 (23 February 1917).

40 Hansard, HC Deb. (series 5), vol. 90, col. 1600 (23 February 1917).

41 On women's work in the *Georgics* see Oliensis (1997) 301 and Perkell (2014).

42 See also D'Agostino (1957) in favour of *nepotes*.

43 Markland (1728) 26, Ribbeck (1894). See also Funaioli (1947) vol. 2, part 1, 380–1 in favour of *penates*.

44 Ottaviano and Conte (2013) 101: 'Plurimum pollent ad textum constituendum Mediceus et Palatinus, at neuter eorum contra alterum praecellere aperte uidetur, quamquam Mediceum puto aliquanto frequentius lectiones seruauisse ueras' (The Mediceus and Palatinus [codices] are of great importance in establishing the text, but neither of them seems clearly to surpass the other, although I think the Mediceus has a little more frequently preserved correct readings'). See also the review of Conte's text by Heyworth (2014).

45 Markland (1728) 26.

46 For a brief biography of Warren see Bailey (2004).

47 Warren (1916).

48 Warren (1916).

49 Warren (1916).

50 Warren (1916).

51 Whetham (1978) 83–7.

52 'Mr. Lloyd George on His Task', *The Times*, 25 November 1918, p. 13.

53 'Mr. Lloyd George on His Task', p. 13.

54 'Mr. Lloyd George on His Task', p. 13: 'You also have forest lands which are unsuitable for higher cultivation. You have no idea how we were handicapped because we had to bring timber from Norway and Sweden and Canada, when you have plenty of land in this country that in the old days used to grow fine timber. There is no healthier occupation for the people than the planting, looking after, and cutting down of trees. Those of you who have lived amongst trees know that you get to love them. Life among trees is an ideal life.'

55 'Mr. Lloyd George on His Task', p. 13.

56 Whetham (1978) 169–71.

57 Whetham (1978) 137–9.

58 Whetham (1978) 137–9.

59 Warren (1916): 'Everyone knows his "purple passages", the most splendid and lasting ornament which the "purple Caesars" ever wore: the laudation of labour and of the happy husbandman's lot – "Oh all too fortunate, did they know their luck, / The tillers of the soil!" [*G.* 2. 458–9] – the praise of Italy – "Mother of increase, mighty mother of men" [*G.* 2. 173–4], the picturesque romance of her hill-towns and "rivers gliding under ancient walls" [*G.* 2. 157]'.

60 Warren (1916).

61 Warren (1916).

62 Sellar (1897) 236.

63 Warren (1916), quoting *G.* 1. 509 and 497.

64 See Irish (2015) 28–9 on the case of British academics, where he discusses a book published by a group of leading Oxford historians, entitled *Why We Are at War: Great Britain's Case*. In September 1914 the Foreign Office purchased 3,000 copies for circulation among British embassies around the world.

65 Bailey (2004).

66 The history is Clark (2013); for a recent review of historiography relating to the conflict see Mulligan (2014).

67 On which see Morrow (2014), esp. p. 430, already quoted in Chapter 5, n. 61: 'In January 1919 the British Empire reached its zenith, with more than a million additional square miles, primarily in former Ottoman domains, as [British Prime Minister] Lloyd George laid claim to dominance in the Middle East. In April 1920 the British and French agreed secretly to monopolise the oil supplies of the Middle East and in July the French took control of Syria and would later rule in Syria and Lebanon. After riots in Egypt and Egyptian demands for complete independence in 1919 and revolt in Iraq in 1920, an over-extended British government granted both limited autonomy in 1922. That same year, Britain assumed the League [of Nations] mandate over Palestine, west of the River Jordan, while Eastern Palestine became Jordan.'

Conclusion: Towards a Decolonizing Pedagogy of Latin Literature

1 Chomsky, quoted in Chomsky and Casleton (2019), speaking on anarchism: 'I've always understood the core principle of anarchism to be the recognition that structures of domination and control are not self-justifying. They carry a burden of proof, and when that cannot be met, as is commonly the case, they should be dismantled, a principle that holds from families to international affairs.'

2 Compare Rabinowitz (1993) 7: 'Classics has been political by defining the epic and tragic genres as presenting great *human* truths. We continue to ask whose experience is validated by these generalizations, and whose is excluded in order to make antiquity the neat whole it appears to be' [emphasis original].

3 See Verg. *Aen.* 8. 678–728, Hor. *Epod.* 9. 11–16 and *Carm.* 1. 37, Prop. 3. 11. 39–46 and 4. 6. 65–6 with Wyke (1992) and Quint (1993).

4 Quint (1993) 21–51.

5 Here are three things I've found useful in imagining the *Aeneid* from a post-colonial perspective. First, the archaeological evidence discussed in Mattingly (2006) pointing to the 'advanced Saharan state' (p. 189) of the Garamantes people, the same people described as subject to Octavian's power at *Aen.* 6. 794–5. Second, Virgil's 'awareness of African rituals and cultural values' in his treatment of Dido, as argued by Haley (2009) 34–40. And third, the comparative study of Roman and South Asian imaginings of political power in Pollock (2006) 259–81, which highlights the contingency of the *Aeneid*'s nationalistic and imperialist framework. See p. 279: 'At the beginning of the *Aeneid*, Vergil "sings of arms and the man", the flight from Troy to Italy, the origins of the Latin people (*genus latinum*), the high walls of Rome, and *imperium sine fine*, power without limit. In his *Raghuvaṃśa*, Kālidāsa bows down to the mother and father of the universe, who are "fused together like a word and its meaning", in order that he might more deeply understand word and meaning when he tells the story of a universalistic political power, *diganta rājya* – power as far as the horizons – and the dynasty of the mythopoetic Raghus. Two visions of "cosmo-politan" order are offered here, and they differ profoundly.'

6 Adams (2016). I owe my interest in informal Latin to Anna Chahoud.

7 See Chapter 1, n. 33, above, the *OLD* s.v. *augustus*[1] and the *TLL* 2. 1379. 55–6, 1381. 34–6. The title 'Augustus' in Latin means something like 'majestic one', 'revered one'. As Barchiesi (2005: 281) writes, 'Our acceptance of the Augustan age as a well-defined period of history is deeply collusive with strategies of self-representation in Rome during the watch of Octavian-Augustus.'

8 hooks (1992) 4–5, quoted in the Introduction.

Appendix: The Geography of the *Georgics*

1 Because Latona gave birth to Apollo and Diana there (Mynors (1990) 179).

2 The translation here is that of Fairclough (1999); the bit in square brackets is my own.

3 I've translated *uenenum* as 'dye', but the Latin word's primary meaning is a medicinal or poisonous substance.

4 See the *OLD* s.v. *Hellespontiacus*: 'Of the Hellespont: often with reference to Priapus as having been born at Lampsacus.'

5 'a name given to several different streams, [it] is bracketed with Phasis by Strabo 11. 14. 7 as the other important river of Armenia' (Mynors (1990) 306).

6 'Media' and its inhabitants the Medes were by Virgil's time historic designations, probably connoting Parthia and its empire: 'to a reader of contemporary Roman poetry the somewhat antiquarian term "Medes" (like "Persians") was becoming a familiar way of referring to the contemporary hostile state of Parthia' (Harrison (2008) 232).

7 Panchaia was the largest of a group of mythical islands in the Indian Ocean, associated with the Ἱερὰ ἀναγραφή (*Sacred Scripture*) of Euhemerus of Messene, a novel which included a journey to Panchaia, and fragments of which are preserved in the work of Diodorus Siculus. See the *OCD* s.v. 'Euhemerus' with Diod. Sic. 5. 41–6 (= Jacoby (1923) 303–8).

8 'Thymbra is an otherwise obscure place in the Troad mentioned at *Il.* 10. 430 and famous for a shrine to Apollo' (Thomas (1988) 2: 205).

9 *Ausonius* is a poetic word for 'Italian': see *OLD* s.v. *Ausonius*.

10 Cyrene in the *Georgics* is Aristaeus's mother, but her name connotes the area of North Africa (in what is now Libya) to where she was taken having been abducted by Apollo, and to which she gave her name. For one version of the story see Ap. Rhod. 2. 500–10.

11 'Busiris, an Egyptian king who killed strangers in order to put an end to a nine-year draught and was eventually killed by Hercules' (Harder (2012) 2: 369–70).

12 This translation is that of Fairclough (1999).

13 *R(h)aetica* denotes the province of Raetia in the Alps, but this vine is placed by Pliny just to the south, in the *ager Veroniensis*. See Plin. *HN* 14. 16, 67 with Mynors (1990) 114.

14 Thule was an island located, according to Strabo (1. 4. 2 = 63 C), six days' sail north of Britain, and it was associated in ancient Greek and Roman geography with the Massiliot explorer Pythias. For more see Thomson (1965) 143–51, Cunliffe (2002) 130–1 and the *OCD* s.v. 'Thule' and 'Pytheas'.

15 Cecrops was a mythical king of Athens. Both Thomas ((1988) 2: 181) and Mynors (1990) 281) suggest that the reference is specifically to the honey of Mt. Hymettus in Attica.

16 See [Probus] on *G.* 3. 19 (= Callim. *Aet.* fr. 60c Harder = fr. 54 Pfeiffer) in Thilo and Hagen (1986) 3: 321–90 with Thomas (1988) 2: 42: 'The specific triumph is conveyed by the words *lucosque Molorchi*, an apparent periphrasis for Nemea. In fact it is a reference to the opening of the third book of Callimachus' *Aetia*, the epinician to Berenice … whose inner panel is the epyllion on the impoverished Molorchus, who entertained Hercules before he killed the Nemean lion and established the games.'

17 'for Olympia, as *lucosque Molorchi* at line 19 stood for Nemea' (Thomas (1988) 2: 74).

18 'Olympus' in Latin can refer to the sky or heavens in general: see *OLD* s.v. 'Olympus'.

19 *OLD* s.v. 'Pelethronius'[1]: 'The name of the district of Thessaly inhabited by the Lapiths and Centaurs.'

20 *OLD* s.v. 'Tempe': 'The valley of the Peneus between Ossa and Olympus in Thessaly, noted for its beauty; (transf.) any beautiful valley.'

21 Calabria in Roman geography denoted what is now southern Apulia, or the heel of Italy; modern Calabria, the toe, was known as the *ager Bruttius*.

22 For more on the mythical Eridanus and its association with the Po, see Myers (2019).

23 The translation here is that of Thomas (1988) 2: 214; on the depiction of river gods as bulls see Jones (2005) 43–4.

24 My translation here takes a phrase from Mynors (1990) 281.

25 Macrob. *Sat.* 3. 20. 7 (beginning a list of the different varieties of grape): 'sicut uuarum ista sunt genera: Aminea – scilicet a regione, nam Aminei fuerunt ubi nunc Falernum est' (In the same way, these are the varieties of grape: Aminean – evidently from that region, for where the Aminei lived is now the Falernian district).

26 For the argument, accepted here, that this phrase is a periphrasis for Herculaneum, see Gigante (2004) 88–91.

27 'strictly Latium' (*OCD* s.v. 'Italy').

28 'Narycum, a principal town of Epicnemidian Locris in mainland Greece, was the mother-city of Locri Epizephyrii, the port of *ager Bruttius*, the "toe" of Italy, from which the pitch tapped from the pine-forests of the interior was shipped to Rome.' (Mynors (1990) 159).

29 Servius's note to *G.* 4. 563 quotes an historian called Lutatius, who says that Naples was first known as Parthenope after the siren of the same name, whose body was buried there. For more on this fragment see Cornell (2013) 2: 713.

30 Arethusa was rescued from the river god Alpheus by Diana, who changed her into water and then opened an underground passage from Elis to Ortigia – the small island in the harbour of Syracuse – to allow her to escape. Arethusa reached Ortigia and took up residence as a famous spring. She features in Verg. *Ecl.* 10; for the story see Ov. *Met.* 5. 572–641. As Mynors notes ((1990) 304), there were several springs in Greece known by her name, but it seems reasonable to suggest that the word here would have connoted the most famous, Syracusan one.

31 'Oebalus was a king of Sparta, and the poets use *Oebalides*, *Oebalius* freely for "Spartan"'. 'Lacedaemonium Tarentum (Hor. *Carm.* 3. 5. 56, 2. 6. 12, Strabo 6. 3. 2), was founded by Spartan colonists under Phalanthus' (Mynors (1990) 275).

32 The *OLD*, s.v. *Syrius*[1], gives: 'Of Syria, Syrian'; b: 'as the name of a dark-skinned variety of pear'. But see Columella, *Rust.* 5. 10. 18 for a possible Tarentine provenance: '[pira] Tarentina, quae Syria dicuntur' (Tarentine pears, which are called 'Syrian').

33 *OLD* s.v. 'Sarra': 'An old name for the city of Tyre'.

34 Ionian intellectuals including Hecataeus and Herodotus inherited and engaged with a tradition, first visible on the shield of Achilles in *Iliad* 18, which conceived of the earth as a disc surrounded by an encircling river, called *Oceanus* (Romm (1992) 12–13). As geographical theory in succeeding centuries advanced to recognize a spherical earth divided into five zones, this disc-shaped image did not fully disappear – an ambiguity, Vogt argues ((1960) 151–5), implicit in the Latin phrase *orbis terrarum*, literally the 'circle of lands', with 'disc' and 'sphere' also attested meanings of *orbis* (see *OLD* s.v. 'orbis' with *TLL* 9. 913–20). *Orbis terrarum* thus seems to have defined the inhabited world in Roman Republican discourse, cognate with the Greek οἰκουμένη and denoting a world stretching from the Straits of Gibraltar to India and centred on the Mediterranean.

35 This could refer to one of two rivers called *Hypanis* in ancient Greek and Roman geography: either the Southern Bug in modern Ukraine (see Hdt. 4. 52), or the Kuban in modern Russia, which flows into the Sea of Asov.

36 The translation here is that of Fairclough (1999) 201.

37 Rhesus is the Thracian king who features at Hom. *Il.* 10. 474–502, where he is killed by Diomedes.

38 A people of the south-eastern coast of the Black Sea, who appear in literature as archetypal forgers of iron. See Aesch. *PV* 714–15, Hdt. 1. 28, Ap. Rhod. 2. 1001–8, Callim. *Aet.* fr. 110. 48 Harder.

39 *OLD* s.v. 'Cicones': 'A people of southern Thrace, whom Ulysses attacked when returning from Troy, and among whom Orpheus met his death.' See Hom. *Od.* 9. 39–61, Hdt. 7. 110.

40 Thomas (1988) 2: 176: 'Virgil has conflated the role of the bees with that of the *Curetes*, the inhabitants of Crete who were said to have covered the cries of the infant god by dancing around him and clashing their shields'.

41 As Pieri (2011) 36 argues, *Gangaridum* in line 27 can also be taken with *ex auro solidoque elephanto*. The phrase would then mean that the carvings on the temple doors are made 'with the gold and solid ivory of the *Gangaridae*'; in this case the battle (*pugnam*) refers to Actium rather than one with the *Gangaridae*.

42 'the seven chief stars of Ursa Major, if not read as forming the outline of a plough, a wagon or a dipper, could be seen, on their circular course round the pole, as seven oxen threshing, *septem triones*' (Mynors (1990) 237).

43 The adjective *leuis* in Latin has a range of meanings, many of which could be used to colour the translation of this phrase: 'lightly armed', 'fickle', etc.

44 *Persis-idis* in Latin is attested for both 'Persia' and 'Persian' (see *OLD* s.v.) and so the reference here is ambiguous. I read it as 'Persian' and have classified it accordingly. The word by Virgil's time was archaic and would, like the term 'Mede', have connoted to Roman readers the Parthian Empire (Mynors (1990) 297, Harrison (2008) 232).

45 *OLD* s.v. 'Quirites': 'A name given to the citizens of Rome collectively in their peacetime functions (esp. in solemn addresses and appeals)'.

References

'A Plea for Apples', *North Devon Journal*, 14 March 1918, p. 7, last accessed via The British Newspaper Archive (britishnewspaperarchive.co.uk), 28 November 2019.

'ART V: *Oceana; or England and Her Colonies*', *The Edinburgh Review* 163(334), April 1886, 405–36, last accessed via the British Periodicals Database (proquest.com/products-services/british_periodicals.html), 28 November 2019.

'ART VI: *The Competition Wallah*', *The Calcutta Review* 39(78), April 1864, 307–44, last accessed via the British Periodicals Database (proquest.com/products-services/british_periodicals.html), 28 November 2019.

'Cheese', *Gloucester Chronicle*, 5 May 1917, p. 2, last accessed via The British Newspaper Archive (britishnewspaperarchive.co.uk), 28 November 2019.

Editorial Article, *The Times*, 31 August 1869, p. 6, last accessed via *The Times* Digital Archive 1785–2013 (gale.com/intl/c/the-times-digital-archive), 28 November 2019.

'Farming in Tuscany', *The Times*, 6 November 1935, p. 17, last accessed via *The Times* Digital Archive 1785–2013 (gale.com/intl/c/the-times-digital-archive), 28 November 2019.

'Foreign Intelligence', *The London Evening Standard*, 25 July 1859, p. 5, last accessed via The British Newspaper Archive (britishnewspaperarchive.co.uk), 28 November 2019.

'Italy After the War', *The Aberdeen Daily Journal*, 13 May 1921, p. 4, last accessed via The British Newspaper Archive (britishnewspaperarchive.co.uk), 28 November 2019.

'Italy at Work', *Dublin University Magazine* 74(441), September 1869, 273–9, last accessed via the British Periodicals Database (proquest.com/products-services/british_periodicals.html), 28 November 2019.

'Jemila: A Roman City in Algeria', *The Times*, 19 October 1925, p. 13, last accessed via *The Times* Digital Archive 1785–2013 (gale.com/intl/c/the-times-digital-archive), last accessed via the British Periodicals Database (proquest.com/products-services/british_periodicals.html), 28 November 2019.

'Leamington Institute: The Rev. W. C. Furneaux on "Life in the East"', *Leamington Spa Courier*, 24 January 1885, p. 7, last accessed via The British Newspaper Archive (britishnewspaperarchive.co.uk), 28 November 2019.

'Literature: Oceana', *The Observer*, 21 February 1886, p. 6, last accessed via ProQuest Historical Newspapers: *The Guardian* and *The Observer* (https://search.proquest.com/hnpguardianobserver/index), 28 November 2019.

'Mr. Lloyd George on His Task', *The Times*, 25 November 1918, p. 13, last accessed via *The Times* Digital Archive 1785–2013 (gale.com/intl/c/the-times-digital-archive), 28 November 2019.

'Notes on Trade and Finance', *The Speaker: The Liberal Review*, London, 8 November 1902, p. 156, last accessed via the British Periodicals Database (proquest.com/products-services/british_periodicals.html), 28 November 2019.

'Obituary: Mr. C. W. Brodribb', *The Times*, 22 June 1945, p. 7, last accessed via *The Times* Digital Archive 1785–2013 (gale.com/intl/c/the-times-digital-archive), 28 November 2019.

'O, Fortunatos Nimium', *The Saturday Review of Politics, Literature, Science and Art* 127(3313), London, 26 April 1919, p. 396, last accessed via the British Periodicals Database (proquest.com/products-services/british_periodicals.html), 28 November 2019.

'Roman Africa: From Jemila to Timgad', *The Times*, 22 October 1925, p. 15, last accessed via *The Times* Digital Archive 1785–2013 (gale.com/intl/c/the-times-digital-archive), 28 November 2019.

'Roman Africa: The Georgics of Algeria', *The Times*, 27 October 1925, p. 17, last accessed via *The Times* Digital Archive 1785–2013 (gale.com/intl/c/the-times-digital-archive), 28 November 2019.

'The Allotment Garden: Seasonable Notes of an Expert', *The Newcastle Daily Journal*, 18 May 1917, p. 3, last accessed via The British Newspaper Archive (britishnewspaperarchive.co.uk), 28 November 2019.

'The Irish Land Question', *The Times*, 25 August 1869, p. 8, last accessed via *The Times* Digital Archive 1785–2013 (gale.com/intl/c/the-times-digital-archive), 28 November 2019.

'Virgil', *Encyclopaedia Britannica*, vol. 21: 653–7, 7th edn (1842), Edinburgh: Adam and Charles Black.

Aberson, M., M. C. Biella, M. Di Fazio and M. Wullschleger, eds (2014), *Entre Archéologie et Histoire: Dialogues sur divers Peuples de l'Italie Préromaine*, Bern: Peter Lang.

Acosta-Hughes, B. and S. A. Stephens (2012), *Callimachus in Context: From Plato to the Augustan Poets*, Cambridge: Cambridge University Press.

Adams, J. N. (2016), *An Anthology of Informal Latin, 200 BC–AD 900: Fifty Texts with Translations and Linguistic Commentary*, Cambridge: Cambridge University Press.

Addison, J. (1709), 'An Essay on the *Georgics*', in J. Dryden (1709), *The Works of Virgil: Containing His Pastorals, Georgics and Aeneis*, 3 vols., 3rd edn, 1: 77–92, London: Jacob Tonson.

Addison, J. (1718), *Remarks on Several Parts of Italy, etc. In the Years 1701, 1702, 1703*, 2nd edn, London: Jacob Tonson.

Alpers, P. J. (1996), *What is Pastoral?*, Chicago: University of Chicago Press.

Ando, C. (2002), 'Vergil's Ethnography and Politics in First-century Rome', in
D. S. Levene and D. P. Nelis (eds), *Clio and the Poets: Augustan Poetry and the
Traditions of Ancient Historiography*, 123–42, Leiden: Brill.

Asheri, D., A. Lloyd and A. Corcella (2007), *A Commentary on Herodotus Books I–IV*,
English edn, O. Murray, A. Moreno and M. Brosius (eds), Oxford: Oxford
University Press.

[Ashworth, J. H.] (1851), *The Saxon in Ireland: Or, the Rambles of an Englishman in
Search of a Settlement in the West of Ireland*, London: John Murray.

Astbury, R., ed. (2002), *M. Terentius Varro Saturarum Menippearum Fragmenta*, 2nd
edn, Munich: Teubner.

Austin, C. and G. Bastianini, eds (2002), *Posidippi Pellaei quae supersunt omnia*,
Milan: LED (*Edizioni Universitarie di Lettere Economica Diritto*).

Ayres, P. (1997), *Classical Culture and the Idea of Rome in Eighteenth-Century England*,
Cambridge: Cambridge University Press.

Badian, E. (1968), *Roman Imperialism in the Late Republic*, Oxford: Blackwell.

Badian, E. (1972), *Publicans and Sinners: Private Enterprise in the Service of the
Roman Republic*, Ithaca, NY: Cornell University Press.

Bailey, C. (2004), 'Warren, Sir (Thomas) Herbert (1853–1930)', revised by
M. C. Curthoys, *The Oxford Dictionary of National Biography*, online edn, Oxford:
Oxford University Press, last accessed via oxforddnb.com, 28 November
2019.

Barchiesi, A. (1979), 'La vendetta del silenzio. Uno schema esegetico antico e una
pretesa correzione d'autore in Virgilio, *Georgiche*, 2, 225', *ASNP* 9(2): 527–37.

Barchiesi, A. (2005), 'Learned Eyes: Poets, Viewers, Image Makers', in K. Galinsky (ed.),
The Cambridge Companion to the Age of Augustus, 281–305, Cambridge:
Cambridge University Press.

Barchiesi, A. (2008), 'Bellum Italicum: L'Unificazione dell'Italia nell'Eneide', in G. Urso
(ed.), *Patria diversis gentibus una? Unità politica e identità etniche nell'Italia antica*,
243–60, Pisa: ETS.

Batstone, W. (1997), 'Virgilian didaxis: value and meaning in the *Georgics*', in
C. Martindale (ed.), *The Cambridge Companion to Virgil*, 125–44, Cambridge:
Cambridge University Press.

Beard, M. (2007), *The Roman Triumph*, Cambridge, MA: Harvard University Press.

Begley, V. and K. D. De Puma, eds (1991), *Rome and India: The Ancient Sea Trade*,
Madison, WI: University of Wisconsin Press.

Behrendt, K. A. (2004), *The Buddhist Architecture of Gandhāra*, Leiden: Brill.

Benjamin, W. (1999), 'Theses on the Philosophy of History', in H. Arendt (ed.),
Illuminations, trans. H. Zohn, reprinted edn, 245–55, London: Pimlico.

Bennett, B. T., ed. (1980), *The Letters of Mary Wollstonecraft Shelley*, 2 vols., Baltimore, MD: John Hopkins University Press.

Berger, J. (1972), *Ways of Seeing*, London: Penguin.

Bernard, S. G., C. Damon and C. Grey (2014), 'Rhetorics of Land and Power in the Polla Inscription (*CIL* I² 638)', *Mnemosyne* 67: 953–85.

Bhattacharya, S. (1977), 'The Indigo Revolt of Bengal', *Social Scientist* 5(12): 13–23.

Bispham, E. (2007), *From Asculum to Actium: The Municipalization of Italy from the Social War to Augustus*, Oxford: Oxford University Press.

Bispham, E. (2014), 'The Lucanians: historical perspective', in M. Aberson, M. C. Biella, M. Di Fazio and M. Wullschleger (eds), *Entre Archéologie et Histoire: Dialogues sur divers Peuples de l'Italie Préromaine*, 311–30, Bern: Peter Lang.

Black, J. (1992), *The British Abroad: The Grand Tour in the Eighteenth Century*, London: Sutton Publishing Limited.

Blackwood, F. T. (1866), 'Irish Emigration', *The Times*, 11 December 1866, p. 8, last accessed via *The Times* Digital Archive 1785–2013 (gale.com/intl/c/the-times-digital-archive), 28 November 2019.

Blackwood, F. T. (1867), 'An Answer to the Question Put To The Kilkenny Parliament', *The Times*, 2 January 1867, p. 6, last accessed via *The Times* Digital Archive 1785–2013 (gale.com/intl/c/the-times-digital-archive), 28 November 2019.

Boase, G. C. (2007), 'Peel, Sir Robert, third baronet (1822–1895)', revised by H. C. G. Matthew, *The Oxford Dictionary of National Biography*, online edn, Oxford: Oxford University Press, last accessed via oxforddnb.com, 28 November 2019.

Bond, D. F., ed. (1970) *Critical Essays from the Spectator by Joseph Addison, with four Essays by Richard Steele*, Oxford: Oxford University Press.

Bose, S. (1993), *Peasant Labour and Colonial Capital: Rural Bengal Since 1770*, Cambridge: Cambridge University Press.

Bosworth, A. B. (1988), *From Arrian to Alexander: Studies in Historical Interpretation*, Oxford: Clarendon Press.

Bosworth, A. B. (1996), 'The Historical Setting of Megasthenes' Indica', *CPh* 91(2): 113–27.

Bourdin, S. (2012), *Les Peuples de l'Italie Préromaine: Identités, Territoires et Relations Inter-Ethniques en Italie Centrale et Septentrionale (VIIIᵉ-Iᵉʳ s. av. J.-C.)*, Rome: École Française de Rome.

Bowman, A. K. (1996), 'Egypt', in A. K. Bowman, E. Champlin and A. Lintott (eds), *The Cambridge Ancient History Volume 10: The Augustan Empire, 43 B.C.–A.D. 69*, 2nd edn, 676–702, Cambridge: Cambridge University Press.

Boyle, A. J. (1979), '*In Medio Caesar*: Paradox and Politics in Virgil's *Georgics*', in A. J. Boyle (ed.), *Virgil's Ascraean Song: Ramus Essays on the Georgics*, 65–86, Berwick: Aureal Publications.

Bradley, G., E. Isayev and C. Riva, eds (2007), *Ancient Italy: Regions without Boundaries*, Liverpool: Liverpool University Press.

Bradley, K. (1994), *Slavery and Society at Rome*, Cambridge: Cambridge University Press.

Bradley, M., ed. (2010), *Classics and Imperialism in the British Empire*, Oxford: Oxford University Press.

Brady, C. (2013), *James Anthony Froude: An Intellectual Biography of a Victorian Prophet*, Oxford: Oxford University Press.

Braund, D. (1994), *Georgia in Antiquity: A History of Colchis and Transcaucasian Iberia 550 BC–AD 562*, Oxford: Oxford University Press.

Braund, S. M. (2017), *Understanding Latin Literature*, London: Routledge.

Braund, S. M. (2019), 'Women and Earth: Responses to the *Georgics* in the Twentieth and Twenty-First Centuries', in B. Xinyue and N. Freer (eds), *Reflections and New Perspectives on Virgil's* Georgics, e-book edn (no page numbers), London: Bloomsbury.

Brodribb, C. W. (1913), 'Manilius II: 189–191', *CR* 27(3): 93.

Brodribb, C. W. (1917), 'War and the *Georgics*', 1 March 1917, *The Times Literary Supplement*, p. 106, last accessed via *The Times Literary Supplement Historical Archive 1902–2014* (gale.com/intl/c/the-times-literary-supplement-historical-archive), 28 November 2019.

Brodribb, C. W. (1922), 'Aeschylus, *Supplices*, 1012–3', *CR* 36(7/8): 162.

Brodribb, C. W. (1928), *Virgil: The Georgics: In English Hexameters*, London: E. Benn.

Brodribb, C. W. (1946), *Poems*, London: Macmillan.

Broughall, Q. J. (2015), *Assuming the Purple: The Rehabilitation of Ancient Rome in Victorian Culture, 1837–1901*, PhD thesis, Maynooth: National University of Ireland.

Brunt, P. A. (1971), *Italian Manpower 225 B.C – A.D. 14*, Oxford: Clarendon Press.

Brunt, P. A. (1978), '*Laus Imperii*', in P. D. A. Garnsey and C. R. Whittaker (eds), *Imperialism in the Ancient World*, 159–91, Cambridge: Cambridge University Press.

Buckland, C. E. (1901), *Bengal under the Lieutenant-Governors*, 2 vols., Calcutta: S. K. Lahiri and Co.

Bull, P. (2009), 'Butt, Isaac', in J. McGuire and J. Quinn (eds), *Dictionary of Irish Biography*, online edn, Cambridge: Cambridge University Press, last accessed via dib.cambridge.org, 28 November 2019.

Butler, S., ed. (2016), *Deep Classics: Rethinking Classical Reception*, London: Bloomsbury.

Butler, S. J. (2012), *Britain and Its Empire in the Shadow of Rome: The Reception of Rome in Socio-Political Debate from the 1850s to the 1920s*, London: Bloomsbury.

Butt, I. (1834), *Virgil's* Georgics, Dublin: William Curry Jun. and Co.

Butt, I. (1847), *A Voice for Ireland. The Famine in the Land: What Has Been Done and What Is to be Done. Reprinted from the Dublin University Magazine*, Dublin: James McGlashan.

Butt, I. (1866), *Land Tenure in Ireland: A Plea for the Celtic Race*, Dublin: John Fowler.

Butt, I. (1867), *The Irish People and the Irish Land: A Letter to Lord Lifford; with Comments on the Publications of Lord Dufferin and Lord Rosse*, Dublin: John Falconer.

Cadili, L. (2001), *Viamque adfectat ad Olympo: Memoria ellenistica nelle 'Georgiche' di Virgilio*, Milan: LED.

Cartault, A. (1899), 'Un contre-sens traditionnel sur Virg. *Georg.* i. 489–92', *RPh* 2(23): 232–7.

Carter, J. M., ed. (1982), *Suetonius: Divus Augustus*, Bristol: Bristol Classical Press.

Casson, L., ed. (1989), *The* Periplus Maris Erythraei: *Text with Introduction, Translation, and Commentary*, Princeton, NJ: Princeton University Press.

Chalker, J. (1969), *The English Georgic: A Study in the Development of a Form*, London: Routledge and K. Paul.

Chambers, D. D. C. (1993), *The Planters of the English Landscape Garden: Botany, Trees, and the Georgics*, New Haven, CT: Yale University Press.

Chard, C. (1999), *Pleasure and Guilt on the Grand Tour: Travel Writing and Imaginative Geography, 1600–1830*, Manchester: Manchester University Press.

Chichester, H. M. (2004), 'Harris, Sir William Cornwallis (*bap.* 1807, *d.* 1848)', revised by J. Falkner, *The Oxford Dictionary of National Biography*, online edn, Oxford: Oxford University Press, last accessed via oxforddnb.com, 28 November 2019.

Chomsky, N. and S. Castleton (2019), 'Choosing Hope', *Boston Review: A Political and Literary Forum*, 4 June, last accessed via bostonreview.net/politics/noam-chomsky-scott-casleton-choosing-hope, 28 November 2019.

Chuanxi, Z. (2012a), 'Creation and development of a unified multi-ethnic centralized state system', in Y. Xingpei, Y. Wenming, Z. Chuanxi and L. Yulie (eds), *The History of Chinese Civilization*, 4 vols., English translated edn, 2: 42–94, Cambridge: Cambridge University Press.

Chuanxi, Z. (2012b), 'Growth of the feudal economy', in Y. Xingpei, Y. Wenming, Z. Chuanxi and L. Yulie (eds) *The History of Chinese Civilization*, 4 vols., English translated edn, 2: 139–95, Cambridge: Cambridge University Press.

Citroni, M. (2015), 'La vittoria e il tempio: intrepretazione del proemio al III libro delle *Georgiche*', in P. Fedeli and H.-C. Günther (eds), *Virgilian Studies: A Miscellany Dedicated to the Memory of Mario Geymonat*, 39–88, Nordhausen: Traugott Bautz.

Claridge, A. (2010), *Rome: An Oxford Archaeological Guide*, 2nd edn, Oxford: Oxford University Press.

Clark, C. (2013), *The Sleepwalkers: How Europe Went to War in 1914*, London: Penguin.

Clausen, W., ed. (1994), *A Commentary on Virgil: Eclogues*, Oxford: Clarendon Press.

Collings, J. (1906), *Land Reform: Occupying Ownership, Peasant Proprietary and Rural Education*, London: Longman, Green and Co.

Conington, J. and H. Nettleship, eds (2007), *Conington's Virgil: Georgics*, reprint of the 1898 5th edn, Bristol: Bristol Phoenix Press.

Cooley, A. E., ed. (2009), Res Gestae Divi Augusti: *Text, Translation and Commentary*, Cambridge: Cambridge University Press.

Cooper, H. (2015), 'Pastoral and Georgic', in P. Cheney and P. Hardie (eds), *The Oxford History of Classical Reception in English Literature Volume 2 (1558–1660)*, 201–24, Oxford: Oxford University Press.

Cornell, T. (1989a), 'Rome and Latium to 390 BC', in F. W. Walbank, A. E. Astin, M. W. Frederiksen and R. M. Ogilvie (eds) *The Cambridge Ancient History Volume 7 Part 2: The Rise of Rome to 220 B.C*, 2nd edn, 243–308, Cambridge: Cambridge University Press.

Cornell, T. (1989b), 'The Conquest of Italy', in F. W. Walbank, A. E. Astin, M. W. Frederiksen and R. M. Ogilvie (eds) *The Cambridge Ancient History Volume 7 Part 2: The Rise of Rome to 220 B.C*, 2nd edn, 351–419, Cambridge: Cambridge University Press.

Cornell, T. (1995), *The Beginnings of Rome: Italy and Rome from the Bronze Age to the Punic Wars (c. 1000–264 BC)*, London: Routledge.

Cornell, T. and K. Lomas, eds (1997), *Gender and Ethnicity in Ancient Italy*, London: Accordia Research Institute.

Cornell, T. (2004), 'Deconstructing the Samnite Wars', in H. Jones (ed.), *Samnium: Settlement and Cultural Change: The Proceedings of the Third E. Togo Salmon Conference on Roman Studies*, 115–32, Providence, RI: Center for Old World Archaeology and Art, Brown University.

Cornell, T., ed. (2013), *The Fragments of the Roman Historians*, 3 vols., Oxford: Oxford University Press.

Cornwallis Harris, W. (1844), *The Highlands of Æthiopia*, 3 vols., London: Longman, Brown, Green and Longmans.

Cramer, R. (1998), *Vergils Weltsicht: Optimismus und Pessimismus in Vergils* Georgica, Berlin: De Gruyter.

Crawford, M. H. (1974), *Roman Republican Coinage*, 2 vols., Cambridge: Cambridge University Press.

Crawford, R. (1998), 'English Georgic and British Nationhood', *English Literary History* 65(1): 123–58.

Crosby, T. L. (2011), *Joseph Chamberlain: A Most Radical Imperialist*, London: I. B. Tauris.

Cunliffe, B. (2002), *The Extraordinary Voyage of Pytheas the Greek*, London: Penguin.

Curti, E., E. Dench and J. R. Patterson (1996), 'The Archaeology of Central and Southern Roman Italy: Recent Trends and Approaches', *JRS* 86: 170–89.

D'Agostino, V. (1957), 'A Virgilio, *Georgiche* 2, 317 s. e 514', *Rivista di Studi Classici* 5: 153–5.

Davenport, T. R. H. and C. Saunders (2000), *South Africa: A Modern History*, 5th edn, London: Macmillan.

De Bruyn, F. (2004), 'Reading Virgil's *Georgics* as a Scientific Text: The Eighteenth-Century Debate between Jethro Tull and Stephen Switzer', *English Literary History* 71(3): 661–89.

De Saint-Denis, E., ed. (1956), *Virgile: Géorgiques*, Paris: Les Belles Lettres.

Degrassi, A., ed. (1947), *Inscriptiones Italiae*, 13: *Fasti et elogia*, fasc. 1: *Fasti consulares et triumphales*, Rome: Libreria dello stato.

Degrassi, A. ed. (1954), *Fasti Capitolini*, Turin: G. B. Paravia.

Dench, E. (1995), *From Barbarians to New Men: Greek, Roman, and Modern Perceptions of Peoples of the Central Apennines*, Oxford: Clarendon Press.

Dench, E. (1997), 'Sacred Springs to the Social War: Myths of Origins and Questions of Identity in the Central Apennines', in T. Cornell and K. Lomas (eds), *Gender and Ethnicity in Ancient Italy*, 43–52, London: Accordia Research Institute.

Denoon, D. and M. Wyndham (1999), 'Australia and the Western Pacific', in A. Porter (ed.), *The Oxford History of the British Empire Volume III*, 546–71, Oxford: Oxford University Press.

Dexter, J. P. (2013), 'The Reception of Phanocles at *Georgics* 4. 507–27', *Mnemosyne* 66: 303–11.

Dominik, W. J. (2009), 'Vergil's Geopolitics', in W. J. Dominik, J. Garthwaite and P. A. Roche (eds), *Writing Politics in Imperial Rome*, 111–32, Brill: Leiden.

Dryden, J. (1709), *The Works of Virgil: Containing His Pastorals, Georgics and Aeneis*, 3 vols., 3rd edn, London: Jacob Tonson.

Duggan, C. (2008), *The Force of Destiny: A History of Italy since 1796*, London: Penguin.

Edelstein, L. and I. G. Kidd, eds (1989), *Posidonius Volume I: The Fragments*, 2nd edn, Cambridge: Cambridge University Press.

Egan, R. B. (2001), 'Orpheus and the Ciconian Women: The Crux at Vergil, *Georgics* 4. 520', *Mouseion* 1(1): 55–68.

Ehrenberg, V. and A. H. M. Jones, eds (1976), *Documents Illustrating the Reigns of Augustus and Tiberius*, 2nd edn, Oxford: Clarendon Press.

Ernout, A., ed. (1949), *Pline L'Ancien: Histoire Naturelle Livre XII*, Paris: Les Belles Lettres.

Erren, M., ed. (1985–2003), *P. Vergilius Maro: Georgica*, 2 vols., Heidelberg: C. Winter.

Fairclough, H. R. (1999), *Virgil: Eclogues, Georgics, Aeneid: Books 1–6*, revised by G. P. Goold, Cambridge, MA: Harvard University Press.

Fantuzzi, M. and R. Hunter (2004), *Tradition and Innovation in Hellenistic Poetry* Cambridge: Cambridge University Press.

Farrell, J. (1991), *Vergil's* Georgics *and the Traditions of Ancient Epic: The Art of Allusion in Literary History*, New York: Oxford University Press.

Ferguson, J. (1978), 'China and Rome', in H. Temporini and W. Haase (eds), *Aufstieg und Niedergang der römischen Welt*, 2. 9. 2: 581–603, Berlin: De Gruyter.

Ferriss-Hill, J. L. (2011), 'Virgil's Program of Sabellic Etymologizing and the Construction of Italic Identity', *TAPA* 141(2): 265–84.

Fischer, R. (1968), *Das ausseritalische geographische Bild in Vergils Georgica, in den Oden des Horaz und in den Elegien des Properz*, Zürich: Juris.

Fitzgerald, R. (1984), *Virgil: The Aeneid*, London: Harvill Press.

Fitzpatrick, M. P. (2011), 'Provincializing Rome: The Indian Ocean Trade Network and Roman Imperialism', *Journal of World History* 22(1): 27–54.

Foley, C. (2014), *Of Cabbages and Kings: The History of Allotments*, London: Frances Lincoln.

Foot, M. R. D., ed. (1968), *The Gladstone Diaries. Volume II: 1833–1839*, Oxford: Clarendon Press.

Formicola, C. (2008), 'Il poeta e il politico. Virgilio e il potere', *GIF* 60 (1–2): 65–89.

Forth, A. (2017), *Barbed-Wire Imperialism: Britain's Empire of Camps, 1876–1903*, Berkeley, CA: University of California Press.

Foster, J. (1988), 'The End of the Third *Georgic*', *PVS* 19: 32–45.

Foster, R. F. (1989), *Modern Ireland 1600–1972*, London: Penguin.

Foulon, A. (2014), 'Quand les poetes écrivent l'histoire; Auguste vu par Virgile, Ovide et Horace', *REL* 92: 99–121.

Fronda, M. P. (2010), *Between Rome and Carthage: Southern Italy during the Second Punic War*, Cambridge: Cambridge University Press.

Froude, J. A. (1886), *Oceana, or England and its Colonies*, new edn, London: Longmans, Green and Co.

Funaioli, G. (1947), *Studi di Letteratura Antica: Spiriti e Forme, Figure e Problemi Delle Letterature Classiche*, 2 vols., Bologna: Nicola Zanichelli.

Gabba, E., ed. (1958), *Appiani Bellorum civilium liber primus*, Florence: La nuova Italia.

Gabba, E. (1989), 'Rome and Italy in the Second Century BC', in A. E. Astin, F. W. Walbank, M. W. Frederiksen and R. M. Ogilvie (eds), *The Cambridge Ancient History Volume 8: Rome and the Mediterranean to 133 B.C.*, 2nd edn, 197–243, Cambridge: Cambridge University Press.

Gabba, E. (1994), 'Rome and Italy: The Social War', in J. A. Crook, A. Lintott and E. Rawson, (eds), *The Cambridge Ancient History Volume 9: The Last Age of the*

Roman Republic, 146–43 B.C, 2nd edn, 104–28, Cambridge: Cambridge University Press.

Gagliardi, P. (2009), '*Fortunatus* in Virgilio', *REL* 87: 92–113.

Gale, M. R. (1998), 'War and Peace in Lucretius and the *Georgics*', *PVS* 23: 101–28.

Gale, M. R. (2000), *Virgil on the Nature of Things: The* Georgics, *Lucretius and the Didactic Tradition*, Cambridge: Cambridge University Press.

Galeano, E. (2009), *Open Veins of Latin America: Five Centuries of the Pillage of a Continent*, trans. C. Belfrage, new edn, London: Serpent's Tail.

Gardner, H. C. (1904), *The* Georgics *of Virgil: Translated in English Verse by Lord Burghclere*, London: J. Murray.

Gardner, H. H. (2014), 'Bees, Ants, and the Body Politic: Vergil's Noric Plague and Ovid's Origin of the Myrmidons', *Vergilius* 60: 3–31.

Geue, T. (2018), 'Soft Hands, Hard Power: Sponging Off the Empire of Leisure (Virgil, *Georgics* 4)', *JRS* 108: 115–40.

Geymonat, M., ed. (1973), *Opera P. Vergili Maronis*, Turin: Paravia.

Gibbons, L. (2000), 'Race Against Time: Racial Discourse and Irish History', in C. Hall (ed.) *Cultures of Empire: Colonizers in Britain and the Empire in the Nineteenth and Twentieth Centuries*, 207–23, Manchester: Manchester University Press.

Gigante, M. (2004), 'Vergil in the Shadow of Vesuvius', in D. Armstrong, J. Fish, P. A. Johnston and M. B. Skinner (eds), *Vergil, Philodemus, and the Augustans*, 85–99, Austin, TX: University of Texas Press.

Giusti, E. (2019), 'Bunte Barbaren Setting Up the Stage: Re-Inventing the Barbarian on the *Georgics*' Theatre-Temple (*G.* 3. 1–48)', in B. Xinyue and N. Freer (eds), *Reflections and New Perspectives on Virgil's* Georgics, e-book edn (no page numbers), London: Bloomsbury.

Glover, T. R. and W. Y. Sellar (1911), 'Virgil', in *The Encyclopaedia Britannica*, vol. 28: 111–16, 11th edn, Cambridge: Cambridge University Press.

Glover, T. R. (1912), *Virgil*, 2nd edn, London: Methuen.

Goff, B., ed. (2005), *Classics and Colonialism*, London: Duckworth.

Goodfellow, M. S. (1981), 'North Italian Rivers and Lakes in the *Georgics*', *Vergilius* 27: 12–22.

Goukowsky, P., ed. (2014), *Diodore de Sicile: Bibliothèque Historique Fragments Tome IV Livres XXXIII–XL*, Paris: Les Belles Lettres.

Graham, [no first name given] (1844), 'Report on the Agricultural and Land Produce of Shoa. By Captain Graham, Bengal N.I of the Mission to Abyssinia', *Journal of the Asiatic Society of Bengal*, 13(148): 253–96, Calcutta: Bishop's College Press.

Graham, W., ed. (1941), *The Letters of Joseph Addison*, Oxford: Clarendon Press.

Grant, M. (1971), *Herod the Great*, London: Weidenfeld and Nicolson.

Gray, P. (2018), 'The Great Famine, 1845–1850', in J. Kelly (ed.), *The Cambridge History of Ireland Volume III 1730–1880*, 639–65, Cambridge: Cambridge University Press.

Grayzel, S. R. (2002), *Women and the First World War*, Harlow: Pearson.

Green, P. (1978), 'Caesar and Alexander: *Aemulatio, Imitatio, Comparatio*', *AJAH* 3(1): 1–26.

Griffin, J. (1985), 'The Fourth *Georgic*, Virgil and Rome', in *Latin Poets and Roman Life*, 163–82, London: Duckworth [= K. Volk (ed.), *Vergil's* Georgics, 225–48, Oxford: Oxford University Press].

Grueber, H. A. (1970), *Coins of the Roman Republic in the British Museum*, 3 vols., London: British Museum.

Gruen, E. S. (1984), *The Hellenistic World and the Coming of Rome*, 2 vols., Berkeley, CA: University of California Press.

Gruen, E. S. (1996), 'The Expansion of the Empire under Augustus', in A. K. Bowman, E. Champlin and A. Lintott (eds), *The Cambridge Ancient History Volume 10: The Augustan Empire, 43 B.C. – A.D. 69*, 2nd edn, 147–97, Cambridge: Cambridge University Press.

Guest, R. and A. V. John (1989), *Lady Charlotte: A Biography of the Nineteenth Century*, London: Weidenfeld and Nicolson.

Hagerman, C. A. (2013), *Britain's Imperial Muse: The Classics, Imperialism, and the Indian Empire, 1784–1914*, Basingstoke: Palgrave Macmillan.

Haley, S. P. (1993), 'Black Feminist Thought and Classics: Re-membering, Re-claiming, Re-empowering', in N. S. Rabinowitz and A. Richlin (eds), *Feminist Theory and the Classics*, 23–43, New York: Routledge.

Haley, S. P. (2009), 'Be Not Afraid of the Dark: Critical Race Theory and Classical Studies', in L. Nasrallah and E. Schüssler Fiorenza (eds), *Prejudice and Christian Beginnings: Investigating Race, Gender, and Ethnicity in Early Christian Studies*, 27–49, Minneapolis: Fortress Press.

Harder, A., ed. (2012), *Callimachus: Aetia*, 2 vols., Oxford: Oxford University Press.

Hardie, F. (1974), *The Abyssinian Crisis*, London: Batsford.

Hardie, P. R. (2004), 'Political Education in Virgil's *Georgics*', *SIFC* 2: 83–111.

Hardwick, L. (2003), *Reception Studies*, Oxford: Oxford University Press.

Hardwick, L. and C. Gillespie, eds (2007), *Classics in Post-Colonial Worlds*, Oxford: Oxford University Press.

Hardwick, L. and C. Stray, eds (2008), *A Companion to Classical Receptions*, Oxford: Blackwell.

Harmsworth, C. (1916), 'Labour on Farms', *The Times*, 27 December 1916, p. 4, last accessed via *The Times* Digital Archive 1785–2013 (gale.com/intl/c/the-times-digital-archive), 28 November 2019.

Harris, W. V. (2011), 'The Roman Economy in the Late Republic, 133–31 B.C.', in
    Rome's Imperial Economy: Twelve Essays, 257–87, Oxford: Oxford University Press
    [= W. Scheidel, I. Morris and R. Saller, eds (2007), *The Cambridge Economic History
    of the Greco-Roman World*, 511–39, Cambridge: Cambridge University Press].

Harrison, S. J. (2004), 'Virgil's *Corycius senex* and Nicander's *Georgica*: Georgics 4.
    116–48', in M. Gale (ed.) *Latin Epic and Didactic Poetry*, 109–23, Swansea:
    Classical Press of Wales.

Harrison, S. J. (2005), 'Vergil and the *Mausoleum Augusti*: Georgics 3. 12–18', *Acta
    Classica* 48: 185–8.

Harrison, S. J. (2008), '*Laudes Italiae* (Georgics 2. 136–175): Virgil as a Caesarian
    Hesiod', in G. Urso (ed.), *Patria diversis gentibus una?: Unità, politica e identità
    etniche nell'Italia antica*, 231–42, Pisa: ETS.

Harrison, S. J. (2017), *Victorian Horace: Classics and Class*, London: Bloomsbury.

Heerink, M. A. J. (2011), 'Ovid's Aeginetan Plague and the Metamorphosis of the
    Georgics', *Hermes* 139(4): 464–72.

Heitland, W. E. (1921), *Agricola: A Study of Agriculture and Rustic Life in the Greco-
    Roman World from the Point of View of Labour*, Cambridge: Cambridge University
    Press.

Henkel, J. (2011), 'Nighttime Labor: A Metapoetic Vignette Alluding to Aratus at
    Georgics 1. 291–296', *HSPh* 106: 179–98.

Henze, P. B. (2000), *Layers of Time: A History of Ethiopia*, London: Hurst and Co.

Herklotz, F. (2012), '*Aegypto Capta*', in C. Riggs (ed.), *The Oxford Handbook of Roman
    Egypt*, 11–21, Oxford: Oxford University Press.

Heyworth, S. J. (2014), 'Review Article: Silvia Ottaviano, Gian Biagio Conte (ed.),
    P. Vergilius Maro: Bucolica; Georgica', *BMCRev* 2014.02.47, last accessed via The
    Bryn Mayr Classical Review (http://bmcr.brynmawr.edu/), 28 November 2019.

Hinds, S. (1998), *Allusion and Intertext: Dynamics of Appropriation in Roman Poetry*,
    Cambridge: Cambridge University Press.

Hirtzel, F. A., ed. (1900), *P. Vergili Maronis Opera*, Oxford: Clarendon Press.

Hoblyn, R. (1825), *A Translation of the First Book of the Georgics of Virgil, in Blank
    Verse*, London: W. Phillips.

Hobson, J. A. (1902), *Imperialism: A Study*, London: James Nisbet.

Hollingsworth, T. H. (1983), 'The Influence of Malthus on British Thought', in
    J. Dupâquier, A. Fauve-Chamoux and E. Grebenik (eds), *Malthus Past and Present*,
    213–21, London: Academic Press.

Holzberg, N. (2015), *Vergil, Georgica: Eine Bibliographie*, online Word document
    accessed via http://www.niklasholzberg.com/Homepage/Bibliographien.html,
    28 November 2019.

hooks, b. (1992), *Black Looks: Race and Representation*, Boston, MA: South End Press.

Hopkins, K. (1978), *Conquerors and Slaves*, Cambridge: Cambridge University Press.

Horsfall, N. (1997), 'The Geography of the *Georgics*', *Ancient History* 27(1): 7–18.

Horsfall, N., ed. (2000), *Virgil, Aeneid 7: A Commentary*, Leiden: Brill.

Howarth, J. (1994), 'Women', in B. Harrison (ed.), *The History of the University of Oxford Volume VIII: The Twentieth Century*, 345–75, Oxford: Oxford University Press.

Hudson, D. (2004), 'Brodribb, Charles William (1878–1945)', revised by S. Basu, *The Oxford Dictionary of National Biography*, online edn, Oxford: Oxford University Press, last accessed via oxforddnb.com, 28 November 2019.

Hunter, R. (2006), *The Shadow of Callimachus: Studies in the Reception of Hellenistic Poetry at Rome*, Cambridge: Cambridge University Press.

Hurst, I. (2006), *Victorian Women Writers and the Classics: The Feminine of Homer*, Oxford: Oxford University Press.

Hutchinson, G. O. (2008), *Talking Books: Readings in Hellenistic and Roman Books of Poetry*, Oxford: Oxford University Press.

Irish, T. (2015), *The University at War, 1914–25: Britain, France, and the United States*, Basingstoke: Palgrave Macmillan.

Isaac, B. (2004), *The Invention of Racism in Classical Antiquity*, Princeton, NJ: Princeton University Press.

Isayev, E. (2007), *Inside Ancient Lucania: Dialogues in History and Archaeology*, London: Institute of Classical Studies.

Isayev, E. (2014), 'The Lucanians: Archaeological Perspective', in M. Aberson, M. C. Biella, M. Di Fazio and M. Wullschleger (eds), *Entre Archéologie et Histoire: Dialogues sur divers Peuples de l'Italie Préromaine*, 331–48, Bern: Peter Lang.

Jacob, C. (1999), 'Mapping in the Mind: The Earth from Ancient Alexandria', in D. Cosgrove (ed.), *Mappings*, 24–49, London: Reaktion.

Jacoby, F., ed. (1923), *Die Fragmente der griechischen Historiker, Erster Teil: Genealogie und Mythographie*, Berlin: Weidmann.

James, L. (1917), 'Public Schools and Farm Work', *The Times*, 9 January 1917, p. 13, last accessed via *The Times* Digital Archive 1785–2013 (gale.com/intl/c/the-times-digital-archive), 28 November 2019.

James, L. (1997), *Raj: The Making and Unmaking of British India*, London: Abacus.

Jenkyns, R. (1989), 'Virgil and Arcadia', *JRS* 79: 26–39.

Jerram, C. S., ed. (1892), *Virgil: Georgics*, 2 vols., Oxford: Clarendon Press.

Johnson, W. R. (1981), 'The Broken World: Virgil and His Augustus', *Arethusa* 14(1): 49–57.

Jones, P. J. (2005), *Reading Rivers in Roman Literature and Culture*, Oxford: Lexington Books.

Jones, S. P. (2009), 'Maguire, John Francis', in J. McGuire and J. Quinn (eds), *Dictionary of Irish Biography*, online edn, Cambridge: Cambridge University Press, last accessed via dib.cambridge.org, 28 November 2019.

Kaster, R. A. (2002), '*Invidia* and the End of *Georgics* 1', *Phoenix* 56(3/4): 275–95.

Katz, J. T. (2008), 'Vergil Translates Aratus: *Phaenomena* 1–2 and *Georgics* 1. 1–2', *MD* 60: 105–23.

Katz, J. T. (2016), 'Another Vergilian signature in the *Georgics*?', in P. Mitsis and I. Ziogas (eds), *Wordplay and Powerplay in Latin Poetry*, 69–86, Berlin: De Gruyter.

Keay, J. (2000), *India: A History*, London: HarperCollins.

Keble, J. (1912), *Keble's Lectures on Poetry*, trans. E. K. Francis, English edn, Oxford: Clarendon Press. First published in Latin, Oxford: 1844.

Keightley, T. (1846), *Notes on the Bucolics and Georgics of Virgil*, London: Whittaker and Co.

Kelly, J., ed. (2018), *The Cambridge History of Ireland Volume III 1730–1880*, Cambridge: Cambridge University Press.

Keppie, L. (1981), 'Vergil, the Confiscations, and Caesar's Tenth Legion', *CQ* 31(2): 367–70.

Keppie, L. (1983), *Colonisation and Veteran Settlement in Italy: 47–14 B.C.*, London: British School at Rome.

Kincaid, J. (1988) *A Small Place*, London: Virago Press.

Kling, B. (1966), *The Blue Mutiny: The Indigo Disturbances in Bengal, 1859–1862*, Philadelphia, PA: University of Philadelphia Press.

Kramer, A. (2014), 'Blockade and Economic Warfare', in J. Winter (ed.), *The Cambridge History of the First World War*, 3 vols., 2: 460–89, Cambridge: Cambridge University Press.

Krebs, C. B. (2006), '"Imaginative Geography" in Caesar's *Bellum Gallicum*', *AJP* 127(1): 111–136.

Kronenberg, L. J. (2000), 'The Poet's Fiction: Virgil's Praise of the Farmer, Philosopher, and Poet at the End of *Georgics* 2', *HSPh* 100: 341–60.

Laroui, A. (1977), *The History of the Maghrib: An Interpretative Essay*, trans. R. Manheim, English edn, Princeton, NJ: Princeton University Press.

Letta, C. (1972), *I Marsi e il Fucino Nell'Antichità*, Milan: Cisalpino-Goliardica.

Lewis, C. T. and C. Short, eds (1969), *A Latin Dictionary*, reprint of the 1870 first edn, Oxford: Clarendon Press.

Lintott, A. (1994), 'Political History, 146–95 B.C.', in J. A. Crook, A. Lintott and E. Rawson (eds), *The Cambridge Ancient History Volume 9: The Last Age of the Roman Republic, 146–43 B.C*, 2nd edn, 40–103, Cambridge: Cambridge University Press.

Lomas, K. (2014), 'Italy during the Roman Republic, 338–31 BC', in H. Flower (ed.), *The Cambridge Companion to the Roman Republic*, 2nd edn, 233–59, Cambridge: Cambridge University Press.

Low, A. (1985), *The Georgic Revolution*, Princeton, NJ: Princeton University Press.

Lowrie, M. (2015), '*Rege Incolumni*: Orientalism, Civil War, and Security at *Georgics* 4. 212', in P. Fedeli and H.-C. Günther (eds), *Virgilian Studies: A Miscellany Dedicated to the Memory of Mario Geymonat*, 321–42, Nordhausen: Traugott Bautz.

Ludlow, F. and A. Crampsie (2018), 'Environmental History of Ireland, 1550–1730', in J. Ohlmeyer (ed.), *The Cambridge History of Ireland Volume II 1550–1730*, 608–637, Cambridge: Cambridge University Press.

Lyne, R. O. A. M. (1974), '*Scilicet et tempus ueniet . . .*: Vergil, *Georgics* 1. 463–514', in T. Woodman and D. West (eds), *Quality and Pleasure in Latin Poetry*, 47–66, Cambridge: Cambridge University Press [= R. O. A. M. Lyne (2007), *Collected Papers on Latin Poetry*, 38–59, Oxford: Oxford University Press].

MacGóráin, F. (2014), 'The Mixed Blessings of Bacchus in Virgil's *Georgics*', *Dictynna* 11, online edn (no page numbers), accessed via https://dictynna.revues.org/1069, 28 November 2019.

MacNeice, L. (1966), *The Collected Poetry of Louis MacNeice*, E. R. Dodds (ed.), London: Faber and Faber.

Mackail, J. W. (1895), *Latin Literature*, London: C. Scribner's Sons.

Mackail, J. W. (1923), *Virgil and His Meaning to the World of To-day*, London: G. Haarp and Co.

Majumdar, R. C. (1960), *The Classical Accounts of India*, Calcutta: Firma K. L. Mukhopadhyay.

Malcovati, H., ed. (1953), *Oratorum Romanorum Fragmenta Liberae Rei Publicae*, 3 vols., Turin: Paravia.

Mandelbaum, A. (1981), *The Aeneid of Virgil*, Berkeley, CA: University of California Press.

Markland, J., ed. (1728), *P. Papinii Statii Silvarum Libri Quinque ex vetustis exemplaribus recensuit et notas atque emendationes adjecit*, London: William Bowyer.

Markovitz, C. (2002), *A History of Modern India 1480–1950*, trans. N. George and M. Hardy, London: Anthem.

Marsh, P. T. (1994), *Joseph Chamberlain: Entrepreneur in Politics*, New Haven, CT: Yale University Press.

Martindale, C. (1993), *Redeeming the Text: Latin Poetry and the Hermeneutics of Reception*, Cambridge: Cambridge University Press.

Martindale, C. and R. F. Thomas, eds (2006), *Classics and the Uses of Reception*, Oxford: Blackwell.

Martindale, C. (2013), 'Reception – A New Humanism? Receptivity, Pedagogy, The Transhistorical', *Classical Receptions Journal* 5(2): 169–83.

Martinengo-Cesaresco, E. (1911), *The Outdoor Life in Greek and Roman Poets, and Kindred Studies*, London: Macmillan.

Martyn, J. (1741), *Pub. Virgilii Maronis Georgicum Libri Quatuor. The Georgicks of Virgil, with an English Translation and Notes*, 1st edn, London: R. Reily.

Marx, K. and F. Engels (1996), *Collected Works Volume 35: Karl Marx, Capital, Volume 1*, London: Lawrence and Wishart.

Mattingly, D. J. (2006), 'The Garamantes: The First Libyan State', in D. Mattingly, S. McLaren, E. Savage, Y. al-Fasatwi and K. Gadgood (eds), *The Libyan Desert: Natural Resources and Cultural Heritage*, 189–204, London: The Society for Libyan Studies.

Mattingly, D. J. (2011), *Imperialism, Power, and Identity: Experiencing the Roman Empire*, Princeton, NJ: Princeton University Press.

Maurenbrecher, B., ed. (1967), *C. Sallusti Crispi Historiarum Reliquiae*, 2 vols., Stuttgart: Teubner.

Mayhoff, C., ed. (1875), *C. Plini Secundi Naturalis Historiae Libri XXXVII: Vol. II, Libri VII–XV*, Leipzig: Teubner.

Mbembe, A. (2017), *Critique of Black Reason*, trans. L. Dubois, Durham, NC: Duke University Press.

McCoskey, D. E. (2012), *Race: Antiquity and its Legacy*, London: I. B. Tauris.

McDonald, L., ed. (2003), *The Collected Works of Florence Nightingale, Volume 5*, Waterloo, Ontario: Wilfrid Laurier University Press.

McGushin, P., ed. (1994), *Sallust: The Histories*, vol. 2, Oxford: Clarendon Press.

McKay, A. G. (1970), *Vergil's Italy*, Bath: Adams and Dart.

McLaughlin, R. (2014), *The Roman Empire and the Indian Ocean: The Ancient World Economy and the Kingdoms of Africa, Arabia and India*, Barnsley: Pen and Sword.

McLaughlin, R. (2016), *The Roman Empire and the Silk Routes: The Ancient World Economy and the Empires of Parthia, Central Asia & Han China*, Barnsley: Pen and Sword.

McWilliams Tullberg, R. (1998), *Woman at Cambridge*, revised edn, Cambridge: Cambridge University Press.

Meban, D. (2008), 'Temple Building, *Primus* Language, and the Proem to Virgil's Third Georgic', *CPh* 103(2): 150–74.

Meiksins Wood, E. (2015), *The Pristine Culture of Capitalism: A Historical Essay on Old Regimes and Modern States*, new edn, London: Verso.

Merivale, C. (1850–82), *History of the Romans Under the Empire*, 7 vols., London: Longmans, Green and Co.

Merkelbach, R. and M. L. West, eds (1967), *Fragmenta Hesiodea*, Oxford: Clarendon Press.

Miller, W. (1904), 'A Tour Through the Peloponnesos', Part 1, *The Westminster Review* 162(6): 639–48, last accessed via the British Periodicals Database (proquest.com/products-services/british_periodicals.html), 28 November 2019.

Miller, W. (1905), 'A Tour Through the Peloponnesos', Part 2, *The Westminster Review* 163(1): 74–90, last accessed via the British Periodicals Database (proquest.com/ products-services/british_periodicals.html), 28 November 2019.

Mills, W. (1780), *The Georgics of Virgil*, London: W. Richardson.

Montagu, E. S. and F. J. N. Thesiger (1918), 'East India (Constitutional Reforms). Report on Indian Constitutional Reforms', Command Paper no. 9109, 3rd Series (1900–18), last accessed via the ProQuest UK Parliamentary Papers database (parlipapers.proquest.com/parlipapers), 28 November 2019.

Morgan, J. D. (1992), 'The Origin of Molorc(h)us', *CQ* 42(2): 533–8.

Morgan, L. (1999), *Patterns of Redemption in Virgil's* Georgics, Cambridge: Cambridge University Press.

Morrow, J. H. (2014), 'The Imperial Framework', in J. Winter (ed.), *The Cambridge History of the First World War*, 3 vols., 1: 405–32, Cambridge: Cambridge University Press.

Mouritsen, H. (1998), *Italian Unification: A Study in Ancient and Modern Historiography*, London: Institute of Classical Studies.

Müller, C., ed. (1882), *Geographi Graeci Minores*, 2 vols., Paris: A. Firmin Didot.

Mulligan, W. (2014), 'The Trial Continues: New Directions in the Study of the Origins of the First World War', *The English Historical Review* 129(538): 639–66.

Murphy, T. (2004), *Pliny the Elder's Natural History: The Empire in the Encyclopedia*, Oxford: Oxford University Press.

Murray, A. T. (1999), *Homer: Iliad*, 2 vols., revised by W. F. Wyatt, Cambridge, MA: Harvard University Press.

Myers, F. W. H. (1908), 'Virgil', in *Essays Classical*, 106–76, London: Macmillan (first published London: Macmillan, 1883).

Myers, M. Y. (2019), 'From Cumae to the Po: Italian Itineraries in *Aeneid 6*', *Dictynna* 16, online edn (no page numbers), last accessed via https://dictynna.revues. org/2021, 20 December 2019.

Mynors, R. A. B., ed. (1969), *P. Vergili Maronis Opera*, Oxford: Clarendon Press.

Mynors, R. A. B., ed. (1990), *Virgil:* Georgics, Oxford: Clarendon Press.

Nadeau, Y. (1984), 'The Lover and the Statesman: A Study in Apiculture (Virgil, *Georgics* 4. 281–558)', in T. Woodman and D. West (eds), *Poetry and Politics in the Age of Augustus*, 59–82, Cambridge: Cambridge University Press.

Nadiem, I. H. (2008), *Taxila in Buddhist Gandhara*, Lahore: Sang-e-Meel.

Nappa, C. (2005), *Reading After Actium*, Ann Arbor, MI: University of Michigan Press.

Nelis, D. and J. Nelis-Clément (2011), 'Vergil, *Georgics* 1. 1–42 and the *pompa circensis*', *Dictynna* 8, online edn (no page numbers), last accessed via https://dictynna. revues.org/730, 28 November 2019.

Nelis, D. P. (2004), 'From Didactic to Epic: *Georgics* 2. 458–3. 48', in M. Gale (ed.), *Latin Epic and Didactic Poetry*, 73–107, Swansea: Classical Press of Wales.

Nelis, D. P. (2013), 'Past, Present, and Future in Virgil's *Georgics*', in J. A. Farrell and D. P. Nelis (eds), *Augustan Poetry and the Roman Republic*, 244–62, Oxford: Oxford University Press.

Nelson, S. A. (1998), *God and the Land: The Metaphysics of Farming in Hesiod and Vergil*, New York: Oxford University Press.

Newsinger, J. (2013), *The Blood Never Dried: A People's History of the British Empire*, 2nd edn, London: Bookmarks Publications.

Nicolet, C. (1980), *The World of the Citizen in Republican Rome*, trans. P. S. Falla, London: Batsford.

Nicolet, C. (1991), *Space, Geography, and Politics in the Early Roman Empire*, Ann Arbor, MI: University of Michigan Press.

Nicolet, C. (1994), 'Economy and Society, 133–43 B.C.', in J. A. Crook, A. Lintott and E. Rawson (eds), *The Cambridge Ancient History Volume 9: The Last Age of the Roman Republic, 146–43 B.C*, 2nd edn, 599–643, Cambridge: Cambridge University Press.

O'Brien, K. (1999), 'Imperial Georgic, 1660–1789', in G. MacLean, D. Landry and J. P. Ward (eds), *The Country and the City Revisited: England and the Politics of Culture, 1550–1850*, 160–79, Cambridge: Cambridge University Press.

O'Rourke, D. (2011), '"Eastern" Elegy and "Western" Epic: Reading "Orientalism" in Propertius 4 and Virgil's *Aeneid*', *Dictynna* 8, online edn (no page numbers), last accessed via https://dictynna.revues.org/699, 28 November 2019.

Oakley, S. P., ed. (1997–2005), *A Commentary on Livy: Books VI–X*, 4 vols., Cambridge: Cambridge University Press.

Ogilvie, R. M., ed. (1974), *Titi Livi ab Urbe Condita Tomus I, Libri I–V*, Oxford: Clarendon Press.

Oliensis, E. (1997), 'Sons and Lovers: Sexuality and Gender in Virgil's Poetry', in C. Martindale (ed), *The Cambridge Companion to Virgil*, 294–311, Cambridge: Cambridge University Press.

Otis, B. (1963), *Virgil, A Study in Civilized Poetry*, Oxford: Clarendon Press.

Ottaviano, S. and G. B. Conte, eds (2013), *P. Vergilius Maro Bucolica; Georgica*, Berlin: De Gruyter.

Owen-Lee, M. (1996), *Virgil as Orpheus: A Study of the* Georgics, Albany, NY: State University of New York Press.

Page, T. E., ed. (1898), *P. Vergili Maronis Bucolica et Georgica*, London: Macmillan.

Paget, R. F. (1968), 'The Ancient Ports of Cumae', *JRS* 58: 152–69.

Pallottino, M. (1991), *A History of Earliest Italy*, trans. M. Ryle and K. Soper, London: Routledge.

Papillon, T. L., ed. (1882), *P. Vergili Maronis Opera: Virgil, with an Introduction and Notes*, 2 vols., Oxford: Clarendon Press.

Parker, G. (2008), *The Making of Roman India*, Cambridge: Cambridge University Press.

Parker, G. (2011), 'India, Egypt and Parthia in Augustan Verse: The Post-Orientalist Turn', *Dictynna* 8, online edn (no page numbers), last accessed via https://dictynna.revues.org/691, 28 November 2019.

Pati, B., ed. (2010), *The Great Rebellion of 1857 in India: Exploring Transgressions, Contests, and Diversities*, Abingdon: Routledge.

Pellicer, J. C. (2012), 'Pastoral and Georgic', in D. Hopkins and C. Martindale (eds), *The Oxford History of Classical Reception in English Literature Volume 3 (1660–1790)*, 287–322, Oxford: Oxford University Press.

Pellicer, J. C. (2019), 'Georgic as Genre: The Scholarly Reception of Vergil in Mid-Eighteenth-Century Britain', in S. Bär and E. Hauser (eds), *Reading Poetry, Writing Genre: English Poetry and Literary Criticism in Dialogue with Classical Scholarship*, 79–93, London: Bloomsbury.

Pelling, C. B. R., ed. (1988), *Plutarch: Life of Antony*, Cambridge: Cambridge University Press.

Pelling, C. B. R. (1996), 'The Triumviral Period', in A. K. Bowman, E. Champlin and A. Lintott (eds), *The Cambridge Ancient History Volume 10: The Augustan Empire, 43 B.C. – A.D. 69*, 2nd edn, 1–69, Cambridge: Cambridge University Press.

Perkell, C. (2014), 'Women', in R. F. Thomas and J. M. Ziolkowski (eds), *The Virgil Encyclopedia*, 3 vols, 3: 1391–3, Chichester: Wiley Blackwell.

Pfeiffer, R., ed. (1949), *Callimachus*, 2 vols., Oxford: Clarendon Press.

Pieri, B. (2011), 'L'epica in *fieri* e due esegesi vulgate (Verg. *Georg.* III 26s.; 46s.)', in *Intacti saltus: studi sul III libro delle Georgiche*, 31–54, Bologna: Pàtron.

Pitt, W. (1792), untitled speech in the 'Debate on Mr. Wilberforce's Motion for the Abolition of the Slave Trade', 2 April 1792, in *Cobbett's Parliamentary History of England from the Earliest Period to the Year 1803*, 36 vols., London: T. C. Hansard, 1806–1820, vol. 29, cols. 1133–58.

Pollard, A. F. (2004), 'Froude, James Anthony (1818–1894)', revised by W. Thomas, *The Oxford Dictionary of National Biography*, online edn, Oxford: Oxford University Press, last accessed via oxforddnb.com, 28 November 2019.

Pollock, S. (2006), *The Language of the Gods in the World of Men: Sanskrit, Culture, and Power in Premodern India*, Berkeley, CA: University of California Press.

Porter, B. (2004), *The Lion's Share: A Short History of British Imperialism 1850–2004*, 4th edn, London: Pearson/Longman.

Potter, T. (1987), *Roman Italy*, London: British Museum Press.

Powell, A. (2008), *Virgil the Partisan: A Study in the Re-Integration of Classics*, Swansea: Classical Press of Wales.

Powell, J. U., ed. (1925), *Collectanea Alexandrina*, Oxford: Clarendon Press.

Purvis, J. (1991), *A History of Women's Education in England*, Milton Keynes: Open University Press.

Putnam, M. C. J. (1979), *Virgil's Poem of the Earth: Studies in the Georgics*, Princeton, NJ: Princeton University Press.

Quint, D. (1993), *Epic and Empire*, Princeton, NJ: Princeton University Press.

Rabinowitz, N. S. (1993), 'Introduction', in N. S. Rabinowitz and A. Richlin (eds), *Feminist Theory and the Classics*, 1–20, New York: Routledge.

Rackham, H. (1968), *Pliny. Natural History, Volume IV: Books 12–16*, revised edn, Cambridge, MA: Harvard University Press.

Ramsey, J. T., ed. (2003), *Philippics: I–II*, Cambridge: Cambridge University Press.

Rao, A. and B. G. Rao (1992), *The Blue Devil: Indigo and Colonial Bengal*, Delhi: Oxford University Press.

Raschke, M. G. (1978), 'New Studies in Roman Commerce with the East', in H. Temporini and W. Haase (eds), *Aufstieg und Niedergang der römischen Welt*, 2. 9. 2: 604–1378, Berlin: De Gruyter.

Rawson, E. (1985), *Intellectual Life in the Late Roman Republic*, London: Duckworth.

Readman, P. (2008), 'Jesse Collings and Land Reform, 1886–1914', *Historical Research* 81(212): 292–314.

Ribbeck, O., ed. (1894), *P. Vergili Maronis Opera I: Bucolica et Georgica*, 2nd edn, Leipzig: Teubner.

Rich, A. (2001), *Arts of the Possible: Essays and Conversations*, Norton: New York.

Richardson, J. S. (1996), *The Romans in Spain*, Oxford: Blackwell.

Richardson, J. S., ed. (2000), *Appian: Wars of the Romans in Iberia*, Warminster: Aris and Phillips.

Richlin, A. (2014), *Arguments with Silence*, Ann Arbor, MI: Michigan University Press.

Richter, W., ed. (1957), *Vergil:* Georgica, Munich: Max Heuber Verlag.

Roddaz, J.-M. (1984), *Marcus Agrippa*, Rome: École Française de Rome.

Romm, J. S. (1992), *The Edges of the Earth in Ancient Thought: Geography, Exploration, and Fiction*, Princeton, NJ: Princeton University Press.

Ross, D. O. (1987), *Virgil's Elements: Physics and Poetry in the* Georgics, Princeton, NJ: Princeton University Press.

Røstvig, M-S. (1962), *The Happy Man: Studies in the Metamorphoses of a Classical Ideal*, 2 vols., 2nd edn, Oslo: Norwegian University Press.

Roussel, P. and M. Launey, eds (1937), *Inscriptions de Délos. Nos. 1497–2219*, Paris: H. Champion.

Roy, T. (2011), 'Indigo and Law in Colonial India', *The Economic History Review* 64(S1): 60–75.

Royds, T. F. (1914), *The Beasts, Birds, and Bees of Virgil*, Oxford: Blackwell.

Runciman, S. (2004), 'Miller, William (1864–1945)', *The Oxford Dictionary of National Biography*, online edn, Oxford: Oxford University Press, accessed via oxforddnb. com, 28 November 2019.

Said, E. W. (1978), *Orientalism*, New York: Pantheon Books.

Said, E. W. (1994), *Culture and Imperialism*, London: Vintage.

Salmon, E. T. (1958), 'Notes on the Social War', *TAPA* 89: 159–84.

Salmon, E. T. (1967), *Samnium and the Samnites*, Cambridge: Cambridge University Press.

Sambrook, J., ed. (1981), *James Thomson*, The Seasons, Oxford: Clarendon Press.

Sargeaunt, J., C. Brodribb, et al. (1917), 'Classical Metres for English Poetry', *CR* 31(5/6): 123–6.

Saunders, C. and I. R. Smith (1999), 'Southern Africa, 1795–1910', in A. Porter (ed.), *The Oxford History of the British Empire Volume III*, 597–623, Oxford: Oxford University Press.

Sayre, L. B. (2002), 'Locating the Georgic: From the *Ferme Ornée* to the Model Farm', *Studies in the History of Gardens and Designed Landscapes* 22(3): 167–92.

Scott, E. (n.d.), 'Roman Agriculture, Gender and Work, *or* Havesting Women's Work from Roman Landscapes', unpublished paper last accessed via https:// eleanorscottarchaeology.com/unpublished-papers, 28 November 2019.

Seager, R. (1994), 'Sulla', in J. A. Crook, A. Lintott and E. Rawson, (eds), *The Cambridge Ancient History Volume 9: The Last Age of the Roman Republic, 146–43 B.C*, 2nd edn, 165–207, Cambridge: Cambridge University Press.

Seeley, J. R. (1971), *The Expansion of England*, J. Gross (ed.), Chicago: University of Chicago Press (first published London: Macmillan, 1883).

Sellar, W. Y. (1897), *The Roman Poets of the Augustan Age: Virgil*, 3rd edn, Oxford: Clarendon Press (first published Oxford: Clarendon Press, 1883).

Seymour, R. (2012), *The Liberal Defence of Murder*, London: Verso.

Simpson, D. P., ed. (1964), *Cassell's New Latin-English English-Latin Dictionary*, 3rd edn, London: Macmillan.

Skutsch, O., ed. (1985), *The Annals of Q. Ennius*, Oxford: Clarendon Press.

Sonnenschein, E. A. (1897), '*Sabellus*: Sabine or Samnite?', *CR* 11(7): 339–40.

Spencer, D. (2002), *The Roman Alexander: Reading a Cultural Myth*, Exeter: University of Exeter Press.

Spencer, D. (2010), *Roman Landscape: Culture and Identity*, Cambridge: Cambridge University Press.

Spurr, M. S. (1986), 'Agriculture and the *Georgics*', *G&R* 33(2): 167–87 [= K. Volk, ed. (2008), *Vergil's* Georgics, 11–42, Oxford: Oxford University Press].

Steinmayer, O. (1997), 'The Bow in the Groves of India', *Arion* 5(1): 130–42.

Stephens, S. A. and P. Vasunia, eds (2010), *Classics and National Cultures*, Oxford: Oxford University Press.

Storey, N. R. and M. Housego (2010), *Women in the First World War*, Oxford: Shire Publications.

Stray, C. (1998), *Classics Transformed: Schools, Universities and Society in England, 1830–1960*, Oxford: Oxford University Press.

Suerbaum, W. (1981), 'Spezialbibliographie zu Vergils Georgica', in H. Temporini and W. Haase (eds), *Aufstieg und Niedergang der römischen Welt*, 2. 31. 2: 395–499, Berlin: De Gruyter.

Sweet, R. (2012), *Cities and the Grand Tour: The British in Italy, c. 1690–1820*, Cambridge: Cambridge University Press.

Sweet, T. (2002), *American Georgics: Economy and Environment in Early American Literature*, Philadelphia, PA: University of Pennsylvania Press.

Sydenham, E. A., ed. (1952), *The Coinage of the Roman Republic*, London: Spink and Son.

Syme, R. (1939), *The Roman Revolution*, Oxford: Clarendon Press.

Symonds, R. (1991), *Oxford and Empire: The Last Lost Cause?*, Oxford: Clarendon Press (first published London: Macmillan, 1986).

Talbert, R. J. A., ed. (2000), *The Barrington Atlas of the Greek and Roman World*, 3 vols., Princeton, NJ: Princeton University Press.

Tarrant, R. J. (1997), 'Poetry and Power: Virgil's Poetry in Contemporary Context', in C. Martindale (ed.) *The Cambridge Companion to Virgil*, 169–87, Cambridge: Cambridge University Press.

Theiler, W., ed. (1982), *Poseidonios, Die Fragmente*, 2 vols., Berlin: De Gruyter.

Thibodeau, P. (2011), *Playing the Farmer: Representations of Rural Life in Vergil's Georgics*, Berkeley, CA: University of California Press.

Thilo, G. and H. Hagen, eds (1986), *Servii Grammatici Qui Feruntur in Vergilii Bucolica et Georgica Commentarii*, 3 vols., Hildesheim: G. Olms.

Thomas, M. (2005), *The French Empire Between the Wars: Imperialism, Politics and Society*, Manchester: Manchester University Press.

Thomas, R. F. (1982) *Lands and Peoples in Roman Poetry: The Ethnographical Tradition*, Cambridge: Cambridge University Press.

Thomas, R. F. (1986), 'Virgil's *Georgics* and the Art of Reference', *HSPh* 90: 171–98 [= R. F.

Thomas, R. F., ed. (1988), *Virgil: Georgics*, 2 vols., Cambridge: Cambridge University Press.

Thomas, R. F. (1999), *Reading Virgil and His Texts*, Ann Arbor, Michigan: University of Michigan Press.

Thomas, R. F. (2001a), *Virgil and the Augustan Reception*, Cambridge: Cambridge University Press.

Thomas, R. F. (2001b), 'The *Georgics* of Resistance: From Virgil to Heaney', *Vergilius* 47: 117–47.

Thomas, R. F. (2007), 'Didaxis and Aesthetics in the *Georgics* Tradition', in A. Harder, A. A. MacDonald, and G. J. Reinink (eds), *Calliope's Classroom: Studies in Didactic Poetry from Antiquity to the Renaissance*, 71–102, Leuven: Peeters.

Thomas, R. F. (2019), 'Aesthetics, Form and Meaning in the *Georgics*, in B. Xinyue and N. Freer (eds), *Reflections and New Perspectives on Virgil's* Georgics, e-book edn (no page numbers), London: Bloomsbury.

Thomas, W., ed. (2008), *The Journals of Thomas Babington Macaulay*, 5 vols., London: Pickering and Chatto.

Thompson, E. P. (2013), *The Making of the English Working Class*, new edn, London: Penguin (first published London: Victor Gollancz, 1963).

Thomson, J. O. (1951), 'Place-Names in Latin Poetry', *Latomus* 10: 433–8.

Thomson, J. O. (1955), '*Geographica Vergiliana*', *G&R* 2(2): 50–8.

Thomson, J. O. (1965), *History of Ancient Geography*, new edn, London: Biblo and Tannen.

Thorley, J. (1969), 'The Development of Trade between the Roman Empire and the East under Augustus', *G&R* 16(2): 209–33.

Townshend, C. (1983), *Political Violence in Ireland: Government and Resistance since 1848*, Oxford: Clarendon Press.

Toynbee, A. J. (1965), *Hannibal's Legacy: The Hannibalic War's Effects on Roman Life*, 2 vols., Oxford: Oxford University Press.

Trevelyan, G. O. (2010), *The Competition Wallah*, new edn, Cambridge: Cambridge University Press (first published London: Macmillan and Co., 1864).

Trilling, D. (2019), 'Britain is Hoarding a Treasure No One is Allowed to See', *The Atlantic*, Washington, D.C., 9 July, last accessed via https://www.theatlantic.com/international/archive/2019/07/why-britain-wont-return-ethiopias-sacred-treasures/593281/, 28 November 2019.

Turner, F. M. (1993), 'Virgil in Victorian Classical Contexts', in *Contesting Cultural Authority: Essays in Victorian Intellectual Life*, 284–321, Cambridge: Cambridge University Press.

Van Minnen, P. (1991), 'Lentils from Pelusium: A Note on Vergil's *Georgics* I 228', *Mnemosyne* 44: 167–170.

Vance, N. (2000), 'Imperial Rome and Britain's Language of Empire, 1600–1837', *History of European Ideas* 26(3–4): 211–24.

Vance, N. (2015), 'Classical Authors, 1790–1880', in N. Vance and J. Wallace (eds), *The Oxford History of Classical Reception in English Literature Volume 4 (1790–1880)*, 29–56, Oxford: Oxford University Press.

Vasunia, P. (2005), 'Greater Rome and Greater Britain', in B. Goff (ed.), *Classics and Colonialism*, 38–64, London: Duckworth.

Vasunia, P. (2009a), 'Greek, Latin, and the Indian Civil Service', in J. P. Hallett and C. Stray (eds), *British Classics Outside England*, 61–96, Waco, TX: Alban [= *PCPhS* 51: 35–71].

Vasunia, P. (2009b), 'Virgil and the British Empire, 1760–1880', *Proceedings of the British Academy* 155: 83–116, Oxford: Oxford University Press.

Vasunia, P. (2013), *The Classics and Colonial India*, Oxford: Oxford University Press.

Vaughan, W. E., ed. (1989), *A New History of Ireland V: Ireland Under the Union, Part I 1801–1870*, Oxford: Clarendon Press.

Vermes, G. (2014), *The True Herod*, London: Bloomsbury.

Vogt, J. (1960), '*Orbis Romanus*: Ein Beitrag zum Sprachgebrauch und zur Vorstellungswelt des römischen Imperialismus', in *Orbis: Ausgewählte Schriften zur Geschichte des Altertums* 151–71, Freiburg: Herder.

Volk, K. (2008), *Vergil's Georgics*, Oxford: Oxford University Press.

Wakefield, E. (1886), 'New Zealand and Mr. Froude', *The Nineteenth Century: A Monthly Review* 20(114): 171–82, last accessed via the British Periodicals Database (proquest.com/products-services/british_periodicals.html), 28 November 2019.

Walbank, F. W., ed. (1957–79), *A Historical Commentary on Polybius*, 3 vols., Oxford: Clarendon Press.

Warren, H. (1916), 'The Empire and the Land', *The Spectator*, London, no. 4, 602, 9 September 1916, p. 8, last accessed via *The Spectator* Archive (http://archive.spectator.co.uk/issues), 28 March 2018.

Warton, J. (1763), 'Reflections on Didactic Poetry', in C. Pitt and J. Warton, *The Works of Virgil in English Verse*, 4 vols., 2nd edn, 1: 291–335, London: R. and J. Dodsley.

Weeda, L. (2015), *Vergil's Political Commentary in the* Eclogues, Georgics, *and* Aeneid, Berlin: De Gruyter.

Whetham, E., ed. (1978), *The Agrarian History of England and Wales Volume VIII: 1914–1939*, Cambridge: Cambridge University Press.

Whitcomb, K. (2018), 'Vergil, Octavian and Erigone: Admiration and Admonition in the Proem to *Georgics* 1', *CJ* 113(4): 411–26.

White, H. (1912), *Appian. Roman History, Volume II*, Cambridge, MA: Harvard University Press.

White, R. (2017), *The Man on the Land: Classics in Colonial Australia*, DPhil thesis, Oxford: University of Oxford.

Whittaker, C. R. (1996), 'Roman Africa: From Augustus to Vespasian', in
A. K. Bowman, E. Champlin and A. Lintott (eds), *The Cambridge Ancient History
Volume 10: The Augustan Empire, 43 B.C.–A.D. 69*, 2nd edn, 586–618, Cambridge:
Cambridge University Press.

Wilkins, H. M. (1874), *The Georgics of Vergil: With a Running Analysis, English Notes,
and Index*, London: Longmans, Green and Co.

Wilkinson, L. P. (1963), 'Virgil's Theodicy', *CQ* 13(1): 75–84.

Wilkinson, L. P. (1969), *The Georgics of Virgil: A Critical Survey*, Cambridge:
Cambridge University Press.

Willis, I. (2011), *Now and Rome: Lucan and Vergil as Theorists of Politics and Space*
(London).

Wiseman, T. P. (1987a), 'Viae Anniae', in *Roman Studies: Literary and Historical*,
99–115, Liverpool: Francis Cairns [= *PBSR* 32: 21–37].

Wiseman, T. P. (1987b), 'Viae Anniae Again', in *Roman Studies: Literary and Historical*
116–25, Liverpool: Francis Cairns [= *PBSR* 37: 82–91].

Wyke, M. (1992), 'Augustan Cleopatras: Female Power and Poetic Authority', in
A. Powell (ed.) *Roman Poetry and Propaganda in the Age of Augustus*, 98–140,
London: Bristol Classical Press.

Xinyue, B. and N. Freer, eds (2019), *Reflections and New Perspectives on Virgil's
Georgics*, London: Bloomsbury.

Zanker, P. (1988), *The Power of Images in the Age of Augustus*, Ann Arbor, MI:
University of Michigan Press.

Ziolkowski, T. (1993), *Virgil and the Moderns*, Princeton, NJ: Princeton University
Press.

Index of Passages from the *Georgics*

Index